THE WORLD
ACCORDING TO
ERATOSTHENES

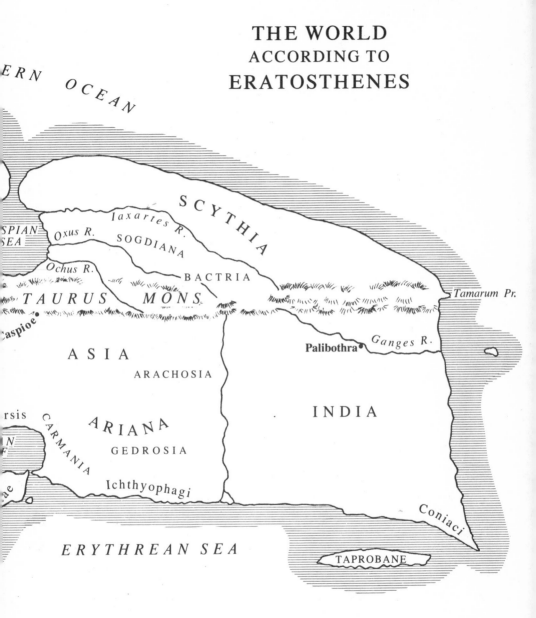

ERN OCEAN

SCYTHIA

Iaxartes R.

Oxus R.   SOGDIANA

SPIAN
SEA

Ochus R.

BACTRIA

TAURUS   MONS

Tamarum Pr.

Caspioe

Ganges R.

ASIA

Palibothra

ARACHOSIA

rsis

N
F

CARMANIA

ARIANA

GEDROSIA

INDIA

Ichthyophagi

ae

Coniaci

ERYTHREAN SEA

TAPROBANE

Scholar, farmer, poet, novelist, and inventor, Howard Baker was born in Philadelphia in 1905 and educated at Whittier College, Stanford University, the Sorbonne, and the University of California, Berkeley, where he took a Ph.D. In Paris in 1929 he became one of the circle of American and British writers around Ford Madox Ford, who helped him to publish his first book, *Orange Valley*, a novel. He has also published *Induction to Tragedy;* two collections of poetry, *From the Country* and *Ode to the Sea;* and numerous essays. He has taught at Harvard University and as a visiting professor at Berkeley and the University of California, Davis.

PERSEPHONE'S CAVE

Persephone's Cave

Cultural
Accumulations
of the
Early Greeks

HOWARD BAKER

The University of Georgia Press

ATHENS

Published by the University of Georgia Press, Athens 30602
Copyright © 1979 by Howard Baker

Set in 11 on 13 point Times Roman type
Printed in the United States of America

ACKNOWLEDGMENTS

The author and the publisher are grateful to the original copyright holders for permission to reprint the following material.
"A Portrait of Aesop," "Pythagoras of Samos," "The Ionians
and the Housing of Their Gods," and "Eudoxus of Cnidus"
first appeared in the *Sewanee Review;* copyright 1969, 1972, 1973
by the University of the South; reprinted by permission of the
editor. Chapter 5 was first published under the title "Pray Thee
Who Was the Artificer? What the Fabric?" in the *Michigan Quarterly Review*, vol. 14 (1975), and chapter 1 was first published
under the title "The Tunnel of Eupalinus" in the *Michigan Quarterly Review*, vol. 15 (1976); copyright 1977 by Howard Baker.

LIBRARY OF CONGRESS
CATALOGING IN PUBLICATION DATA

Baker, Howard, 1905–
  Persephone's cave.
  Bibliography.
  Includes index.
    1. Civilization, Greek—Addresses, essays, lectures.
I. Title.

DF77.B25   938   77–11162
        ISBN 0–8203–0438–7

CONTENTS

Les corps sont souvenirs, les figures
sont de fumée.

—Paul Valéry

PREFACE

IT HAS NOT BEEN my intention to write a book expounding a controversial theme. I am not equipped, either professionally or temperamentally, to take part in the debates in which scholars are presently engaged, certainly not to try to add systematically to the knowledge of antiquity which their diligence has accumulated and on which I have drawn freely, with great satisfaction, during the past two decades. My studies have been formed from an angle which is more personal than that which is normal in a scholarly treatise.

Nevertheless, just because of this obliquity, I hope that the collection of notes on the Works and Days of some of the earlier Greeks which is assembled here will have a certain vitality of an uncommon sort and also an underlying coherence which will gradually make its character felt. I am also aware that a train of thought with innovative quirks in it will collide now and again with the thinking of a certain number of readers. For this reason I have made every effort to give justification for noticeable departures from traditional points of view. Moreover, since what may appear to be acceptances by common consent often fall far short of being unanimous, I have persuaded myself that my general course is not far off the beaten track.

More difficult to explain is the wayward structure, as it may seem, of the book itself. Earlier drafts of a manuscript which was entitled "The Ionians . . . etc." in several variant forms, simply would not flow along consecutively when I tried to give proper place to the Greeks who lived on the Aegean coast to the north and the south of the strictly Ionian settlements, not to mention those who had transported elements of their Ionian civilization into the Italiote west. Just how a figure like Pythagoras, who had lived his life partly in Samos, partly in Croton, would fit into a sequential account of the Ionians was a question to which I could find no ready answer.

A passable solution seemed to emerge, however, after a painful scrutiny of another question: why should there have been for me a sense of a genuine need for a book dealing with horizontal materials which were a part of the Greek experience?

A long time ago in connection with other studies in seminars at several universities, the germ of the idea for this book came into being, and little by little the idea took on some semblance of a coherent whole. The memory of all this, this step by step growth of what ended by being a project for research and writing, stood out like the profile of a distant landscape in my mind: why, therefore, should not the outline of the acquisition of the subject matter be the basis for a good and quite unarbitrary plan for the presentation of the project I had in mind? It would give polarity to topics and prevent them from blurring too much into one another. This principle has governed the structure of the book which follows.

Consequently, in this already unorthodox preface it would seem to be only appropriate to include a description of the origins to which I refer.

The book began with Shakespeare, or rather with the drama of Shakespeare, and what lay behind it in its own time and place and helped to infuse in it its intricate character. The tragedies came first to my attention, and with them came the drama of Seneca. Although the translated tragedies of the Roman master were better known in Elizabethan England than were other ancient tragedies, they were too effete, too metaphysically rhetorical, I soon realized, to have moved the subsequent great works in English toward their tremendous level of success. On the other hand, in contrast with the Roman stage pieces, the translations of Plutarch's *Lives* by Thomas North and Ovid's *Metamorphoses* by Arthur Golding were beautifully substantial bridges extending back into antiquity. These literary triumphs seemed to prove that the robust subjects of Elizabeth had a lusty appetite for the best menu of classics that the scholarship of the Renaissance could set before them.

This brought up some urgent questions. Why was it that Seneca was a poor provider in comparison with Ovid? The problem was worrisome. It led by routes which I do not remember now toward scrutinizing Seneca's *Medea* side by side with the *Medea* of Euripides and the discovery of how one-dimensional the Roman treatment was in comparison with the Greek. Further study brought out the great variety of forces that was contained within the body of Greek mythology, of which Euripides could take full advantage but which for Seneca was practically nonexistent. It was as if a Roman determinism had crushed the native sense of freedom which the Greeks enjoyed.

Thus began further inquiries into the Greek past that lay, in the

sixteenth century, more or less shrouded within the archives of documents which were still unavailable in English but were only waiting to
emerge into a world which was intuitively awaiting them, and which
did succeed in bringing them rapidly into light as the sixteenth century
passed into the next.

These initial observations argued that Shakespeare's tragedies could
be grasped with better perspective if one could visualize some of them
beside some of the great Greek tragedies: *King Lear*, for example,
beside Euripides' *Phoenissae*. In this comparison *King Lear* did not
come off second best, as Seneca's *Medea* obviously did in the first
comparison. But in spite of startling, unexpected similarities, the differences in the dramatic conventions which shaped each play—the size
of the audience, the expectations of the audience—were so great that
to try to tabulate similarities would be an idle pastime. And yet in this
there was also an illumination. Shakespeare had drawn on a legendary
accumulation surrounding the story of Lear which was as complete,
with its threads of history and mythology, twisting villainy and explosive heroics, as the stuff that had made up the memories of the Greeks.
England's own archaic past looked all the more rich and energetic for
its exposure beside the past of Greece. This was worth pursuing. But
first came the need to know antiquity better.

My efforts toward that end began early and have proved to be un-
ending. At first, in those early seminars, everything seemed to be within reach. It did not take long, however, to discover that some things,
especially mythology, though obviously a golden heritage among all
people, was not likely to submit to the precepts of systematic study.
There will be no chapter on mythology per se in this book. The reliance
on mythology will be motivated by narrative fragments which, I trust,
will be self-explanatory. Instead there will be a chapter on Aesop and
the Aesopic fables. In practical terms some of the fables are the sky-
stories of mythology brought down to earth and sufficiently tamed to
become manageable. When animals speak, and speak plainly about the
errant ways of gods and kings, farmers and fishermen and metalsmiths,
and other animals, they enjoy the freedom of mythic action and yet
keep it in touch with the homely everyday business of human beings.
The fable called "The Cat and Aphrodite," for example, is a stunning
variant on the Medea myth reduced to ten lines. Myths themselves
were probably no more remote than common fables for a people who

had spent their lives living with memories of their mythological past. It takes no great act of the imagination to tell us how myths, unstable though they may have been, served as mnemonic devices for shepherds and sailors, and as mimetic tools for resolute or irresolute adventurers.

I am persuaded that the Aesopic fable illustrates the human psyche at the substructure level—the archetypal quandries which are reflected more evasively in the skyward-reaching mythic compositions. And beside that, the fable and the fabulous episode in whatever literary form each may have assumed, as every student of the Northern Renaissance in Europe soon discovers, were without doubt the most vital of direct ties coming down from ancient times. Dreams, shades of the dead, monsters and prodigies, soothsayers, mourners for Philip Sparrow, celebrants with Gargantua (a hero born in the mind of a celebrated university lecturer on Hippocrates and Galen)—these represent Greek and Roman infiltrations into the bookstalls and schools of London and Paris, though they entered by obscure routes and were often quaintly disguised. As for Aesop himself, it suffices to say that his fables served as textbooks for boys learning their languages when Shakespeare was a boy.

Lucian of Samosata, in his high-spirited *Dialogues* and other sophistical pleasantries, served similarly as a pedagogic mine for teachers of Greek. With Lucian we come to a later artificer of myths, and to another center of study where this present book found some of its origins: the home of Sir Thomas More with Erasmus as his guest. The Greeks, looked at from the point of view of these collaborators in the rebirth of the past, are no longer gowned in the paraphernalia of the Middle Ages, though they sometimes, as in *The Praise of Folly,* which Erasmus wrote in the house of Sir Thomas, use a Lucianic cast of characters to satirize the present social and ecclesiastical scene. Or in the *Adages,* which Erasmus made popular, or in the *Utopia* these intellectual adventurers imposed a Greek manner and a Greek sanity on the hurly-burly of their times. On their pages, thanks to them, Plato confronts brutal monarchs, and Aristophanes, the inhuman generals of armies. And soon thereafter, the Greeks of Erasmus and More became the easygoing companions of wily young scribblers, of George Gascoigne, of John Lyly, of Thomas Nashe, for instance.

In the context of these seminars the name Jacques Amyot, little remembered though it may be, ought to be somewhere near the forefront. The translator of that "stupid Boeotian with a golden mind," Plutarch, on whose works, the *Moralia* no less than the *Lives*, all of the Northern Renaissance pastured, leads us most directly to Montaigne, and to Thomas North and the drama, then to Philemon Holland and the rebirth of philosophical curiosity. The haunting memory of things that had been said with uncomplicated appreciation about the classics at the beginning of the modern era quickens the desire to resay it all, as far as would be possible with the few necessary revisions, in essentially that way once again.

From the two points of departure which the seminars brought out— the first, an English archaic tradition with its own peculiarities of mythology and religion, civil wars and roaming ships; and the second, a direct influx of Greek literature in the sixteenth century—from these there followed several closer studies. First of all of the ever-blessed Ben Jonson who *ate* his books when, running short on food, he had to sell them back to a book dealer. Whatever eventually happened to the books, he appears to have digested them before parting with them. We become aware of how deeply Jonson was immersed in multiform traditions; the best traditions then, the best traditions now: the local and immediate, the far off yet still immediate. And in particular to his credit was this, that in restoring Latin poetry to its proper place of honor, he freed it from the mistakes of the Senecans, and gave it in his English the vibrant tones of its Greek heritage. This was very impressive and disturbing: we found ourselves compelled to try to follow those roving footsteps of Ben Jonson's back into the "life of Memorie," deep into the cave where Persephone sits enthroned.

I hope this book will show its derivations from those not too distant authors who I would like to think are to some degree its sponsors. Among them I hope I may include Francis Bacon, Lord Verulam. For it is true that, if only in superficial sessions, the *Novum Organum* and *The Advancement of Learning* began opening the way to what was to be taken up in greater detail later on. "As to the opinions of the ancient philosophers, for example those of Pythagoras, Philolaus, Xenophanes"—how magnetic the names! and how well the passage continued!—"we could therefore wish there were, with care and judgment, drawn up a book of ancient philosophies, from the lives of the old philosophers . . . so that each philosophy would be drawn out and continued separate, and not ranged under titles and collections, as

Plutarch has done. For every philosophy, when entire supports itself, and its doctrines thus add light and strength to each other; which, if separated, sound strange and harsh.''

Sad to say, Lord Bacon's wish has not been fully gratified. We have reason to fear now that it never can be, in view of the fragmented condition of the source materials. Nevertheless the industry of scholars, preponderantly German scholars, at the beginning of the present century has produced with ''care and diligence'' the volumes which approach Bacon's requirements. But even so, with good collections at hand, there remains a never ending challenge to sort over again and again the pieces of philosophy that have survived, the way archaeologists arrange and rearrange the marble and terracotta and bronze pieces which have been brought up from underground, and most especially there remains an obligation to detect the *idola,* of Bacon's aphorism, of the tribe or the den, the marketplace or the theater, that may be lurking in any too plausible an interpretation of them.

The wish to combine the ''harsh and strange'' transmissions of Pythagorean doctrine and to see whether they might be fitted together in a single doctrine ''strong enough to support itself'' is a motive behind a great deal that is said in the course of this book. Not that Francis Bacon was the lonely instigator of an emphasis on Pythagoras. The name Pythagoras shines like the brightest of stars in the darkest of black-print pages that one comes across in the collections of the great libraries of Renaissance books.

So much for the more obvious studies of literature and science which led to what is contained in the chapters that follow. But to recollect those seminars as if the documents which were put to use told the whole story would be to mutilate the events of that time. There were individual people with individual minds presenting the materials and others working with what was being presented in a flow of exchanges. For many of us Francis Bacon was a creation emanating principally from the mind of Professor William Dinsmore Briggs of Stanford. As for the evasive works which I have referred to with affection as ''archaic'' in England: there goes with them the image of the bemused glance and deft wit of Professor Willard Farnham of Berkeley, California. The adventurous sessions on how the French reached back into the past for their own enrichment and then passed their gains on for everyone to enjoy were not exactly seminars. They were scenes in which a number of pages, printed and manuscript, were worked over on a round table shared with a cat in the apartment of Professor Emile Legouis in Paris.

Thus an induction leading to a fairly confident sense of Euripides and Aristophanes, Herodotus and Plutarch, with a handful of lyrics, some odds and ends of epics, came about in a fairly normal way. And then, at some point, normal studies became more and more like retracing an eroded caravan route which finally came out on a coastland with cities and valleys beautiful beyond compare. From the wayplaces where this book began, its migration was ended in the provinces of high archaism among the Greek-speaking peoples. And that is where it has been enjoying its long sojourn.

A great proportion of the beginning of these investigations was derived, as I say, from a good routine university curriculum. Not so several other topics which loomed just as large as literary topics on archaic horizons: the physical sciences, for example, and architecture, mathematics, philosophy, medicine. Here there was to be encountered one of the commonest of intellectual embarrassments. General histories, general lectures, insofar as they are general, are formed from a point of view which is post-Hellenic; they may become grand studies once they get launched, but often they are very feeble at the start, treading the archaic age as if it were a quagmire. Those which are not general are inclined to end where they began, not extending far enough down to reach us, not finding the ties to connect one science with another. There are exceptions; there are also ways to select and combine a certain number of titles. The comments in the appended reading list reflect an attempt to deal with this problem.

Perhaps skepticism about the worth of a good many reference works is a cavil. It may very well be impossible for any human being to produce a totally inclusive history of philosophy or of mathematics, when the best of philosophers and mathematicians seem to have come to an impasse in their search for truth, which requires a new language, a new set of symbols, a new form of notation. These refinements make communication even among colleagues difficult. Inevitably so, perhaps. Perhaps that is the way of truth. Certainly, as Parmenides found out, it is somewhat lonely up there. The present author will not be so foolish as to attempt a thoroughly coherent and extended argument. From fragments he will attempt to piece out just enough of the pot to give an idea of what it may once have looked like.

Archaeology is another science which invites a prolonged and shapeless pursuit if the layman attempts to study it in and for itself. But fortunately attention given even by a layman to a few sites will bespeak a great deal about neighboring sites, and, especially if it is in Asia Minor, the design of the plan of the city and the design of the life that was lived there. But in another way archaeology, or rather the view out over the rough sunlit expanse of a freshly cleared site, has been for the purposes of this book the one seminar that has been matched by no other. When highly visible materials lie directly under the eye and the unrehearsed commentary of a trained voice strikes the ear, then, in those moments, remembered passages that have been read and photographs that have been committed to memory cease being documents imprinted on sheets of paper; they start expanding into three, no, four dimensions, with the bright light of the Aegean dancing around them.

One other gentle, admirable force is responsible for the shape of the pages which, I hope, you are about to read. It is hard for me to speak of it with detachment. But in that period in Paris now long past, a novel, a simple fictional story about my home in California, came out of a little folding Corona typewriter when studious pages on the classical heritage should have been coming out of it. The novel, however, came out of that awkward small contraption rapidly, in a matter of months only. I inject this remark: I am now horrified at the notion of a young man thinking he could divide the forces within himself and write a book in so short a time.

In any event, a most generous older man, Ford Madox Ford, found a good deal of merit in the manuscript. He commended it to my publisher. What he did not mention to the publisher, he told me privately. "Bahkair," he said, choosing for some reason to affect a French pronunciation of my name, "you must, you really must try to do something about your style!" Well, to the shade of a dear, incredible man, I can say I have tried. Although I have learned, though unfortunately much too slowly, that trying too hard only makes matters worse, at least I have become reconciled to the condition that for some of us writing a book takes a long time.

A question has come up more than once. "Who do you think," I

have been asked, "will want to read a book like this?" I could understand perfectly what was implied. Had I not taken over a large field
which I had plowed and sowed to a crop like, let us say, saffron, without inquiring into the market for a product of exotic interest but of
dubious commercial value at the present time? For whom did I write
this? I wrote it, for example, for Caroline Gordon and her abiding loy-
alty to good workmanship wherever, whenever it may have occurred,
in whatever century; and for several editors whose attention always
turned toward these same values: for Andrew Lytle and William H.
Ralston; for Radcliffe and Eileen Squires; for my literary agent, Lucile
Sullivan, a woman who has observed many things with Hellenic clarity. There are many others; I know that there are more than I know.
Each is a unique reader, not one of them belonging to any category that
I have ever been able to imagine.

To the question "Who will read this book?" there was added a second question: "What is the book really about?" The book is, I shall
have to reply because of some inner necessity, a study in the foundations of a quite Pythagorean philosophy—an idealistic pragmatism or
a pragmatic religion—which I must claim as my own. If the reader
examines my remarks on mathematics under item 133 in the bibliographical essay, he will find as explicit a description of this Pythagoreanism as any I can manage to make. The gist of the matter is an
adjustment of the individual personality to a universal context into
which the personality merges and loses itself.

The readers to whom I may convey something of a philosophic character are exactly the same, I am sure, as the readers with the historical
and aesthetic sensitivities to whom I have just referred: they are individuals whose imperatives are not constrained to the here and now.

For them I have tried to write a narrative that takes the present back
into the past and brings the past down into the present. My only hope
is to review some old, turbulent years pleasantly; to set forth

> Sweet mix'd with sowre for the Reader, so
> As doctrine and delight, together go.
> —Horace, *De Arte Poetica*: trans. Jonson

Terra Bella, California

Opposite—The interior of the tunnel of Eupalinus. *This is a study in negative rendition of a photograph made in 1961 by Stephen Toulmin for Photo Tenis in Samos. I am grateful to Aline Moran for the extraordinary prints she has put at my disposal.*

1 · SAMOS: THE TUNNEL OF EUPALINUS

Scene: Hades. SOCRATES *and* PHAEDRUS.

PHDR. Do you remember the building of the walls at the Piraeus?

SOC. Yes.

PHDR. All that heavy machinery and heavy labor, while the flutes were leading the complicated motions with their music? The precision of the progress, how mysterious it was? And how evident? What a confusion at first! what a settling down to bold orderliness! what solidity, what rigor, were begotten between the string of the plumbline and the string stretched to level the flat tiers of the stones!

SOC. I cherish the memory. Those beautiful materials, those heavy stones! How much too, too light we have now become!

PHDR. And the temple near the Boreas altar? Do you remember it?

SOC. The temple of Artemis Huntress?

PHDR. Yes, that one. One day when we were resting near there, we talked about Beauty.

SOC. Yes, yes. Alas!

PHDR. I've become friend to the man who built that temple. He was an architect from Megara. His name was Eupalinus.

SOC. I wonder what an architect could find to do down here, where every project is only a memory. But, left as we are to endless conversation, I'd like to hear what he might say in favor of his profession.

PHDR. I've learned a few precepts from him. I don't know whether they would please you. As for me, they fascinate me.

SOC. Can you give me an example?

PHDR. What would you make of this? He is fond of saying: *No details ever remain in the final execution.*

SOC. I understand that, and I do not understand it.

PHDR. My temples, he says, must move people in the same way that some beloved object moves them. "Phaedrus," he said to me, "the more I think about my art, and the more I study it, the more I suffer and rejoice in architecture:—and the more I can feel what I was. I recognize that myself that I have been, with pleasure and certainty. I am amazed at the scope of my expectations, and at the exact correspondence between the promises I made in my head and the strength I found in my hands to accomplish my purposes, each and all.''

—Paul Valéry, *Eupalinos ou l'Architecte*

IN THE SUMMER OF 1964 Eupalinus of Megara, in my mind, was one of the most haunting and evasive of ancient phantoms. I knew that he had been called, during his time on earth, to the court of Polycrates, the tyrant of Samos, to design and oversee the building of a tunnel which Herodotus describes as one of the three greatest works—all of them Samian, as it happened—that he had seen in any Greek land. The commission to build the tunnel, which Eupalinus took over in about 540 B.C., required the drilling of an aqueduct five-eighths of a mile long through the solid rock of the ridge which mounts above Samos, the ancient capital and naval basin on the south side of the Ionian island. The magic of the tunnel consisted in this, that from hidden springs through hidden conduits it delivered water into the channel under the mountain for deployment on the seaward side to the fountains of the city. Waterworks like these were an extremely important asset in the everyday life of the inhabitants of the dry shelf above the harbor; in wartime they were the most indispensable of the resources necessary for withstanding a siege. In addition to the ingenious design of Eupalinus's tunnel and its harmonious conformity with the landscape, it was conceived on a truly heroic scale. It had been dug simultaneously from both ends, moving resolutely into the heart of the ridgerock and missing direct connection so narrowly that only a small bend and horizontal correction were required to join the flumes together.

How was it done? How could it possibly have been done? I must explain that as one who has lived most of his life in an arid coastland, with another sea washing its borders, the flow of water in artfully contrived channels has held a primitive fascination for me. My hills show too here and there the healed-over scars of a wandering pioneer ditch; and now also, here and there, enormous reservoirs at the mouths of giant tunnels. But what could have been possible in the sixth century before Christ?

In 1964 June Goodfield and Stephen Toulmin had finished their intensive study of the masterly engineering of Eupalinus. Their investigations demolished a fantasy that had been passed down among the gullible learned from the time of Hero of Alexandria. The Toulmins

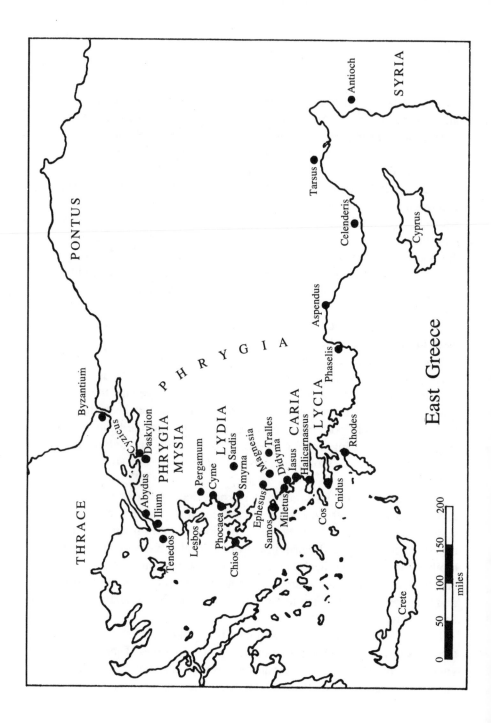

PONTUS

SYRIA

Antioch

Tarsus

Celenderis

Cyprus

Aspendus

PHRYGIA

Byzantium

Phaselis

Cyzicus

Daskylion

LYCIA

CARIA

Abydus

Pergamum

Sardis

Tralles

Rhodes

Ilium

PHRYGIA

LYDIA

Magnesia

Jasus

MYSIA

Cyme

Didyma

Halicarnassus

THRACE

Smyrna

Miletus

Cos

Tenedos

Phocaea

Ephesus

Cnidus

Lesbos

Samos

Chios

East Greece

Crete

miles

0   50   100   150   200

were able to show that by the very nature of the terrain—because of its exceeding roughness—no one could possibly have chased a series of elegantly constructed Pythagorean triangles in a survey around the mountain in order to establish the proper elevations and directions at the ends of the tunnel. Theirs was a wholly constructive finding. Pythagoras of Samos was far too great a mathematician to be saddled with a conjurer's flight of fancy.

Then there was a problem about the person of Eupalinus himself. An architect? The great architect in Samos was Theodorus, the builder of the tall-columned temple of Hera: after the tunnel, the second of the great works of the Greeks according to Herodotus, the third being the deep-water mole that protected the haven of Polycrates' boar-snouted battle fleet. But Paul Valéry insists, with an eloquence that haunts me, on the superb powers in the art of making fine buildings that Eupalinus the Megaran must have brought with him to these Aegean coasts. Now here again there is something that I should explain. I am Paris educated, somewhat deeply so, though in a sadly constricted way, after having been born and bred to these arid coastlands. As all the world knows, Paul Valéry wrote a poem in architectural periods about the fecund-sterile sea: I too had attempted something of a similar sort, though so far as I knew, my sea was only that of a particular wave-washed immobile beach of Baja California in a particular moment in history. I say, so far as I knew. Once, when I had newly gone over to Harvard, a Junior Fellow named Harry Levin asked me about the submerged ties that make one person take, if not his sustenance, then his courage; if not his substance, then his forms, from another—in my case, Valéry. In this suggestion I am glad to believe; it is hopeful, like an act of faith, but still I do not know. My beaches have always been desert beaches, more like those of Samos than of the French Mediterranean. Under the same rule I must say that, though I hope my worship of architecture is as faithful as Valéry's, I know it lacks that profusion of lovely detail in which his abounds. Mine is hardly more than a pavement-and-façade construction with something incalculable in it which wants to spring up into the high sunlight, like the wild bamboo.

Samos and Baja California: they are wildly disparate. The Ionians were decorative and articulate, while we, like our Indians, have been rudely covered and almost silent. But there are the strongest of ties among all of us. The religions of the Mediterranean world have been

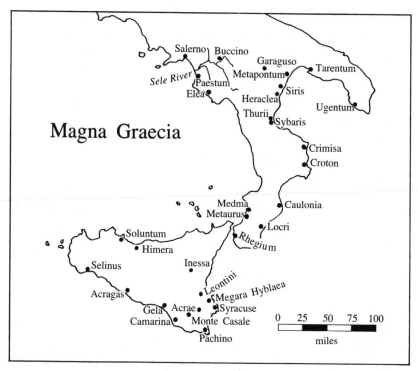

ever-renewing, like the rhizomes of the Heavenly Ailanthus which the Chinese miners scattered far and wide along the silent gold-veined draws in the foothills of my country. And the underground phenomena of history have produced sequences of outshoots which are clearly visible: Valéry and La Fontaine and Racine, Euripides and the Ionians, for example; Valéry and Viollet-le-Duc and Vitruvius and Theodorus of Samos; Shakespeare and Montaigne, Plutarch and Egypt and Aesop and the Seven Sages. But Eupalinus of Megara, and of Samos, stems from a particularly obscure root of history—unless it was a sort of orientalizing stock which combined the plastic aesthetics of Megara and Corinth with the fieldwork of Thales and the Milesians.

Which would not have been impossible! But it was puzzling when in 1964 the overnight steamer brought me and my family suddenly within sight of Samos itself. It was early morning when we went up on deck. There, across a bright band of sunlit blue water, a steep hillside bristled with spare scattered pines. A fellow traveler, our neighbor at the ship's rail, sighed aloud, aloud enough to make him sure we heard him. "Samos! Samos," he said, "for me it is the home to which I return!" I nodded sympathetically; but I noticed that he was addressing himself more to my daughters, who were bright-haired, fresh young women, than to me. One of them asked him where he had been living. He named a city in New Jersey, and added that he had been a big boy, grown up and yearning to fly off on his own, when he had left Samos. Now he was happy to return; he thought that he might never leave his native island again.

On the open dock at Karlovassi, where the ship called before proceeding to the modern capital of the island, Vathy, a small crowd churned slowly, the welcomers seeking out the ones to be welcomed, embracing and parting like motes in a sunbeam. Off to one side stood the young man and woman who had come aboard at one of the island stops the evening before. Their baby was in its mother's arms; their dog was on a thong beside them. The reed roof of their house, with a bundle topped by a pot and a pair of shoes, lay in a roll at their feet. Though obviously prepared for some vast new adventure, they seemed to be content just to stand on the dock, with their treasures and their heir close at hand, fascinated by the sight of a steamer preparing to depart. The man returning from New Jersey, after leaving us with ceremonious farewells, had stopped, lingering near a group of cafe tables where a pale plume of charcoal smoke and steam from octopus flesh rose from a brazier. It looked as if he made a small genuflection before he hurried on with his bulging suitcase toward a taxi.

All this went on as if it were happening in total silence despite the visible evidence to the contrary. The tumult of the ship's gear and tackle and the low organ chords of the Aegean winds blotted out momentary small clamors. This is the way it had been through the centuries, no doubt about it; this was the pattern of the human choreography that had always been enacted with the arrival of a ship at one landing place or another up and down the Mediterranean.

Before we cast off, the three bright-eyed Samian ladies who had boarded the ship in the Piraeus were already tilting and shimmering in their white dresses in the first of the switchbacks on the hillside track above the waterfront. Their little donkeys were almost invisible beneath them. A fourth donkey carried the black-clad old woman who had led the animals to the dock to meet them. A fifth followed. Its

The Vale of the Imbrasos: *on the island of Samos, above the port of Karlo-vassi. The uplands roll out in broad undulations, with many an olive grove on the hillsides and many of the famous vineyards crowded into the valleys. From the crest this is the view looking southward, down the course of Imbrasos, at the foot of which in the hazy distance there are deep springs beside a cluster of the willowy sacred lygos. Here, from the springs, the birth of the goddess Hera is said to have taken place. Later her sanctuary beside the Aegean embraced a great altar with the lygos still growing from its farther wall.*

saddle baskets were stacked high with sparkling, paperwrapped packages, the plunder that the ladies had fetched home from Athens.

II

Vathy is tiered on a hillside. At first glance there appears to be no hint or trace of Eupalinus to be seen here. The capital city presides over a broad harbor like many another small center of population in the islands; but this city is more open than most, and it has this difference: the mosaic of the white housefronts and the red-tiled rooftops is studded with orange trees. They stand out like plump green buttons, and along with them every so often a palm lifts an explosive green spangle. The effect is Asiatic.

Vathy is an unexcited city. An imponderably wealthy museum, on

Odos Aristarchoy, Vathy. *Aristarchus Street is one of the graceful flights of steps which hang like pendants against the slopes surrounding the harbor. The names given these streets bespeak the long memories of the Samians. There is a Herodotus Street, a Pythagoras Street; but this one celebrates the most astonishing genius of ancient times. Aristarchus initiated a Copernican description of the solar system and a theory of real but disembodied numbers which is now, and only now, beginning to make sense once again.*

the upper boundary of a humid botanical garden, is never overrun by visitors. On the pale stone towers of the abandoned windmills, no sails are set flying to attract tourists. The famous Samian wine, announced in large modern scrip on a sign across the bay, appears to be the product of a gleaming cooperative winery; otherwise activity on the waterfront is limited to local traffic. Caiques come in peddling vegetables; ferries permit the gregarious Greeks to go back and forth, visiting from island to island. The esplanade itself is jaunty with cafes and small shops, and the activities of pack animals, bicycles, and auto buses.

A block or two inland from the central square on the esplanade, the streets are likely to turn suddenly into a flight of stone steps at the foot of the hill or into narrow white-paved passages which seem to lead nowhere. Sometimes an avenue comes to a stop in a dead end, where garden walls flank wrought-iron gates, and above them Victorian houses with quizzical tall windows face toward the world, looking puzzled about the accidents of their origins and wondering about their proper present identities.

But Vathy is a city in which nothing ought to be taken for granted. The new and the old, the West and the Orient, blend mysteriously together. A narrow stone-paved mule track, dating perhaps from the time of Eupalinus, goes up and around the scrubby mountain to the south, and its course is roughly paralleled by a black-topped highway which follows along in expansive sweeping curves leading the motor-car comfortably to the shrunken scenes of the very early triumphs of the island and of Ionia.

Although Vathy has a reserved, inscrutable life of its own, centering as it seemed to me in the obscure festivals of the Eastern calendar, still it is a place where the passing stranger is honored and if he lingers on the island he is led into the living rooms of the houses. The visitor will become acquainted with prominent Samians, with Costas Ptinis, for instance, publisher of the newspaper and student of Ionian culture who will reveal, perhaps unintentionally, the feelings of triumph and despair in Samian patriotism: so many have been the victories, so numerous the debacles in twenty-five hundred years of recorded history. But on the other hand Dr. Serandos will be the picture of golden calm. For him there is no contradiction at all between his crisply modern hospital and his unagitated, politically neutral, pastoral island.

And here again there emerges another instance of the coherences which tie our past into a single whole. Dr. Serandos's white, red-roofed hospital rises behind a wall which is sheltered at one end by a thicket of olive trees. Within so recognizable a product of local architecture, no one should imagine that there may be ignorance of anti-biotics or an absence of modern apparatus. What is impressive in the hospital, however, is a philosophy of moderation in resorting to the latest in available prescriptions. Sometimes I have suspected that at home we often have recourse to the newest drugs almost automatically, without forethought as to what may ensue sooner or later for the patient. In Samos a law of ancient medicine—Nature must be finally "sufficient in all for all"—seems still to be respected.

The philosophy of Dr. Serandos I visualize as extending back to that of Democedes, who, like Eupalinus, was summoned (from Croton) by Polycrates. This philosophy would be related therefore to the philosophy of Alcmaeon and Pythagoras. It would have travelled with the archaic caiques in interchanges with the Cnidus of Eudoxus and the Cos of Hippocrates. And when Democedes was taken to Persia, it would have been transmitted—or retransmitted as revised—back to Egypt, and from there by the Moors in slow stages to Spain; thence to the New World, Baja California, Santa Barbara, Monterey. All this is of a piece. It can be read in its full coherence in the architecture of the Spanish missions which still stand; in their function and design, in their use of heavy materials which mount behind a wall that is shaded by the lithe, enduring, pale green leaves of the olive, all is of a piece.

III

Fortunately for us there happened to be visitors from Athens in Vathy, university people, and with them a daughter, Mary Burness, a beautiful young graduate student in archaeology, of an age and of a discipline which matched the vital facts about my daughters. But there was a profound difference between them and us. These people knew our language perfectly, as we certainly did not know theirs. We were limited to some ludicrous—to their ears—antique perversions of their words. *Eupalinus* was a name Mary would have nothing to do with. We could pronounce an ancient inscription as we saw fit; but as for the proper names which Greeks still remembered and often used, it had to be *Efpalinos*, no other way.

In the volubility all around us, the greatest share often came from Mr. Ptinis; but always only in Greek. A witty, exceedingly learned, outgoing man, he was exasperatingly unintelligible to us: we often flanked ourselves with our friends and tried to attend to interpretations coming from all directions.

This was the scene in which we found ourselves when at last we stood at the entrance of the tunnel of Eupalinus. It was to the northwest, on the edge of a ragged thin olive grove, above the sea-port village of ancient Samos, now Pythagorion. Fragments of the wall of Polycrates climbed the steep, brush-covered hillside above us, and in the other direction over the village and the narrow blue Strait of Samos lay Mycale, one of the most westerly of the rugged outthrusts from the Asiatic continent. The tunnel itself could be reached by descending a narrow set of stone stairs within a small square portal building. The

Eupalinus's Descent into the Tunnel. *With the architectural methods of Tiryns still lingering in his mind, Eupalinus built a corbeled ceiling to cover the stairs that led down to the mouth of the tunnel. This photograph was taken from below with the aid of flash equipment. The light on the steps is the sunlight that enters through the modern portal.*

staircase had been discovered more or less recently, late in the past century, Mr. Ptinis wanted the Burnesses to tell us. Before that time the entrance, with the tunnel behind it, had lain in total darkness for more than a thousand years; but then that was the way things went, we were assured, on an island which had been passed over and over again from the hands of one masterly thief to another.

Down the short flight of steps we went, one following another, picking our way with the help of the beams of flashlights, and on down through a passageway which was roofed over in the archaic style in which one stone slab is tilted against the top of its opposite number. For a while daylight filtered in behind us, and then darkness gathered itself thickly around the small animate electric beams. Suddenly, beyond a curve in the passage, a blinding column of sunlight fell in front of us from a sort of chimney which rose into the brightness of the out-

Archaic Goddess in Full Dress. *Hera, in her oriental extraction, was one of a number of east Greek variants on Cybele. She wears a tall, horned miter; her canes support her extended arms, her traditional peacocks are at her side. This photograph is a copy of one of the large bronze coins which the Romans permitted the Samians to issue during the Imperial period. The original for the iconography on the coin was probably a fairly small and crude wooden figure which was elaborately decorated.*

side world. After that, came the tunnel and complete darkness again. It was a squarish burrow, about the size of a man's reach overhead and from side to side. All that our darting lamps showed to us was a pathway on the ledge to the left, and to the right a deep slot, far down in the bottom of which was the tiled conduit which had once carried water from the secret springs to Samos, the renowned metropolis. The horizontal ledge and the perpendicular narrow chasm continued as far as we cared to pursue them, always leading onward into the gloomy inwards of the mountain.

Outside the sun had never poured down on the world with such brilliance.

Then Mr. Ptinis, waving his arms and refusing to believe that we could not understand what he was saying, conducted us via crowded taxi to the Heraion. There in that massive ruin antiquity was over-

Landfall at Cape Colonna: *the solitary column which dominates the horizon. All around it on the site of the early sanctuary, Venus bushes are creeping over the litter of marble that came from the great temple and altar of Hera and the secondary shrines dedicated to Apollo and Artemis and to Hermes and Aphrodite; from treasuries and monuments, even a Byzantine church. Only Mount Mycale, rising from Asia in the background, stands secure.*

whelming. After the rattling taxi and the cross-cutting voices, the voice of our host had slowed down noticeably and had fallen into the gentle tones which usually go along with colloquial speech. Interpretations were delivered quietly to our ears. This low patchwork of stones was prehistoric, we learned, while this higher one which stretched out quite a little more was part of the great altar. Once in the protection of this altar the lygos had grown; it was that particular willow tree which was sacred to Hera and her more primitive forerunners, or perhaps we should call them her earlier incarnations. Close by were parts of the floors and foundations of archaic temples, elegant structures which had created a setting for the colossal Ionic temple, built by Theodorus, to honor Hera.

With one exception all buildings are completely leveled alike. One column from the great structure which dates from the time of Poly-

crates remains standing; the drums are imperfectly aligned, some of
the top ones have fallen, but still the column which has survived is so
conspicuous a white shaft that sailors have named this bulge in the
coastline Cape Colonna.

On every side are the exquisitely worked drums of other columns,
capitals and lathed bases, moldings and revetments—all are stacked in
the neat arrangements in which the German archaeologists left them.
But coarse tall weeds crowd round both the remnants of gigantic architecture and the small human being who seeks to intrude. Nature it may
be enjoys the ugliness of weeds; it seems obviously to prefer darkness.
It intends beyond all doubt to lay an overgrowth on the glittering ruins
of the sanctuary of Hera, turning the site once again, if possible, into a
gloomy meadow of asphodel.

Mr. Ptinis was not content until we had inspected the third of the
architectural wonders that had impressed Herodotus so decisively.
Here again antiquity—or more particularly—the Archaic Age is still
coolly visible in the deep-sea mole which Polycrates caused to be
thrust far out, half-enclosing the bay around which his peerless civilization had fashioned its dwelling place. This barrier is constructed on
a base of cyclopean stonework. Although the narrow top has been
paved and perhaps a stone replaced here and there, the structure is as
it was two and a half millennia ago. But the great marvel is not the
massive fitted stones which come in sight as a swell recedes, nor the
often measured great depth of the water, but something very different
from all that, as a man of Costas Ptinis's intelligence knew very well.
It is what you see when you look down on it from a little height up on
the hill. The famous, enduring mole is actually a slender, delicately
curving string of masonry reaching out into the sea. In architectural
terms it is a perfect example of what the ancient Ionic order intends
to be: a combination of the opposites of lightness in appearance with
enormous actual weights, marrying the pairs, water and air, darkness
and sunlight.

After so generous and intensive a tutoring from my contemporaries,
the Samians and the experienced visitors alike, what does a man do?
A man, I mean, who has been half-blinded by sun and marble in the
Heraion, who has squinted at the lean geometry of a deep-water mole,
and has peered like Tiresias into a tunnel—what does he do to find the

A Haven for the Fleet of Polycrates. *The mole which sheltered the naval base curves outward in the center of the picture; the ancient city is lying huddled in its very modest contemporary guise at the foot of the mole. This is the scene as it looks now from a portal in the sixth-century B.C. fortifications, some halfway up the ascent of Mount Castro. The tunnel of Eupalinus, beginning on the edge of the flatland below, pierced the mountain which rises on the left.*

axiom which will fit at least the general pattern of his experience, and keep it fresh? He lies awake at night more than he likes to; he tries retracing his steps in the daytime.

Take the harbor mole, for instance. It is one thing when viewed with the perspective which the observer ordinarily gives it. It is another thing when the observer pokes around on the broad quailike base from which it takes off into the outer waters. Here he finds himself in a shipyard and in an important way closer to the sea than the mole itself has taken him. Six or eight boats are propped on stays in no particular order. Mostly they are of the caique type, exciting in their shape, high in the stem and stern, "like the horns of oxen," as Homer describes them. Some were in need of repair, one was in the process of being built, and one was the strangest boat I had ever noticed. It had a flat stubby prow which became a wicked beak at deck level. While I was wondering about it, visualizing it as a boat which could attack and quickly put a boarding crew onto the deck of another boat—consciously designed perhaps to be a cove-lurking pirate ship—the image of the caique which was under construction began dominating my images of the other boats. Without a thought in my head but a curiosity in my legs I wandered back toward the shipwrights who were attaching and smoothing the new planking on the underside of the hull.

One of the carpenters was using an adz, a short-handled, moderately lightweight, curved-bladed adz to smooth out the sheeting on the bottom of the boat. Once Odysseus, on Calypso's island, built a great raft. He used an adz to shape the timbers, as Homer is at pains to tell us, and along with it several other tools: the mortising, drilling and pinning, being the crux, according to Homer, of the shipwright's art. "That," I said to myself, "that is an adz!" And then naturally I hastened to look at the joints in the rib structure of the caique.

Since the planking was only partly in place, the mortising was in plain sight. I wondered why I hadn't seen it in my first glance, it was so remarkable a feature in the design of the boat. Under the stern the ribs rose up quite high from the kelson, flattened out, and then rose sharply upwards again. But as the sequence of ribs proceeded forward the upwards lift from the kelson became less and less high while the curve of the hull became broader and broader. From midships forward the sequence of shapes followed a reverse pattern. The shape achieved was that of the oxen-horned, "well-curved, broad-beamed freight

Homeric Craftsmanship in the Twentieth Century: caique under construction in Pythagorion in 1964. On the left is a view of the framework and planking from the stern; on the right, the swelling midships and rising bow. On the ribs the mortised joints and the trail marks of the adz may be seen. The knots and unevennesses of the local materials are also visible, but with caulking and paint the humble Aleppo boards are metamorphosed into the hide of a faithful barque.

ship," again in the appreciative words of Homer. The well-curved structure was accomplished in the two-man shipyard in Pythagorion by lapping tenon and mortise at each of the sharper bends and pegging the joints together. The ax, the adz, and the auger were still the skilled shipwright's tools; and the mortise, though eventually it gets planked in, is still his prettiest piece of showmanship.

Homer does not give Odysseus a saw, possibly because Odysseus didn't need one to build a raft, possibly because he couldn't have worked a suitable one alone. On the mole at Pythagorion they ripped the planking with a saw. The logs were never straight; so the sawyers followed along with the curves of their materials. They came out with crooked boards of course; but crooked boards, with picking and choosing, are easier to fit to the hull of a boat than straight ones.

Planking the ship in any event is a relatively simple matter; framing the hull is a challenge to the builder's art. In this phase of the construction of ships there were problems which led me to discover that Theophrastus in his *History of Plants* speaks with praise of the *torneia* or crooked timbers which are selected for shipbuilding. Here is a realm in which the crooked is preferred to the straight, and the stockpile of logs bent in all directions made a scene which I found hard to adjust to. But they have a beautiful archaic logic about them. Each rib, and each section of each rib, differs in size and curvature from any other, except for its mate on the opposite side. So the builders look over the curves in each log, assign it to a place in the design, square it off with ax and adz, cut the mortises which will tie it in with its neighboring member, leaving extra thickness to round out and reinforce the fitted joints.

There still must be men who can go out into the scantily wooded mountains of Samos and see an endless variety of shapes in the wind-bent Aleppo pines; and among them there will be some unique forms which they will take possession of and build into a good but modest ship, following Homeric procedures all the way. By seeking out their particular hamadryads, rather than denuding one slope after another, they may have won the good will of the minor divinities who have rewarded them with an island that has remained green.

For just plain attractiveness, the tree-shaded waterfront of Pythagorion, with its tiny shops and pleasant cafes, is without compare. We often went over from Vathy just to sit there in the late afternoon.

Sometimes someone came along, or went over with us, with whom we made conversation. But often the quai and the other cafe tables were all but deserted. And so was the harbor. The old basin, which had sheltered some of the great fleets of the world in times past, has begun looking so empty in recent centuries, its banks so uncluttered, that someone, noticing the shapeliness which the famous mole had given it, nicknamed it the frying pan, *Tigani*. And the name *Tigani*, wry as it must have sounded, stuck to it until quite recently, when the twenty-five hundredth birthday of Pythagoras came round and the honored name *Pythagorion* was conferred upon it.

On the waterfront, just outside the lesser, eastern mole, Pythagorion has an attractive small beach where it is quite possible that Pythagoras demonstrated number theories with pebbles on a flat ledge and used his staff to trace out a triangle in a semicircle in the sand at the edge of the wavelets. It is quite possible, it is much more than quite possible, that Cleopatra dabbled a golden foot in these limpid waters. The world may never have seen festivities so lavish as those which Eastern dependent kings proffered before those semisecluded lovers, Anthony and Cleopatra. Here, here on the rim of the frying-pan.

One evening we took a walk around the esplanade to see how progress was going on the new caique. All seemed to be in order; several new pieces of sheeting had been put in place during the day. Then we entered a minor street leading up an incline toward the Church of the Metamorphosis, which inevitably must stand on the site of one or another of the most important early structures, possibly the citadel, probably a citadel which housed the long-remembered palace of Polycrates. The street, I soon realized, was very narrow. Many people were out, enjoying the evening breeze which was coming up off the harbor and sea. They were sitting on their threshold stones, talking back and forth with neighbors; their children were bunched together, playing their games. In another few moments the street made a turn and was more narrow and more and more filled with people. There were chairs and tables, clothes on clotheslines overhead, old women in black dresses, children everywhere, men in workclothes, and the workclothes seemed to be the kind that were worn in the fields in the country. The last stretch under the church looked, to my eye, impassable. But not so. Room was made for us to slip through, everybody smiled and nodded cordially to us and then reconverged into their groups as before. No one likes to intrude. We simply were not prepared to blunder into a tiny congested island of humanity in the center of a small village.

Even in that moment though, I think we felt we had not intruded. We had been looked at with what had seemed to be some pleasure and interest and hardly even with surprise. Later I imagined that we had encountered people who had not as yet broken the habit of living in a walled city. But why hadn't they? They plainly weren't poverty stricken. They may have preferred a compact, snug society. But as congenial as they appeared to be, nevertheless, in that fading daylight, in that narrow passage, they seemed to be so unreal that I continued to wonder about them, until studying the life of Eudoxus suggested at last an answer.

A vision which had to do, in some obscure way at first, with the tunnel of Eupalinus came to me in the night. I think that what suggested this byplay of ideas was a recollection of the dazzling points of light which came from the fairly distant shore of Samos after our ship had left Karlovassi that first Sunday morning. Someone with binoculars said there were people; well, obviously, they were boy scouts on the beach and they were playing a mirror against the passing ship.

Eventually this incident came back to me to resolve itself into a brilliantly gleaming silver coin in the center of a very dark, perfectly circular setting. But after another moment I could see the head of a child brightening the dark rim and at the same time eclipsing the shining coin. And then came the memory of the sunny day in a much earlier year, a year that had been so dry that we planned to set up a new pump on an abandoned well. But a problem was troubling us. What was the condition of the metal casing that lined the well? Was it still intact, or had the walls caved in? Since inspection was in order, someone got a mirror from the bathroom, brought it to the car and we drove off. Standing around the open well-head, we turned a stream of pure sunshine down into the bore, and the sunlight revealed the silver coin of water, perfectly circular, perfectly centered in its encasement, looking like a silver Delia in her full glory, until one of my own young Delias got her head in the way. She bounced back, instantly removing the concavity. It was magical. And yet sometimes we had also inspected a horizontal pipeline, reflecting the sun from one mirror onto another and projecting the beam forward into the pipe; that was more magical but ordinarily too awkward to be of much use.

Light Well that Dates from the Sixth Century B.C.: *possibly the oldest struc-*
ture of its kind in the world. Sunlight from above ground drops directly on
the beginning of the bore, which enters the mountain at this point and con-
tinues straight north until it emerges near the springs of Agiades. Whatever
else may have been its purpose, the shaft of light forms an orientating beacon
for anyone following the narrow ledge beside the sunken aqueduct.

Now that I thought about it, I considered the mirror to be one of the
glories of the Archaic Age. Amasis of Egypt, as the museum bore
witness, had presented Polycrates of Samos with some splendid examples of the mirror-maker's art. And as for the art of thinking about
things, things such as mirrors, Anaxagoras had put in articulate form,
early in history, the explanation of a phenomenon which had doubtless
been descried more or less clearly even earlier. The moon, he maintained, is a mirror reflecting the light of the sun, and registering in the
form of an eclipse the fact that from time to time the head of Gaia gets
in the way.

A day or so later we returned to the old tunnel of Eupalinus, armed
with two modern mirrors, the best we could find. Now it was possible
to stand above the light-well which had surprised us and impressed us

on the occasion of our first visit, and with one mirror in hand to pick up the image of the sun and reflect it down the flue, catching it on the second mirror and turning the streak of pure sunshine into the depths of the tunnel. Now, now indeed, we had the beam which would pierce the darkness. At will we could make the ray lose itself in the distance, while casting a warm glow in the bluish walls, so straight was the bore; or we could make it paint an area here and there with a brightness which showed in the ribbons of shadow, the gentle irregularities that had crept into the carving of the ceiling and sides and deeply cleft floor.

And so, with fire stolen from Helios playing on the undulating crystalline surfaces, we could read in the tilt of the walls and the angle of the ceiling that the tunnel diggers had gone along with the natural cleavages of the strata in the stone, giving and taking and rounding off their progress as dancers might. That's the way the work had gone forward, leaning a little, swaying a little, following the rhythm of the material. This was workmanship which is understandable. It was like the shipbuilders' work. And it is our comfort to know that workmen who work like that can never be remote from us.

A mirror, as I say, is as simple as it is wonderful. I have no doubt that the man from Megara, Eupalinus, set up a mirror of his own under the light-well, establishing it on an immovable base at a fixed angle so that it could throw out ahead of his miners a target spot, which the men digging were always in pursuit of. Nor do I doubt that, following a guide-line of surveyor's pickets transversing the ridge, with a mirror and a long water-level he checked the levels and directions which the layout of a double attack on both ends of the tunnel required.

For me, when we dragged the fire of the sun into the darkness under the earth, the effect was both bizarre and uncanny. The likeness of what had been shown me here with what had been shown me in so personal a way years before, when my children were small, came as a shock. I had to ask myself how unbroken the tradition behind the mirror trick might be and whether the boy scouts had been trying to spell out in centaur language some message for my benefit. At the same time I had to wonder whether violating the lower, properly sunless depths of the earth was right. If I was trying to recover something that belonged to the dead of two and a half thousand years ago, I very nearly succeeded. The ways of men effectively at work came awesomely to life in the bedazzled tunnel. For the moment it was as if I were a guest in Persephone's own luminous cave.

But the ways of men coming awesomely to life out of the depths of bygone centuries is also a victory for us who for the moment at least do not stand nakedly in the fearful isolation of the present.

We came up the steps and paused near the entrance portal. I was not quite ready and willing to move on out into the full blaze of sunlight pouring so abruptly and brusquely upon the face of the world.

"Look, Daddy! Candles!" My younger daughter was tugging at my arm. "Votive candles!"

"Yes, candles!" I said. There were more than a few small candles, some burned down almost to stubs, deposited in the crevices in the rough wall just inside the entrance.

"I think they show it's sort of a shrine. They're here for people to light when they come in. How else would they ever be able to go down to the tunnel?" my daughter said.

As for me, I suppose I will never know what was the truth about the candles. Were they there only in recognition of the practical fact that the passing visitor, Samian or other, would be unlikely to have a flashlight at hand? Or was it that he, the same passing visitor, might have felt it only proper to make the return to the past with the aid of a candle, one that has been used before and left behind, as he would use it and leave it behind again, to help someone else find the way to make the descent?

It is said that the walls of the Piraeus rose to the music of flutes. For the first time, only after having gone in and out of the tunnel, have I felt confidence in my sense of the poetry of Anacreon and of the poet's place in the affairs of Samos. His flute led in the rich adventurous architecture, both above and below ground. At least for me it is important to know that when Eupalinus came down the hill he could have taken his place with Anacreon in the men's dining hall, and Anacreon would have reminded him of his buildings; if they are to sing, how troubling and beautiful they must be!

> A ball struck me on a sunny bounce
> When tow-headed Eros batted it
> Straight at me, double-daring me
> To make love to the girl in the vivid slippers.

The Strong Coastline of an Ancient Thalassocracy: *the straits of Mycale viewed from the east. On these waters occurred the scenes of Polycrates' long-remembered naval enterprises. However, since a temple of Poseidon dominated the point of land in the center of the picture and since the twelve Ionian cities all honored this god in particular, these waters must also have brought caiques here with visitors in a festive mood, like that which prevailed on occasion at Delos. At present there is hardly more to catch the eye than an empty channel of the dark-shaded sea, with Turkey on the farther side: only that, but a sight of perfect, dramatic, Mediterranean beauty.*

> A beauty from urban Lesbos, she!
> She scowled at my hair—it is white—
> Picked up the ball and scampered back
> To smirk at a beauteous girl-friend.

Roughness and grace and honey making. When the busy moles are at work in the tunnel and the lofty temple of Hera is rising, the whole hive may be heard singing.

IV

The whole hive could be heard singing, and the oars splashing through the sea. This is a myth that a young Samian told us about the great days of Samos. He owned a '58 Chevrolet and was our friend and taxi driver. Mary Burness translated his words for us.

We were to observe carefully, very carefully, he said, a flat rock of an island a short distance offshore at Daphnis, near the pavilion where we were having lunch. This was the landing place that had once served the luxurious caiques of temple visitors and the rafts of fine marble coming to the Heraion.

Samos once had the best ships in the world, the tale began. Their ships were fastest, their oarsmen were without rivals. They ruled the sea.

"A thalassocracy," I said carefully.

"Keep still, Daddy," said my younger daughter.

The Samians had great confidence and daring when they took their ships to sea. They made boasts when they came home. One day, finding no one who would enter into contest with them, they challenged Helios. They would take one of their swift black ships out and row around the island, they told Helios, and return it to its harbor before he could take his car to the end of its course in the western seas. So in the morning they sped from their harbor toward Helios at the very moment when he rose out of Asia. They rowed mightily through the day, turning the western end of the island in the early afternoon. But Helios drew ahead of them. He disappeared below the horizon just as they reached Daphnis. At that moment the ship and the rowers were turned into stone. As we could see for ourselves, they were still sitting there, the boat still pitching forward, the men still straining at the oars.

Opposite—Early Cult Statue of Hera: *the goddess framed in the entrance of a miniature Ionic temple. Roman Imperial bronze coin from Samos. 27 mm. in diameter.*

2 · THE IONIANS AND THE HOUSING OF THEIR GODS

Scene: Hades. EUPALINUS *to Phaedrus*.

O Phaedrus! when I design a dwelling (be it for the Gods, be it for a man), when I search for its form in myself, endeavoring to fashion an object which will best please the eye and excite the mind, harmonizing reason and comfort, —I must tell you this strange thing, *that my own body seems to count in it.* I think, if you please, that the body, just the body, is an admirable instrument, of which the living though they live in it, make but little use. They draw on it for its pleasures, they suffer its pains, they allow it its indispensable acts; they think that their body is they, yet they forget its existence. . . . Nevertheless they are part of what they see and what they touch: they are the stones, and the trees; they have weight, they lift weight. They often sag down, yawning; but often they rise up and eject thunder! So, when asking myself about the justice of my deliberations when I was a living architect, I noticed that all of my resolutions were capable of changing as if of their own accord when they sprang from the materials which came to my hands. What I had thought, could be; and it could be made to spread out so that it uncovered new sorts of order in each new problem. I could begin where I had finished the day before and then go a little farther. I wasted no time in reveries. Never in the shapeless provinces of my soul did I build imaginary edifices, because in comparison with the real they are as chimaeras and gorgons are to the shrewd beasts of the fables.

My little temple—if you only knew! In that little thing, with its four columns and utterly simple style, I built an ever-renewing memory of a very bright day. My delicate shrine is the mathematical image of a temple girl in Corinth, whom I was so fortunate as to have loved. It copied, as in a metamorphosis, her exact proportions and it continued to return to my eye what she had first given me.

—Paul Valéry

With the indulgence of the reader I will claim as the premise for this chapter the sort of proposition which Vitruvius established in his *De Architectura*. Architecture is concerned, as Paul Valéry reasserts, with much more than the foundation, the walls and roof, the columns and pediments, of a building. What goes inside the building, what surrounds it on the outside, has to be regarded as inseparable from its design; and ultimately, from my point of view, if it is a Greek temple, the soul of the people who are building it and fitting it out for their gods presides over the structure. It is a religious expression, and I hope that heaven will forgive me for trying to elucidate it as such.

In thinking closely about Greek temples one has to rely on an imperfect blending of the little that is still to be seen up and down the Mediterranean and the plenty that is to be gathered from reference books. These being the implacable circumstances, it will be convenient, I believe, to give in the notes appended to this book an account of the particular books which seem at the present time to be most representative of the excellences of ancient architecture. The books of greatest interest include a number of exquisitely learned monographs and many brilliantly illustrated volumes, ranging from European booklets and American paperbacks to sumptuous New York and London folios, sometimes in translation, often with the printing and platemaking done in the presses of the Continent. There is material in abundance for the study of the objects in which the ancient world expressed its religious genius.

The new visibility of the past is what I hope to convey in the narrative which follows. It is as if anyone working his way through the new books may sometimes catch the gleam of the flame on the altar and smell the smoke and hear the foot beat and the chant—thanks to archaeology, the camera, and the book industry. Of course the new books require the support of the old books. If Miss Gisela Richter made Pausanius more informative, the contrary is also true. The Loeb Library's *Description of Greece* hangs like a stiff and pleasantly distorted backdrop behind most of what can be learned about the world of the Hellenes.

To have written about "The Ionians and Their Gods" just a few years ago, before the triumphs of archaeology and color photography, was almost inevitably to have been cramped by the tradition of Sir James Frazer and Jane Harrison, in which, it has seemed to me, religion became a complex of ancient myths and rituals, rather murky goings-on, of more interest for their novelty and remoteness than for their pertinence to our own understanding of ourselves in relation to the past. But now the evidence of visible masonry seems to give a more just sense of Greek preoccupations than literary allusions to rituals, which are often confused and hard to date. For example, the temple of Sunium poised on its promontory south of Athens, by its definite compact clarity against the sky, challenges even today the stranger looking up at it from the angle of an approaching ship, reminding him of what were once presumed to be the inviolable prerogatives of Attic citizens; while in a concentration of white shafts at Didyma or on the island of Samos the gigantic marble jewels which have toppled among the Venus bushes and the reeds in the bright sea glitter, bespeak, even today, a beauty and a leisured reasonableness the like of which is hardly to be found anywhere else.

Religion is always the biggest problem. A fresh look at a structure of beliefs which flourished at the beginning of our history as westerners founding a new civilization would surely be pertinent to the uneasy religious temper of the twentieth century. This look would be an attempt to see into an almost forgotten state of mind that prevailed before Plato and Aristotle planted, consecutively, the concepts of eternal Ideas and an eternal Mover which exist beyond space and beyond time: which is to say, quite a while before Christianity undertook to marry these premises with Hebrew monotheism. An inquiry might profitably limit itself to the preclassical period, to the interval which was at once the time of the ripening of the finest archaic arts and of the beginnings of science and philosophy in Ionia. The island of Samos can serve most conveniently as representative of Ionia, and the forms of Greek architecture as the nexus of the whole subject.

II

The ancient Samians, along with all Ionians, were great makers of festivals, great builders of sanctuaries, and great honorers of the gods. With the arrival of archaic times in the seventh and sixth centuries

B.C., their religious observances seem to have shed the grimmer vestments of the primitive cults and to have become relaxed and easy, lavish, elegant, cheerful, though never giving a man much reason to be optimistic about his ultimate end. The human being was turned loose. And left more or less on his own, he could do nicely except for that one last pang, which was inevitable anyhow. The gods often befriended him, and he was happy to render them their dues of gratitude. It was an informal contract, lacking both the fierce spirituality of the creeds with which we have grown familiar and equally the dark sensualism of the earlier rites. It affected all manifestations of eastern Greek life, not excluding the inquiries of the philosophers—the worldly, mimetic, wonder-inspiring, and very social thing that it was. And it is with it in mind as such, as a well-tuned civilizing instrument, that I undertake to describe the affair of the Ionians with their gods and the style of the things with which they thought it proper to surround them.

It has been argued that this affair was not religious, that this breed of east Greeks was not religious at all. Obviously they were a people who were strongly inclined toward irony and skepticism, and toward delight in an erotic "Milesian" sort of tale: "Ionian minstrels were fundamentally irreligious," in the judgment of Martin Nilsson; "the holy wedding of Zeus and Hera is made rather a sensual love affair." Nilsson, however, as a specialist in the most primitive phases of religion, was seeing the problem from an oblique point of view. Burlesque, as in Homer, did no doubt play fast and loose with the ancient sanctities. But from another point of view we can see that Greek society, once it became literate, learned to relish a sort of vivacious profanity, an errant levity, just as many robust societies have enjoyed their own extravagant Feasts of Fools, in which decorum is turned upside down. And contrariwise only the most cramped of republics would consider the expurgation of Homer an ideological necessity. For people of open minds and open temperaments the gods could hardly be taken so literally as to make spoofing a capital offense.

Whether the brighter Ionians were finally religious or irreligious, we won't try to decide, the distinction being at best a matter of lonely, subjective opinion, and of a piece with man's native irrationality toward other men and their beliefs. But the plain objective fact is that celebrations pertaining to the Olympian cults went on and on in Ionia, undiminished and not visibly corrupted in the period of skepticism and mockery. Our purpose is to inquire into the poise that controlled these celebrations and the relation of this poise with other manifestations of these people, such as their disinterested curiosity about the world, their equanimity toward awesome phenomena, their love of beauty, and their devotion to the powers of the mind and the hand and the senses all fused together in the production of buildings and the fittings for buildings. We will try to say who the Ionians were, and how, in the first blaze of our fragile civilization, they consolidated so many things with such enviable success.

III

The people whose ancestors brought their language and customs to the westernmost seaboard of Asia believed that their stock originated on the mainland of Greece—in fact, in Athens itself, according to Herodotus, their Athenian descent being proved by their calendar and their practice of maintaining old clan ties in the annual feast called Apaturia. Other very strong traditions connected some groups with Pylos, Nestor's famous Pylos, and enlightened Argolis, and a few lesser places. The Samians associated themselves with ancient Argos and their Hera with the Argive Hera. The non-Athenian contingents may have consolidated their Ionic characteristics during a half-remembered stopover in Athens. In any event migrants started moving out eastward from the mainland, so that sooner or later Ionians in the broader sense of the name found themselves scattered along the island route between Attica and Asia Minor, with Delos and the temples of Apollo forming the axis on which their comings and goings turned. Most probably they followed a course which travellers have always followed, hopping from island to island as did your steamship of yesterday, touching Syros and Mykonos, making the devout excursion to Delos, continuing on to Icaria and finally Samos, whence they spread out up and down the neighboring coastal lands, taking up their habitations and intermarrying with the native women.

The first migrations must have happened in the earliest Dark Ages, around 1000 B.C., when the Dorians were breaking into the central establishments in the west, and naturally must have included many bypaths. But before long the migrating Greeks had planted themselves firmly in the centers which were soon to comprise the Panionian league, and by archaic times this circle of cities had become Ionia in the narrow sense of the term. The league consisted in an exclusive alliance of twelve brilliant, small and not-so-small places, the resounding roster of which from north to south runs as follows: Phocaea and Clazomenae on the Gulf of Smyrna, now Izmir; Erythrae, opposite Chios; Teos, Lebedos, Colophon, and Ephesus, along the ragged coast above the swampy delta of the Cayster river, now known as the "Little Maeander"; Priene, Myus, and Miletus on the flat lands and marshes of the Greater Maeander above and below lofty Mount Mycale; then, just outside the coastline, the two great islands, Chios and Samos. Eighty-five miles of the globe's surface stretched between the northernmost and the southernmost settlement. Pretty tight quarters, one would think, considering all that was to go on there.

Even in early times the newcomers prospered. One of their number, in a period which is now quite obscure, put precisely everything which was most important to their minds and hearts together for them in the celebrations of those ancestors of theirs who had had to do with the sack of Troy: Homer, if not from Chios then from somewhere not far away, brought them an unlimited wealth of consciousness which they were bound to share promptly with all Greeks and before long with a multitude of barbarians.

In a similarly obscure interval the first of the great works of Samos was taking shape. In the early eighth century a hundred-foot, central-columned structure dedicated to Hera is identifiable as the earliest temple in Ionia, and in view of its size and its subsequent evolution, it appears to be a prototype as well of the great temples of the Greek world. An Ionic way of doing things, which was at once spacious and full of fine detail, took hold of the imaginations of these people. Under the generous unagitated beauty of the goddess Hera, they learned to underscore and enrich the traditions they had brought with them from the plains below Mycenae. They were stimulated by the strange styles of their oriental neighbors. With the clarities of sunlight and sea hanging around them, they were ready to go to work on all sorts of arts.

IV

In the famous days of Samos, particularly during the middle and second half of the sixth century B.C., we can visualize, on the south side of the island, a few miles of marble-sanded, well-watered seashore lying under green steeply-terraced hills, with the cluster of white-columned temples at one end and the gray-walled city of Polycrates at the other. Between the two stretched that remarkable feature of ancient places, a Sacred Way. Today the grandeurs of the Heraion are still sketched out in the drums and blocks of stone scattered on the ground; and though the palace of Polycrates, which provoked admiration for a number of centuries, has now disappeared, there still remains the neat little naval basin which sheltered his boar-snouted warships. But of the Sacred Way and its wonders no sign is left.

It was a broad ribbon of dry pavement which on leaving the city passed tomb and grave monuments that were works of exquisite artistry. As memorials to the dead the stylized portrait statues of naked *kouros* and elegantly draped *kore* would have been impressive; and curiously striking from our point of view, and wonder provoking, would have been the *stelai:* simple tall shafts of marble which seem to bespeak archaic orderliness at its most powerful. The graceful white shaft stood taller than the man it commemorated; usually it was un-decorated on Samos, merely naming the deceased and rising plain and polished to a crowning sculpture. There on the top Ionic volutes in various combinations supported a flat, widely spreading, perfectly symmetrical palmette. It is as if the gravestone wanted to make only one comment: "Just like the race of leaves, is that of man" (*Iliad* 6. 146), recalling vanished life in the summary form of the uplifted palm leaf.

Passing on across a strip of fertile soil where the grape has flourished for no one knows how long, the roadway led among statue groups into the precincts of the temple. Those of the statues which have survived more or less intact, like the Geneleos group in the Vathy museum, are large, forcefully imagined figures. This one comprises a family group in the archaic style. Between a sitting and a reclining person, stood four younger people, all frontally posed, each spaced off clearly from the others with no byplay of story-telling detectable in the whole, and no reference to the quaint aspects of personality. This is the wonder of the art of this period; its effect is that of calm timelessness, and it harmonized perfectly with the open-air setting and the incomparable Aegean scene.

But the Sacred Way most importantly was the avenue for the great

Deathless the Grace of the Well-girded
Ionian Woman: *Philippa, one of the
free-standing statues in the Geneleos
group (Vathy Museum, Samos). This is
one of the line of statues that together
formed a family, sculptured life-size in
marble, which marked off the entrance
to the Heraion. Like the Cheramyes
dedication in the Louvre, it is a monumental achievement, imagined and
executed in a way that leaves the
viewer undistracted by secondary
thoughts. Its steady, gathered, geometric lines stand in powerful variation against the vivacious attire worn
by the korai done in the Athenian style
and presently collected in the Acropolis Museum. The Samian style is
dated from c. 570 B.C.*

processions. Of course when people travelled in groups, bringing large
retinues with them or being part of a retinue (as in Euripides' *Ion*), and
their object was to carry gifts to the temple and dedicate them, then
every day could be a procession day; and judging by the number of
dedicatory objects that have been unearthed in Samos, this must have
been pretty much the case.

There were two great Samian festivals, however, and each had its
procession. The first, centering on the marriage of Zeus and Hera,
came in the springtime; the other was a midsummer event in which,
through a ceremony of washing the cult statue, Hera's virginity would
be restored to her so that she could marry Zeus all over again the following spring, and thus symbolically the repetitious fecund work of

the years would go on and on in its allotted way. Although the enact-
ments of the Hera myths were doubtless brilliant spectacles, what
remained particularly memorable was the procession with which the
festival began.

That old connoisseur of splendors, Athenaeus, writing on the luxurious practices of various peoples, finds Samian luxury summed up
eloquently in the proverb "Marching to the Heraion with braided
hair." From him we can gather that the populace of the city assembled
in the marketplace on the morning of the first day of the festival and
then in the strict and yet elegant style that had become conventional
they marched out the Sacred Way. The young women wore their hair
in carefully formed locks combed down over their breasts and shoulders, with a fillet or embroidered band or golden clasp to keep it perfectly in place. Snowy sheer clinging chitons dropped from their
shoulders in lightly rippling folds to the ground. Golden bracelets of
fine workmanship encircled their arms. The young men, with hair no
less elaborately arranged, went forth bare-limbed in sketchy armor:
"Warriors advancing with light steps, shield-protected," says the
Samian poet Asius (whom Athenaeus quotes), mocking the youths
with the double meanings implicit in a line from a somber battle scene
in the *Iliad* (13. 158). And so they went, girls and boys, men, women
and children. Many carried fruits or small animals, gifts which would
become part of the feast. The ox-drawn car was a fixture in such a
march, along with handsome larger animals which were to be sacrificed to the gods, roasted, and devoured alfresco by the human celebrants.

On one well-remembered occasion things went wrong, as they were
inclined to do from time to time among the Greeks, then as now. The
Samians were at war with some of their neighbors to the north, and
fearing the disaster of a sudden raid upon the procession, they considered cancelling the festivities for that year. Their military commander, however, a certain Syloson who was perhaps the first to bear
that dubious name, assured them complete protection, and the march
took place as usual, quite peacefully. But once Syloson had delivered
the procession to the Heraion, he returned to the city, called in his
sailors from the triremes, and in the night seized the fortifications
which dominated the capital. The next morning out at the Heraion the

Samians were informed that their government had become a military dictatorship.

V

In festival time the Heraion was the center for a sort of camp meeting where various groups lived together intimately under temporary roofs, ranging according to hints in the written record from reed mats to fine tapestries. Innkeepers set up in business, offering specialities in food and drink. Small merchants sold the curious wares that could be brought profitably from afar; an excellent business was to be had, for example, in statuettes and small sculptures for dedications. Money appears to have been exchanged; big deals set up; the mysterious wealthy could dicker with a sculptor over the commission of a colossal statue like those they saw everywhere around them. Strabo later on came out with something like the unchanging facts of the case when he called the Ionian festival of Apollo at Delos a fair: a fair with its shadier aspects as well as its religious connotations. So too doubtless for Samos.

Although the marriage of Zeus and Hera might be reenacted in circumstances which could resemble those in Ben Jonson's *Bartholomew Fair,* still the enormous presence of the main temple, the five or six secondary temples, the statue groups, the dancing plaza and the great altar, the numerous treasure houses would impose a superior style and order on the general liveliness of the holiday. Frivolities could hardly negate the power of the superb architecture in the background. In fact frivolities, as in the epic world of Odysseus, must be construed as a humanizing dimension in the whole.

That dimension, that self-correcting byplay between the solemn and the frivolous, is exactly what is most discernible in the Homeric *Hymn* to the Delian Apollo, which is beyond all doubt the earliest, the most extensive and most authentic, and most pleasant, document dealing with the personality of Ionia—unless it were the utterly complex Homeric epics themselves. As for the *Hymn,* it relates a simple story, telling how many a rich and famous place, knowing the jealousies among the gods, fearfully turned Leto away when she was in travail with Apollo until at last tiny, sea-girt Delos, with its one palm tree, ac-

cepted her; but even then, it was not until Delos had bargained in-
genuously with Leto, forcing her to swear a great oath granting the
island priority over the other sites which would also claim the unborn
god. With that, Leto labored nine days and nights, and at last Apollo
was born.

The *Hymn* starts toward a conclusion with a joyous address to the
grown god Phoebus Apollo, praising him with the brilliant epithets
which he had acquired. Then it tells how the Ionians meet in Delos to
make festival in his honor. The tone of the account with its delicate
mixtures of light and shadow, is altogether important; in the interests
of objectivity I refrain from setting down my own version of the passage in which the Ionians are characterized; this is the Loeb translation
word for word; the translator is H. G. Evelyn-White:

Many are your temples and wooded groves, and all peaks and towering bluffs
of lofty mountains and rivers flowing into the sea are dear to you, Phoebus,
yet in Delos do you most delight your heart; for there the long-robed Ionians
gather in your honor with their children and shy wives, mindful, they delight
you with boxing and dancing and song, so often as they hold their gathering.
A man would say that they were deathless and unaging if he should then come
upon the Ionians so met together. For he would see the graces of them all, and
would be pleased in heart gazing at the men and well-girdled women with
their swift ships and great wealth.

Thus the festival: games, feasting, dancing and song, with many
caiques on the sea and madding crowds on land. The image of the
long-robed Ionian can be studied, still with an animated existence all
its own, in the bronze statue of the flute player from Samos, now in the
National Archaeological Museum, Athens. The women are complimented with an epic expression, "beautifully girdled," which may
refer literally to the Ionic habit of belting the chiton around the waist so
that it falls straight down, in the simple straight-forward way of the
Samian statues. The children are a charming, disruptive, inevitable
part of the commotion of the scene. But the unexpected detail is the
statement that anyone, looking on, might say that these people are
"deathless and unaging," because ordinarily those words are epithets
reserved for the gods. Using them so lightly expresses the wry,
because untrue, and yet smiling confidence of the author of the *Hymn*
in himself and his human species. So too, with a similar imaginative

liberty, the philosophers will use these same words later on to say how the basic stuff of the cosmos seems to be.

"And there is this great wonder besides"—to continue with the Loeb translation—"and its renown shall never perish—, the girls of Delos, hand-maidens of the Far-shooter; for when they have praised Apollo first, and also Leto and Artemis who delights in arrows, they sing a strain telling of men and women of past days, and charm the tribes of men. Also they can imitate the tongues of all men and their clattering speech: each would say that he himself were singing, so close to truth is their sweet song."

Here again solemn rite merges into comedy. The girls sing the renown of the gods, then the renown of men, then they sing about the fantastic manners of the different tribes of men, in particular, about their various odd ways of making the sounds which constitute their speech. "Barbarians," the Greeks called remoter strangers, thinking they were naming them after the vocal noises they made. Even Herodotus is impressed, worldly though he is, by the clash of dialects among the Ionians of Panionia. We may suppose that the girls of Delos made sport for their audiences by singing nonsense syllables which sounded like the grotesque speech of the exotic visitors actually present. It is an entertaining thing to do, as everyone will agree who remembers Sid Caesar's renditions of German oratory and Japanese and Italian operas.

The *Hymn* ends with a vivid small dialogue. There is a perennial question, the poet reminds the girls of the chorus, which is bound to come up sooner or later when strangers appear:

"Whom think ye, girls, is the sweetest singer that comes here, and in whom do you most delight?"

Then, when that question is put to them, the poet tells them to be sure to remember him and to make reply, each and all, with one voice:

"He is a blind man, and dwells in rocky Chios: his lays are ever more supreme."

The exchange evokes the archaic scene. It is something left behind from an ancient festival which is expressive of the gregarious, competitive excitement of the day. Its effect, in its clarity and simplicity, is very much like the effect of the perfectly formed little first-prize award jug, found in Athens, with this wavering, not quite grammatical, ancient inscription on its shoulder: "Who of all the dancers gambols best—THIS. . . ."

The blind singer from Chios did not overestimate himself. His Delian hymn has had a unique progeny in the work of poets of later times and of successive civilizations. Callimachus, in the heyday of culture in Alexandria, took the Delian stuff and blew it up elegantly to twice its size; and in the heyday of elegance in Rome Sextus Propertius invoked Callimachus to be his sponsor in his efforts to translate the Delian dances into Italian revels, an effort which was to be renewed not without brilliant success in the Italian Renaissance. In a small heyday of our own, Ezra Pound in *Homage to Sextus Propertius* revived memories of the pagan celebration in a peculiarly pleasant idiom:

> Shades of Callimachus, Coan ghosts of Philetas
> It is in your grove I would walk,
> I who came first from the clear font
> Bringing the Grecian orgies into Italy, and the dance into Italy.
> Who hath taught you so subtle a measure, in what hall have you heard it;
> What foot beat out your time-bar, what water has mellowed your whistles?

VI

"Some say that the sanctuary of Hera in Samos was established by those who sailed in the Argo," writes Pausanias (7. 4. 4), "and that these brought the image from Argos. But the Samians themselves hold that the goddess was born on the island by the side of the river Imbrasos under the lygos that even in my time grew in the Heraion."

Thus, according to ancient authority, thus in a clash of legends begins the Samian affair with the gods. According to the modern German scientists who have made the island their particular study, the *lygos,* or ancient willow, did in fact rank as the primary object of religious excitement among the early inhabitants. The Imbrasos, though only an unimpressive riverbed while it remains in the hills, waters a luxuriant patch of land as it makes its debouchment on the sea. Here were living springs, beside which grew the great, gentle trees; and it is around the stump of one of these that some of the oldest rockwork has been found—an encircling basin, a flat pavement, and a crude altar. According to Hans Walter, who has condensed most of what is known —and surmised—about the Heraion in his *Das griechische Heiligtum,* the forerunner of Hera was quite apparently a vegetation goddess. She is perhaps to be understood as living earth with all of its growing things taking on immanent form in the lygos tree. Her first image was presumably an unshaped slab of wood, the "rude stock" of old-fashioned parlance, which was dropped from heaven; and the ritual which was associated with her was, in the modern catch phrase, a "fertility rite."

I think that the inadequacy of both the old and the new vocabulary to deal with the Hera of the Ionians must be more or less self-evident. To recite the pedigree of a deity or a ritual, in the manner of the school of Sir James Frazer, is hardly ever to capture the thing as it actually existed. Rather it is often to lose it in the shadows where all divinity and all ways of soliciting divinity are constantly merging together. More to the point perhaps is to recognize that pools of water and flowery groves—and the sea itself—created, and still create, the sort of wonder which builds monuments, be they rough stone altars or great temples or the multiplication of shrines to the nymphs like those which Strabo discovered on the lowlands at the mouth of the river Alpheus. The goddess Hera is to be discovered, if at all, in many an evasive shimmer rather than in the hard abstraction which would either affirm or deny her descent from the vegetation goddess.

Of the two larger festivals of Hera, the first—the marriage with Zeus —speaks for itself. The divine embrace toward which the ceremonies led obviously bespoke creation, reproduction, fertility, the perpetuation of things. It is impossible now to measure the degree of delicate symbolism or gross sensuality which may have crept in and out of this rite, nor are there impeccable standards against which to imagine making the measurement; a marriage feast being what it is, though, the forces that pervade it could hardly have been other than beneficent, mysterious but yet no mystery, as it has been among people always.

The second seems as eccentric as the first centric. The Tonea may be translated as the feast of the binding. The principal activity in it was washing and reattiring the cult statue, a ceremony which had its parallels at other places. In Samos the wooden statue was carried to the sea or to a riverbank, cleansed in ritual fashion, brought back, and clothed with an elegance which contrasted with the simplicity of the underlying figure and then restored to its place in the shrine; but in Samos the rite had a particular logic in that the bath was a preparation for the marriage with Zeus. So in its way it was an opulent variation on the ceremony

An Archaic Wedding Announcement. *This small wood carving, found in the Heraion at Samos, represents the sacred annual marriage of Zeus and Hera. Archaeologists date it back to the last quarter of the seventh century* B.C. *It has now disappeared. See Akurgal (bibliographical essay item 55), pl. 64. Reproduced from D. Ohly, "Holz,"* Mitteilungen des Deutschen Archäologischen Instituts, *1953*.

which normally preceded weddings, like the wedding which Iphigeneia thought awaited her in Aulis, in which there is customary recourse to special springs and streams like the Imbrasos for ceremonial bath waters. The rite in Samos however ended in fantasy. The statue appears to have been tied down with withes from the sacred willow. Once long ago, the historian Menodotos relates, some Tyrrhenian pirates came by in the night and carried off the image; but when they had taken it into their ship they found themselves unable to make the ship budge. So they placed the statue on the beach and fled. In the morning Hera's attendants, finding their goddess far from the place where she was supposed to be, imagined that she had wandered away, and to prevent such a thing from happening again they bound her onto a mat of lygos withes.

The name *Tonea,* along with the myth that explains it, implies a rite of which the exact significance is in doubt. Granted that a connection between binding a woman and securing her virginity may be slyly suggested, granted that fettering a cult image to its base has its parallels elsewhere, still I think that the virtue of the Samian Tonea must lie strictly in the artistry of the whole ceremony, with the finest flourish, lacing the statue down, reserved for the end.

My contention, as against Walter's, is that ritual is more likely to imitate art, than art ritual. For instance, the goddess on the Ludovisi throne, who is being lifted from the sea by gold-filleted attendants, illustrates the Homeric *Hymn* on the birth of Aphrodite, I believe, and not a cult bath. It is significant that Pausanias records several works of art depicting this myth, and thousands depicting other myths, but none or few which illustrate ritualistic activities; and on painted vases mythological scenes outnumber ritual scenes a hundred to one. The distinction is not unimportant. By seeing ritual as most frequently a derivative from narrative art, you preserve Aegean freedom and gayety; by looking at it the other way, you exaggerate the formalistic. In this matter I must follow the French school, as led by Jean Charbonneaux, rather than its rivals.

The lygos persisted, in any event, through all of the stages of worship on the banks of the Imbrasos. The tree and the archaic goddess, on coins which were struck in the ripe years of the Roman Empire, still compose the badge which was most appropriate to Samos. A number of bronze pieces which depict the ancient statue show her standing erect, elaborately costumed, in the entrance of a tiny temple. To one side in front, on one coin, stands a pot containing the tree; it is small of course but unmistakable in its symbolism.

Coins witness other traditional accouterments of Hera, such as her peacocks. On several Imperial coins a pair of these birds stretch their heads up dramatically under the statue's lifted arms. On early silver coins from Samos, Homer's ox-eyed queen of heaven seems to be remembered in the representation of the head and forequarters of a hand-

An Early Profile from the Islands. *Beginning with such a crude, small, but vigorously uplifted countenance as this, the eastern sculptors devised a series of statuettes which culminated in polished lifesize or often colossal marbles. Though most of them have not survived at all—and if they have survived at Samos, they are headless —still the heroic head in Istanbul, the Demeter from Cnidus in the British Museum, the bronze Demeter from Halicarnassus in Izmir, all are assurances of the stature of the sculpture achieved in eastern places. The statuette above was no doubt a dedication among a multitude of modest dedications in a popular shrine. On the other hand our pathetic* kore, *who is only four inches tall, may have been a child's toy or a child's grave ornament.*

some bovine of indistinct gender. But the most common design on the earliest coinage is the likeness of a lion's face. It is a mask really, a face-on view of a lion's head. The connection with Hera seems, according to Callimachus, to be this: the statue was presented to the spectator with a lion's skin spread out at its feet, apparently to dramatize Hera's invincible powers. Moreover the discovery recently of a small marble tripod of the kind called a perirrhanterion, in which lions lie prostrate, under leash, beneath the feet of three goddesslike women, suggests that notions of a kinship between Hera and the old Mistress of Animals reverberated for a long time through Greek minds.

Other temple decorations emphasize the pattern of oriental associations. There were, for instance, a fiercely stylized lion's head cast in bronze with a complacent frog sitting on it serving somewhere in the precincts as a fountain spout; Eastern monsters like the griffin affixed to kettles; bare-bosomed Astarte figurines; the ox head, the frog, the pomegranate, the lion head rimming the shallow pottery offering vessel called the *kernos*. Goddesses, it appears, can be fickle in their choice of attributes and companions; and this one, once she got over her limitations as a vegetation goddess, showed a decided taste for the orientalizing trends of the times of her greatest triumphs.

Lion skin or no, she remained extravagantly feminine. In the Imperial coins she is dressed to the teeth as befits a goddess who is preparing to become a bride. She wears an enormous mantle with large pleats running across her breast. Below this garment is another with a broad crisscross design. From her partly raised arms cumbersome hangings drop to the ground. These may represent or may conceal the lacings of lygos withes which tie her to her base; the hangings at all events seem to fix the image in its position just as the rods or fillets held by the many-breasted Ephesian Artemis fix her in hers. On her head Hera, also in the Eastern fashion, wears a tall miter that becomes broader as it goes up and is elegantly horned. Probably her trappings were brightly colored. From somewhere in the midst of them she seems to be looking out, full-featured and pensive, dedalic in character, slightly asiatic, like the Lady of Auxerre in the Louvre. The goddess, so arrayed, is the creation for the most part, I would guess, of her vivacious attendants, whose assignment it was to make festival of her bath and toilet.

Maybe that is the way it is with gods and goddesses. They start out as rude stocks and stones, magical, omnipotent, but formless, and they remain that way until they are taken up in the human imagination and cared for. Then they become glorious.

VII

It is said that an early civilization to which the Greeks harkened back in important ways, that of Mesopotamia, produced but few statues of note, practically no free-standing images of human beings which are totally enjoyable. Animals, yes; animals that are fanciful and lovely; some engagingly humanized scenes depicted in friezes; but no real statuary. The reasons for this, it is said (my principal authority is Henri Frankfort), are first that there was a dearth of stone suitable for sculpture and second that copies of the human being, when they were made, were regarded as solidifications of the divine, and as such they were to

Terracotta Protome. *Likenesses of women's faces in hollow mask-like terra-cottas turn up often on the coasts below Samos; they are also found on the temple sites at Paestum and Locri in Italy. The archaic smile in this art is accompanied by unusually wide eyes and full lips. As votives they are apparently directed toward Persephone. Since they are studiously constructed as forefaces only, they are technically* protomes, *and as such they stand out in a startling relationship with a similarly self-aware artistry in coinage and in sky-maps. The bovine protome is as prominent on the early silver coins of Samos as the lion's mask; in Miletus at the same time there appear the fore-quarters of a horse and the forequarters of an ibex as the obverses of silver staters. A black-figure Boeotian painter with eastern affiliations showed so much fondness for representing animals in this way that he is known as the Protome Painter. And thus, in protome form, the Eudoxus-Aratus accounts of the heavens advise us to look for the forequarters of certain animals, Pegasus for example, in identifying a constellation. Ptolemy goes so far as to name Eculeus, the Foal,* Hippou Protome. *The importance of all this is that for Pythagoras and Eudoxus the sky was a sketchy mosaic of familiar images.*

be treated as temple furniture. What statues there were represented heaven-gazing priests or semidivinities in the main. Since the populace was excluded from the temples they were seen only by priests, and of the priests only by those of highest rank. Each inner sanctum where a statue might be relegated was more and more remote from the world of sunlight and shadow, embedded deeper and deeper in temple conventions. In these circumstances the art of translating human form into stone naturally dried up.

With the Greeks it was the opposite. They had stone, they made statues, and they set them up for the widest possible view. They kept their temples open. But even so, they made a practice of bringing the cult image out into the plaza for ceremonial occasions. Their art thrived in the daylight, against the background of landscape and seascape with architectural accents. It was consequently a monumental art. In these scenes anything less than the monumental—the naturalistic, for instance—would have been out of place. It had to create human figures which would match the sky and the sea. Therefore it could never quite forget the pure elemental stone in its shapes and it brightened the shapes with color.

Of course, in Asia, with the passing of time, Mesopotamian constrictions began to relax. In the lands of the old Hittite kingdom, among the Assyrians and the Phoenicians, smiths and sculptors began producing a humanized, highly available art which the Greeks envied, imported lavishly into places like Samos, imitated and improved on. Nevertheless the basic black-and-white differences between East and West remained pretty much what they had been. When Babylon becomes, as it does, the counterpart of archaic Samos—Darius subdued both centers in quick succession at the beginning of his reign—the contrast still hinges on opposing religious presuppositions, and the contrast is extreme.

The Greeks had no official theology and no hierarchy of priests; the Babylonians were ridden by both. Simplistic though this assertion may sound, it will stand up for all practical purposes. The pantheon of the Greek gods was as unsystematic and fictive as Homer and Hesiod had happened to make it; which was so loose a structure that a variety of cults—Demeter's at Eleusis would be but one instance—could go charging off along their separate ways without committing anyone, not even a participant in the rites, to a particular creed. Similarly the oracles. The oracle of Apollo at Delphi, the oracle of Apollo at Branchidae, were local extrusions. Their success rested on a carefully nurtured prestige which was political and social in scope and hardly significant in religious ways.

Samos, though rich in temples, seems never to have let any of them put a noticeable imprint on its public life; but Babylon on the other hand was so overawed by its Ziggurat that it sanctioned a great annual New Year's ceremony in which Marduk's priest divested the king of all royal authority and subjected him to humiliating rites before restoring his divine but temporary mandate to him. The dethroning of course seems to symbolize the submission of king to priesthood as effectively as to Marduk. In contrast with the cheerful Tonea in Samos, the Babylonian New Year's festival was accompanied by a sorrowing ritual of expiation; and this in turn was supported by a liturgy of penitence which was read through the year, and by various extensive services to exorcise demons and bring about magical escapes from misfortune.

In order to confront a universe so riddled by the ominous, the Babylonians developed one of the most ambitious disciplines in history, the pseudoscience of divination. But here again a priestly order was in charge, and the ritualistic, conventional methods of forecasting the future were mixed up thoroughly with methods that demanded a basic exercise of the intelligence. Divination by the study of the entrails of a sacrificed animal, which they favored most, is, I think, an irrational discipline; while astrology, which they favored next, is rational, but because of its official perversity failed to be of much value as an introduction to astronomy; there was nothing in it to foreshadow an Aristarchus. Both techniques of reading the future—and still others —flourished through centuries and centuries of careful nurturing and transmission. Diodorus Siculus considered the education of a Babylonian diviner to be superior to the training which could be obtained in any of the Greek schools. And in its oblique way it probably was.

The Greeks were aware of these Babylonian arts and were mildly addicted here and there to the practice of them. They examined the intestines of their sacrifices for the purposes of divination when the occasion ahead of them seemed to be desperate. They reacted, often disastrously, to the peculiarities of the heavens, they were affected by dreams, they found omens even in trivial things, like a pun embedded in a stranger's name. Mostly, though, they did not concern themselves deeply with divination; it looks as if they may have gone through the motions of using it sometimes, as before the battle of Plataea, as a means of controlling the morale of the army. Nevertheless, as the war with Persia came painfully to the long-awaited showdown, Herodotus seems to find the Greeks increasingly concerned with reading omens in their sacrifices. Curiously (perhaps), it was usually the virile Spartans, and not the softer Ionians, who resorted to the artful science.

One Greek diviner, a man named Deïphonos, could stand for many, and for their repute among intelligent Greeks. The following is the treatment which this particular seer gets from Herodotus.

Just before the great, decisive victory over the Persian land and naval forces at Mycale, the Greek fleet had stayed its departure from Delos until Deïphonos, the diviner whom the Spartan command had brought down with the ships, could assure them of a favorable augury. This accomplished, the fleet set sail and made a rendezvous near the temple of Hera off Samos. Finding that the Persian navy had fled from the island, the Greeks pursued; they rounded Mycale and with battle cries of "Hebe!" (if they were thinking of the child of Hera and Zeus, perhaps remembering the Samian marriage festival) or of "Hera!" (if our text needs mending), they fell on their enemies, who had beached their boats and fortified themselves as best they could, and vied mightily with one another in destroying them.

But Herodotus had interrupted his narrative at the beginning of this episode to tell about the diviner Deïphonos (9. 93–95). What he tells and his manner of telling it are typically Ionian, witty, wayward, vivacious, elusive. The bulk of it is a sparkling digression having to do with the diviner's father, Evenius, also a diviner, whose marvelous adventures must lie somewhat outside the province of ordinary history. It seems that back sometime in the past this man, having been assigned guard duty over a flock of sacred sheep which his town was responsible for, fell asleep and allowed the wolves to get into the flock. As a punishment, his fellow townsmen blinded him. But the gods came to his aid, and eventually they made him a sort of back-country Tiresias by awarding him the gift of prophecy.

So much at a little length Herodotus tells us about the father; but this and only this about the son: "I have heard it said that Deïphonos was no son of Evenius, but only traded on his name, and worked for whatever he could get out of it, up and down Hellas." With this disdainful

remark he abruptly dismisses the diviner and the divination and pro-
ceeds to his own sweeping account of the victory at Mycale.

Though in Babylon to the east and Etruria to the west divination
commanded rapt attention, it certainly was not important in Ionia.
Semonides, the poet who led a Samian colony to Amorgas, appears in
a fragment of his to pride himself on his knowledge of ritual and his
skill in handling the sacrifice of an animal:

> The boar, how I roasted him!
> How I cut him in priestly fashion!
> I'm not bad at my craft!
> (Loeb, Fragment 24)

The context for this, however, is feasting, gourmet cooking, high living. Semonides was a bon vivant, a satirist, and quite clearly a scoffer
at divination.

But of course the furious religiosity of the peoples on the Greek
horizons, both east and west, goes back to the deepest of issues—the
problem of man's frail mortality. The Asiatics like the Etruscans seem
to have brooded constantly on death, alternately loathing it and con-
testing against it, as in the story of Gilgamesh, or building artificial
paradises in which to enjoy it, as in the opulent Royal Cemetery of Ur
or the gaudy tombs of Etruria. Either way the emphasis falls on the
supernatural and the possibility of wringing from the gods a few drops
of their immortal powers. With the Greeks, as we have already said,
that the end is death goes without saying. Death is dismal, as dismal
as Achilles reveals it to be in the underworld scene in the *Odyssey*.
But nothing can be done to undo it, and it is madness to make it a constant topic of thought. The question is whether, from any point of
view, the undeluded and unimpassioned acceptances of the Greeks—
and their vital enjoyments in their gods and their temples and their
myths and their world—do not add up to just about all that can be
expected consciously and rationally, of any faith.

VIII

In the worship of Hera the dancing that the lygos and the fresh fountains attracted was most likely at first a vigorous outdoors pleasure,

like May Day among northern people. Then came the refinements. These can be read as accurately I believe in the housing that was built for Hera as in the scanty evidence of the evolution of the cult-image and the cult itself.

The first astonishing innovation was the "hundred-footer" temple of the early eighth century, already alluded to. It was a tall tunnellike building, some 108 feet long, if we use our notion of a foot, and 21 feet wide. Although open-ended and open-gabled toward the plaza and the big altar to the east, the walls were otherwise a continuous band of sun-dried bricks resting on stone foundations. The roof, which was steep and thatched, found support for its ridge-pole on a row of fourteen centrally located wooden posts. Obviously the problem of interior lighting, which was troublesome anyway in archaic buildings, is especially acute in this strangely elongated one. Of course there could have been an opening in the roof in accordance with a primitive stratagem which culminated in the Pantheon in Rome. If hole there were, even a narrow one, the bright Mediterranean sky would have worked wonders. In any event, the cult statue had a base of its own in the open plaza which it occupied in times of ceremony.

The want of openness in the first building is acknowledged in the design of the second. When a flood in the middle of the seventh century wrecked the old building, the plan for rebuilding it on practically the same foundations called for the elimination of the array of central posts. But this entailed emphasizing even further the elongated interior. The width of the area to be spanned was cut down to eighteen feet, while the length was not much less than it had been before. Samian architects from the beginning, whatever their problems with lighting or with timbering a superstructure, insisted on using wonder-provoking dimensions, which are religious in tone. In this case it was the vista that was to be had, with the aid of skylight or of lamps, down through a brilliantly decorated interior. To offset this artfulness, the builders began very early to stretch wide, completely open, post-supported porticoes around the exterior, creating the pattern for the formal colonnade. At the same time they erected open and yet weather-sheltering arcades near the temple, where the business of the precinct could be carried on.

When the giant temple suddenly succeeded these skinny hundred-footers, it seemed all at once to preserve their strangely impressive effect and to solve their problems. The old peculiarly long perspective is recapitulated in the enormous alleys and cross-alleys among the columns, inside and out, in the new architecture. So deceptive were distances and directions in the sight-lines among the rows of columns that the first of the large buildings became known as the Labyrinth: such at least is the name that Pliny applied to it. The illusion of complex spaces was intensified too by the soaring heights of all members, the columns rising probably to forty or more feet. Good lighting went along with such heights, at least in the foreparts of the building, and would have persisted elsewhere as long as roofing the whole structure over remained unaccomplished, whatever the designers' original intentions may have been.

The first colossal limestone-columned temple was the creation of the Samian artist-engineer Theodorus and the pioneer architect Rhoikos. They began work in about 570 B.C. by moving the channel of the Imbrasos to the west in order to give themselves room for the foundations of the building they had in mind, which was to be 350 by 175 feet, approximately. Thus the project called for erecting an airy-appearing structure of incalculable weight on a water-soaked, treacherous terrain. And this in fact was its marvel. A further marvel was the speed with which it was built. It had arrived at least at the point of having some of its roof tiles in place when it was destroyed by fire in about 540 B.C., possibly in the first of the forays of the Persians against the Greeks (see Pausanias 7. 5. 4).

Immediately there began to spring up a similar, even larger structure to take its place. This is the famous temple of the age of Polycrates which Herodotus names as one of the three most wondrous works of his times. From its ruins it is that the single marble column arises like a white finger, visible today, as it has been for centuries, from miles around.

The second Labyrinth tempts everyone to emphasize its bigness. It was big: sixteen feet longer than its predecessor and four or five feet wider. It did have many—133 by one count—towering columns. It did invite comparison with the Artemision of Ephesus. But statistics are delusive, and the aim of the builders could hardly have been to attain a superiority measurable by mere physical size.

Their aim must have been first of all to build a temple which would fit the festivals. With the coming of the first great temple and with it an enormously enlarged altar, the space between structures was much reduced: the dancing plaza was dwarfed and the festival cramped. The new temple was pushed back to the west another 130 feet. The Imbrasos had to be moved again, but a place for dancing was recovered. The scene returned to what it originally had been: open but surrounded by a scattering of monuments and secondary temples, many more of these now than formerly. To this whole scene the temple of Hera itself must remain subordinate, and its dimensions relatively insignificant.

That most desirable of effects, openness, was the striking feature of the second Labyrinth. The main room, or *cella* in the usual structure, remained an unroofed court. This may not have been altogether intentional; time and materials may not have sufficed to get it covered over; a decision to roof or not to roof may never have been really faced up to. Openness and open-endedness are characteristic of the Ionian mind and Ionic works.

Though Herodotus's account of the great temple of Hera has given it its special renown, it was still incomplete in his day. Until Hellenistic times work on it speeded up and slowed down as conditions dictated; but efforts may have gone more willingly into improvements, such as rafting fine marble down the coast and replacing a limestone column with a much better one, than in trying to get the job finished up. At almost any time one segment or another of the vast temple would have consisted in no more than a row of columns, without entablature or roof.

It was never finished. That is the way it was, the way it had to be. The originators of the design, Theodorus and Rhoikos and their successors, were striving for a note which they and all Ionians knew was out of reach. Their plan was the expression of a peculiar aspiration which might be called religious. The Ionic temple was a fabric which could never be rounded off and called done.

And so you will find Dorian temples on stony promontories; heavy, complete, absolute constructions; some of them, particularly in Italy, still nearly intact. But the Ionian vision was of an ever-changing cluster of ornate, slender white shafts, patched here and there with color, standing on well-watered lowlands bordering the sea and reflecting its restlessness.

IX

Openness and mobility: the Heraion of Samos composed a landscape which could not have been otherwise than vivacious. The cult image of Hera was brought forth from its abode on holidays, as we have said, and became the center of the fair. Apollo and Artemis, Hermes and Aphrodite, with temples of their own, instigated further celebrations: we can read about the origin of one nocturnal festival, not in ancient ritual but in a particular recent emergency in which Samian youths and maidens had danced, with sesame cakes in their hands, in and out of the temple of Artemis, feeding a consignment of boy prisoners who had escaped from a Corinthian ship and taken sanctuary there (Herodotus 3. 48). The flow of human traffic on ordinary days is indicated by the remains of paved avenues that linked the temples together, winding among monuments, leading to buildings which housed works of art of incredible variety. In fact the scene taken as a whole, indoors and out, was a series of galleries in some of which a cult image was the incidental axis for the flow of visitors.

Whatever the lygos branch meant to them, or the sesame cake, or the image of the god itself, these were people who in the fullness of archaic times were moved to one clear sentiment: "First fruits are best, and they belong to the gods." As evidence of the power of this persuasion we can cite a broad range of first-fruit offerings in the form of objects dedicated to a deity and inscribed—or otherwise accounted for in the earliest records—in such a way as to make the transaction unmistakable.

To begin with, first-fruit gifts must have been simple things like the first gatherings of a harvest baked into cakes and eaten ceremonially; in such rites vegetation magic connives easily enough with the gregarious feelings that arise when crops are ready to be taken in, a new year is beginning, and the harvest star, Sirius, has reappeared low in the morning sky, bringing heat with it. In time however the magical and propitiating manoeuvre drops out of sight, and the occasion for thank offerings is no longer confined to the round of seasonal events. Rather, it becomes a rule that one should set aside the first of any abundance, great or small, and tithe it back in the form of a temple gift as an expression of gratitude.

Head from the Hera Temple. *This head comes from a nearly lifesize statue in the Hera temple, which burned just before the time of Polycrates. The powerfully sculptured face with its broad, receding and shadowed eye-placement, broad mouth, prominent cheekbones, and elegant framing, produces an effect of gravity and sensuous beauty which is not easy to understand. The effect is hardly appropriate for the goddess Hera or for a dedication to her. If the sphinx-like mystery of the face is to be explained it may be by imagining someone whose role had to do with the dead. Perhaps it is indeed a sphinx, an image of a priestess prostitute, whose beauty is ultimately like that of the figures on the grave stele, an assurance of a sympathetic guardianship over the souls of the deceased (see Richter, bibliog. item 70). The sensuousness here reminds one of the somber beauty of Persephone on a number of coins. The Greeks in their ultimate aesthetic schematics do not easily reduce themselves to formulas, except perhaps for one: they enjoyed life, they knew it was of short duration. Photo from Buschor, fig. 366, bibliog. item 70. Other similar sphinx-like figures in high relief were apparently architectural decorations at Ephesus and Didyma; they are now to be seen in the British Museum and in the Berlin Museum.*

Most conspicuous of the temple gifts of the sixth century were the life-size or far over life-size statues of naked young men, the kouroi, standing with their tall straight-forward bodies and elaborately dressed hair, here and there, even on the rim of the roof of the great temple of Rhoikos and Theodorus. And along with the youths, the maidens, the korai, with their long shimmering festival chitons and short mantles and meticulously shaped braids; and with them, more regal female figures, the counterparts of the colossal young men, such as the Hera of the Louvre, Cheramyes' dedication, who represents not Hera herself but a noble bearer of a gift to the goddess.

Although none of these statues has come down through the centuries intact, enough has been left to show not only what they looked like but what they had seen fit in their time to say for themselves. They bear short, clear-cut inscriptions quite regularly. Often on the front seam of the chiton, on the leg of the kouros or on the base on which he stands, there is incised a hexameter line which names the donor, whom we may call X for the moment, and continues in Homeric language something like this: "X to Hera dedicates from his gains a gift most beautiful." The formula is followed not in Ionia alone but throughout Greece with but little variation, although the language is twisted around and around, and is sometimes elaborated, while staying within the limits of epigrammatic expression. A second dedication of Cheramyes', a Samian statue now in Berlin, bears a typical hexameter on the edge of the chiton: "Cheramyes m' anetheke thei perikalles agalma" (Cheramyes dedicated me to the goddess, a most beautiful statue-gift). Other inscriptions mention the first fruits or tenth parts of windfalls of some kind, unexpected rewards of booty taken in battle, as being the source that funded the dedication. At their best the verses are pristine examples of archaic written language impressing form and order on amorphous religious premises, and likewise, we may presume, on the imaginative intentions of the artist working with the plastic materials. In either case the objective is the creation and the dedication of a thing which is beautiful in terms of the Homeric canon of beauty.

The epithet "a most beautiful gift" (perikalles agalma) in Homer's text is a climactic phrase used to express a peculiarly Greek appreciation of fine workmanship. In the *Odyssey* (18. 290–300) Penelope's wooers are presenting her at last with their formal gifts. The first gift is a magnificent robe, richly embroidered and fitted with golden brooches; the second is a chain, "cunningly wrought" and strung with beads as bright as the sun; the third is a pair of comparably wonderful earrings. Noble gifts, these; but the final one is a necklace with a jewel: this is a superb, a most splendid perikalles agalma. This is the excellence to which the temple dedications aspire. Whether they occur in marble or ivory or wood, or clay or bronze or gold, each was as laudable for the work of the skilled hand of the maker, who often identifies himself, as for the intrinsic value of the material. Ivory after all, in the eyes of the archaic age, could be decorated advantageously with glass; marble with metal, copper or gold.

While many dedicatory gifts were too little or too simple to carry an inscription, those that are inscribed speak for the others, and we can be sure that all were fashioned with epic care and put on display with lyrical composure. A piece of the rim of a very old pottery kettle from the Heraion preserves the ending of an elegiac distich: ". . . in return for great kindness." The words bespeak the gracious manner of Anacreon and the old Ionian elegy. In some other instances, in spite of difficulties, the inscription is present, full force. A very ancient small bronze kouros, possibly from Thebes, manages to recite its message, even though getting it spelled out meant lacerating both legs with a network of letters: "Mantiklos dedicated me to the Far-darter of the silver bow as part of his tithe; do thou, Phoebus, grant him a kind return."

So much language from so unpretentious and bluntly earnest a little man! Though Ionian suavity may be wanting here, the effect of the whole is still Homeric, including the ingenuous prayer for worthy requital. The overloaded figure illustrates the way in which the Greeks fused their arts together; the verses are part and parcel with the statue and there is no reason why they shouldn't be its predominant feature. An inseparability among the kinds of human expression was a practical fact in archaic times. It was not an age of specializations.

X

You can read a brief history of ancient Samos, with its many-sided activities, purposes, and spiritual values, in the variety of its temple dedications. Behind each of the more impressive dedicatory objects, there lay a story which was handed down as a temple tradition and

Man in a Peaked Phrygian Cap: *some aspiring voyager's votive gift. When a terracotta statuette turns up on a foreign site—Cyprus—history seems to tremble for a moment. The bearded old man is an offering-bearer in the conventional Greek pose; his attire is elaborate, as is suitable for an important occasion. Only his hat is unusual. Although this peaked headdress could have happened simply as an accident in the trade in small dedicatory objects around a temple, I am persuaded that it was worn for its value as a badge asserting Phrygian attachments and that it remained symbolical for a long time after it had ceased to serve as a simple twist of any stuff that would protect the head. It is noticeable in figured friezes in Asia Minor through a considerable span of time. In the ancient contexts the wearer seems to be singled out as a distinguished personage. About the implications of the Phrygian cap, I shall add some remarks later in connection with coinage; see the pictures on p. 232. The present figurine is a flat-backed, protome terracotta, 6½ inches tall.*

related by official narrators to temple visitors. Herodotus makes us fully aware of the richness of the oral history that could be sopped up within the precincts of sanctuaries like the Heraion. In fact we can see pretty clearly that he began the investigations, which were to become his lifework, in the Heraion soon after he migrated to Samos as a young man. History became for him, as it turned out, partly the narrative of what had to be said to explain the monuments and the legends left behind from the fighting with the Persians, and partly the theistic and artistic constructions that were necessary to interpret them.

As for Samos, one of the most meaningful events in its earlier history was the voyage which the ship of a sea captain named Kolaios made when bad winds carried him through the Straits of Gibraltar to the Atlantic port of Tartessos, a then unexploited place that controlled rich mines. Kolaios and his shipmates brought a fortune in metals back to Samos. This occurred in the late seventh or early sixth century; it was the first chapter in the history of Samian sea power. The voyage nevertheless could have become a faded legend; it remained a vivid, precise recollection because Kolaios put a tenth part of the ship's profits into a monumental dedication which testified to the greatness of the achievement. He had a bronze Argolic krater made, an enormous bowl decorated with griffins' heads around the rim, and he set it up in the temple of Hera, using a tripod of three kneeling figures of bronze, each eleven feet high, to support it. This huge thing survived several Hera temples. It challenged the imaginations of all comers, Herodotus among them. It aptly signified a shifting of horizons in the Ionian world.

A wine bowl of similar proportions, which found its way into the Heraion by devious means, signified not so much the heroic as the riddling aspects of history. This is one that had been designed as a gift for Croesus. The Spartans, having concluded an alliance with the grand Lydian monarch, made a huge bronze mixing krater which they calculated to be worthy of his magnificence. While they were shipping it to him by boat, the overthrow both of the man and his splendid city took place. At this juncture the Samians either intercepted the ship which was carrying the bowl and seized it, or the Spartan sailors contrived to sell it to them and then claimed that they had been robbed of it. Whatever the truth, the Samians got the bowl and dedicated it to Hera. Herodotus examined it, heard the story about it, and described it in improbable terms. Only the discovery of the huge volute krater in Vix in France in 1953 makes his account of the container with its frieze of figures around the top fairly credible. So spectacular an ornament, extracted by obscure means from the dust cloud that accompanied the downfall of Sardis and Croesus, encouraged an Ionic mood of restiveness when confronted by examples of gross oriental prosperity: the gods are easily made jealous, mortal men are prone to hybris.

As their sea power increased, the Samians certainly did become high-handed in their treatment of other people's shipping. A dedication by Aiakes attests to this fact. It's probably an inevitable sequence: from power to the misuse of power. But the inscription on the dedication reveals the aplomb, the piety even, with which practices strongly resembling piracy could be accepted. The object in question is a beautiful though headless statue of an over life-size seated figure, a regal womanly figure clothed sumptuously, the feet resting on an upholstered stool, the arms lying forward in the lap beside small lions on the throne arms. The master archaeologist Ernst Buschor believed that it represented Hera, the goddess herself. On the side of the throne are inscribed words to this effect: "Dedicated by Aiakes son of Bryson, who swelled the takings for Hera during his directorship." The sentence may mean that Aiakes, the historical tyrant-director of Samos, inflicted tolls on passing shipping in a more or less customary manner, or it may mean that he plundered whoever and whatever came within his reach; it probably means something in between, a little of both, depending on the circumstances. In any event this Aiakes was doubtless the father of Polycrates and Polycrates was known by his rivals in the Aegean as a pirate. Buschor may be right: a magnificent enthroned Hera would be as appropriate to Samos the thalassocracy as the wooden vegetation goddess was to the modest well-watered area around the lygos tree. Gods and goddesses tend, as Xenophanes said, to be of one and the same corpulence and one and the same complexion with their worshippers.

Archaic Hera sponsored no oracles and had no political influence to trade for gifts; the history of her treasures therefore reflects Ionian detachment. True, Amasis of Egypt, in his troubled search for allies against Persian aggression, did woo Samian Hera with "two wooden statues of himself," which Herodotus says stood yet in his day behind the doors in the great shrine. The shrine also possessed a linen breastplate that came from Amasis, which was so wonderfully woven and embroidered that admiring sightseers are reported to have picked it nearly to pieces; but the breastplate was another of the trophies which the Samians had seized from the Spartans. Most of Amasis's gifts to Samos went where they would presumably do most good—directly to the palace of Polycrates; even here, as matters turned out, they met with Ionian detachment and bought Amasis absolutely nothing. Even-

Kneeling Kouros in a Phrygian Belt. *Elegance and worldliness, though often the characteristics of objects consigned to the gods, reflect the ideals of the Samians themselves. The hair, the headband, and the belt, which distinguish this small dedicatory ivory carving, remind us of the traditional luxury of "youths marching to the Heraion with braided hair." An ivory carving in this style, with these adornments, is accepted as evidence of the flow of an orientalizing influence from Anatolia through Phrygia westward to the Hellenic coasts and islands. See Akurgal, bibliog. item 56, p. 215; Buschor, bibliog. item 71, fig. 242, as source of the photograph used here. National Museum, Athens.*

tually his elegant small gifts became part of the temple collections; and not a few returned to light during the excavations.

On the whole the treasures of the Heraion are reflections of the worldliness of the people supporting the cult. Worldliness, though, is a complicated matter. It relishes small splendors, like the molded and engraved mirrors which came originally from Amasis. It enjoys a wayward myth, as is illustrated in the small bronze casting of a jubilant eagle, which is Zeus, carrying off Ganymede. It steps outside itself in its curiosity about other parts of the world and in its awareness of the transitoriness of things. It is not self-preoccupied. That mainly is its difference from otherworldliness. A memento mori is a private and personal possession in a way that no temple gift ever was. The one is an inward symbol, the other looks outward. The gaunt Biblical figures flanking the doorways of the cathedral in Chartres face us with identical abstracted gazes. Detail by detail they differ from one another in many small ways, but yet they merge together; they form one architectural shadow, full of repeated forms, all expressing the same uncomplicated distant mood which is easy to grasp. The Greeks separated their figures. They made surfaces and textures for the light to play on. They attended to the contours of the body and took account of the landscape around it. Their work shimmers in the atmosphere of this world, and strange though it may sound to say it, it is not easy to grasp.

XI

Underlying the simplicity of the sense of gratitude which originally expressed itself in the tithing of first fruits are some darkish and fairly evasive threads of meaning. Extrarational recognitions seem to be involved. First fruits are special fruits, more noticeable than any that are to follow and more unaccountable, like the earliest figs swelling among the unopened leaves; like youth, like springtime. That or some portion of that joyous unstable thing is what belongs to the gods. And therein lies a trouble. The better and the more wonderful the thing that comes one's way, the more insecure one must be in the possession of it.

That or something of the sort is the secret of the genius of the archaic age and of its finest works, the kouroi and the korai. Both types of youth statues it will be remembered were favored as monuments in graveyards and in the gay temples of the gods. The inference must be that youth itself in its pristine form belongs to the lords who rule over life and death. The absolutely naked and defenseless young man, standing straight, carefully combed; or the delicate chiton-trailing maiden—these are appropriate images for the human being in extremis, whether of good fortune or evil.

There has been found a statue base, clearly the support at one time for a large marble kouros, which is inscribed as follows: "Stand and weep by the tomb of Croesus dead, whom rushing Ares destroyed one day as he fought in the forefront." Miss Gisela Richter sees a likely connection of this base and epitaph with the suave, Eastern-looking kouros from Anavysos: the Lydian name Croesus suggests an east Greek origin of the young man being remembered. But no matter exactly who he may have been, the juxtaposition of the upstanding naked fighter contending unequally with a furious god of war is eloquent beyond analysis. The war god changes his style with the passing of time, but the plight of the young soldier remains forever the same.

At Delphi in May, 1893, a party of excavators digging through a bank toward an ancient retaining wall swept away a curtain of earth from in front of an archaic marble kouros, so that all of a sudden they met a survivor from a very distant age face to face. The effect was shocking, as the documentary photographs show. The white marble figure is so compact, so intensely forward-looking, eager, nude, that he makes his discoverers, standing around wonder-struck in their dark formless clothes, look like phantoms.

The following spring a second, almost identical kouros turned up nearby. Inscriptions on the base blocks indicated that the pair of statues had stood one near the other on a common footing and were the work of Polymedes of Argos. They represented Kleobis and Biton, brothers, who were honored, the inscription revealed, "because they drew their mother for forty-five furlongs, putting themselves to the yoke." The full story of this dazzling act of filial devotion figures among the preliminaries which Herodotus attaches to his Histories. In Book 1, chapter 31, Solon, having arrived in Sardis, recounts the legend of the two youths for Croesus's benefit, proffering it to the rich Lydian monarch as an antidote against his self-infatuation as a supremely prosperous man. But antidotes can be evil-tasting medicines. The parable ruffled Croesus's feelings, as it has ruffled the sensitivities of a great many readers ever since.

The problem for Croesus and Solon was to decide what the greatest possible happiness consists in. A good answer will be found, Solon asserts, in the example of Kleobis and Biton. To begin with, they were fine young men, honorable, rich, and champions in the games. Then one day, when there was to be the great festival of Hera at Argos, the oxen that were accustomed to draw their mother's wagon to the temple failed to arrive from the fields. In the emergency the two athletes put their own necks to the yoke and dragged the cart with their mother in it the forty-five furlongs to the temple steps. In the crowd, the men beholding this praised the youths for their strength, while the women praised the mother for having such sons; and she in her elation went straight to the statue of the goddess and prayed that her boys might be granted the best of the blessings which it is possible for mortals to receive. The prayer was answered. That night in the temple Kleobis and Biton died in their sleep: they nevermore would suffer evils, no disasters of fortune, no illnesses, no old age. The mother was properly rewarded and rebuked.

"Then the Argives," the passage ends, "made and set up at Delphi images of them because of their excellence." They were there for Herodotus to consider when his investigations led him to Delphi; and one of them it was, who after being underground for centuries, suddenly confronted the modern world on a spring day in 1893.

In spite of the peculiar dynamics of oral history and of archaic sculpture, the legend and the statues have both been disconcerting to normal human complacency, ancient and modern. The legend is stylish and nonrepresentative of the most popular sorts of fiction; the statues are severely stylized and nonrepresentational of common notions concerning the bodily makeup of young men. In imagery and story telling they show flagrant disregard for the perfections of nature and the benefactions of divine providence. "Oh! Croesus," Solon observes, ". . . the power above us is full of jealousy, and fond of troubling our lot." Wry dialogue like that offends the devout. Among ancients, Plutarch reprehended Herodotus for this passage, common though the ironical, pessimistic sentiment is in early literature. Among moderns, George Rawlinson, gifted translator and churchman, offered to excuse it as a product of Herodotus's "cheerful, childlike . . . mediocrity." Like the problem of the living statue and the phantom spectators, mediocrity of mind is now much more apparent in the commentary than in the passage commented on. All thoughts which we are capable of entertaining about providence and death, I suppose, must be ultimately mediocre; but these ancient flashes coming from the dark sky which Herodotus knew so well may be the least to be despised.

These flashes are not to be taken quite literally either. After all, a debate on the question "what the greatest possible happiness consists in" can hardly be expected to rise above sophistry. Attempts at such major definitions elude language and the structures of language, and whatever epigrammatic thrusts they produce must be more or less of the nature of the quips that brightened the banqueting halls of the Seven Sages.

Nevertheless Herodotus in these probing stabs departs dramatically from the polytheistic system. In the Kleobis and Biton story the power which blessed the youths with death was the god, the *theos* (in his wording), impersonal in its being, and not Hera, the kindly goddess of the festival, to whom the prayer was addressed. This abstract superior power is not a neat monotheistic something, it is not in the least anthropomorphic, it is simply the way of the universe, the way of a structure so strong and so contrary to the minuscule purposes of man that the disproportion in Ionian minds becomes a vast irony. The god, in this sense, is questioned by Herodotus, as by the whole Homeric tradition, not systematically but with wit, with real pain, and with a lightheartedness no less real, human circumstances being what they are. And the Homeric tradition had the peculiarity of embracing all Greeks in an easy and quite harmonious spiritual confederation. Whatever else, they had had Prometheus on their side.

And so in Argos, though Kleobis and Biton did not awake, the festival went on. Meanwhile the festivals go on in all of the other places, yesterday and today and tomorrow, in parish churches and great cathedrals, with only the meagerest questioning of the ways of the universe. As for Samos, in archaic times the silent kouroi and korai were everywhere about, looking out from the tombs at the bright processions, and down on the loud dancing from the heights of the unfinished temple.

XII

There is also a fabulous picture of the Ionic mind, which if it is not too delicate a tapestry to handle, just might prove to be curiously informative. Ancient mythology having designated Ion, son of Apollo and Creusa, as the founder of the Ionian race, Euripides seized on the myth

From the Heights of the Unfinished Temple: *the grandeurs of the Heraion sketched out in drums and blocks of marble. One may pursue the study of the Ionic egg-and-dart moldings and the orbit tracks of massive lathes on base members for the columns, but he will not find it easy to achieve a vision of the whole richly templed scene. In addition to the eloquent hints coming from smaller objects, in literature, a tragedy such as Euripides' Ion has the power to evoke the complex loftiness contained in the ancient temenos.*

fairly late in his career and converted it into the fantastic scenario which he called *Ion*. The play centers on the discovery, the identification, "the coming forth," of the youth who, through his offspring, would establish the Greek nation on the shores of Asia. In this young man's peculiarities can be detected, I am venturing to say, some of the peculiarities of his descendants, the Ionians. The mixture of stormy drama and cheerful poetry in which Ion finds himself caught up will become the style of the realm he will found, Ionia. All of this, I should add, is as it appears to me to be if we look at the action from Euripides' point of view.

As a poet Euripides had been from the beginning notoriously pro-

Ionian. Tradition makes him the student of Anaxagoras, who had come to Athens bringing Ionian philosophy with him. Be the detail of the connection as it may, Euripides' first extant dramas are ordered by an extreme subjectivism in his tragic persons which is a sinister variant on the Ionian's chief premise, the all-forming mind, or Nous. Medea's private reasoning and her cruel pursuit of her compulsive ideas take place in a mind which resembles Anaxagoras's Nous falling afoul of itself. The cosmos for her is finally and absolutely only as she sees it. She says:

> Of all creatures that live and have a soul
> We women are most unfortunate.
>
> (ll. 231–32)

And unfortunate indeed is the woman or the man who feels himself victimized so much and cannot find a way to get beyond the obsessive force of his particular nature. Medea or Phaedra or Hippolytus is destroyed not by the mere tragic flaw of the Aristotelean canon but by the whole complexion of their beings. Which is much more like Herodotus than Sophocles. The purposes of the gods again stand in doubt.

Then midway in his career Euripides began pitting pure intelligence against the passionate mind, such as Medea's, as the orderer of life. In so doing he was obviously fetching back toward the fountainhead of Ionian science. In a memorable, indeed unforgettable passage he makes Hecuba in the *Trojan Women* postulate a new conception of a divine superior power: now the god is in and of the physical cosmos, in and of nature and man's intelligence (ll. 884–88): "You who uphold the earth, whose throne is earth, whoever you are, though far away, beyond our ever finding out,—Zeus,—whether law of nature or man's intelligence, to you I pray: walking noiselessly you lead our destinies to just ends." The god, if discernible, is to be discerned intellectually. He is the object of the same sort of inquiry at which the Ionian thinkers had been laboring.

The new emphasis on the dispassionate scientific mind leads Euripides into denunciations of warfare and its ghastly stultifications, which must be interpreted in part as hopeful missionary work seeking to put an end to the ruinous contest between Athens and Sparta, the long drawn out, utterly enervating Peloponnesian War. In the *Suppliant Women*, for instance, the Argive king Adrastus, having allowed him-

self to be led into a disastrous war by all sorts of blindly passionate
coercions, finds himself having to face up to the scrutinizing mind of
Theseus and hear himself criticized with cold objectivity. Adrastus,
abject in his defeat, can make no defense of his war nor of himself.
When he should have been skeptical, pragmatic, and restrained, he
had been naive, superstitious, and impetuous. He has earned the scorn
which Theseus lays upon him. But he is a suppliant. The women with
him, widows and mothers, the victims of his pig-headedness, are suppliants too and are utterly pathetic. Theseus undertakes to right the
worst of their wrongs; he regains their dead for them so that the dead
may be buried.

But in aiding them, Theseus has had to make war on Thebes. True,
it is a just war, a minor war, a war sanctioned by religious necessities
—and one which will secure Argos as an ally with Athens in the future.
It is war nevertheless; mixed, as is inevitable, in its motives and therefore an uneasy solution to the dilemma confronting the intelligent man
with pacifist leanings, which Theseus is meant clearly to be. Theseus
was most likely meant to have been, in the eyes of the Athenian audience, a mythical equivalent to Pericles himself, and the legendary war
an equivalent to the war in which Athens found itself enmeshed.

The impact of the victory which Theseus wins over Thebes is
strangely and significantly muted. His success is no deterrent to
Evadne's throwing herself on her husband's funeral pyre and no comfort to the procession of Argive mourners. Force, it seems, is pallid
even in triumph over wrongs, and therein lies the tragedy.

Meanwhile the real war between Athens and Sparta did not come to
an end; it gradually carried the Athenian empire closer and closer to
ruin. When the remnants of the great army thirsted to death in the quarries at Syracuse and the fleet was lost and the Ionians were beginning
to rebel, it must have become only too obvious that in desperate straits
partisan intelligence is as deluding as passionate bemusement. For
Euripides in any event the time had come to give up on both. Both
began with one-sided arguments and ended in fanaticism. Just as Hippolytus had been unnaturally devoted to hunting and Artemis, so
Theseus in the *Suppliant Women* may be said to have been abnormally
partial toward rationalizing and Athena, and the time had come to give
up on all that sort of thing.

At this juncture Euripides created a new drama, of which *Ion* is representative. No one knows what to call this group of plays—*Ion*, along with *Helen* and *Iphigenia in Tauris*. Neither tragedy nor comedy describes them; tragicomedy suggests something so synthetic as to be useless; Lesky's "tyche-drama" is too remindful of Fortune's heavy hand. They go beyond romance, and rise far above melodrama. How they work, though, is no mystery. They are sumptuous pieces written for the Great Dionysia in Athens and as such are always dramatizations of the mythological past. They are big, spectacular, intensely poetical. Earlier, the dramatists had plotted their chief works for the festival so that the play ended in the death or near death of the chief player, these terminations being the strongest they knew. But the road toward a particularly appropriate death could be discerned only in certain atmospheres, only in moments of transparent faith, when the protagonist's fault stood out mightily against a background of accepted virtues. These conditions never quite existed for Euripides; Medea, with all those faults of hers, flatly refused to die for him. So now he concentrated on the structure and the overall theatrical effects essential to drama, exploiting grand spectacle and explosive plot and letting the whole thing work itself out, through skepticism and mockery and tenderness, toward a detached but vivacious ending. He brought an Ionian mode brilliantly into the theater.

XIII

Ion dramatizes a festival. It is an impromptu festival to be sure but not an insignificant one, since no less a personage than Creusa, Queen of Athens, has come with the king-consort and an enormous retinue to Delphi on a mission of some moment. The seriousness of the mission is not apparent at first. Creusa's women attendants come in gayly, like all celebrants and temple visitors, commenting on the sculptures, explicating for each other's benefit the myths depicted in the friezes, asking questions of one of the keepers of the sanctuary: "Is it true that Phoebus's house is built over the Earth's navel?" Answer: "Yes, and it's hung with garlands and watched over by Gorgon-eyes."

Into the hubbub comes Creusa, the Queen, smoldering in Euripidean fashion with old wrongs and secret longings. In her the sight of the temple provokes strange agitations which she can neither communicate nor conceal. When Xuthus, the king-consort, appears, it is otherwise.

Coarse in his prosperity as partner in the rule of Athens, he sets about ostentatiously to offer first fruits. He is determined, we soon detect, to wheedle from the god the one thing which he and Creusa lack, that is, offspring.

He succeeds or he thinks he does, and beyond all expectations. The oracle pronounces Ion, the young keeper of the shrine, son to him. Xuthus, trying to interpret the oracle, imagines himself to have been the begetter of a child one riotous night during another festival which he attended several decades before; he remembers enough of his revels to feel himself justified in claiming Ion as his son. Ion accepts this preferment somewhat dubiously. All that he knows about his own birth is that he was a foundling who was discovered in an open cradle on the temple steps. He is obliged in deference to Apollo's oracle to conclude that his father is indeed this stranger from Athens and his mother some totally forgotten Delphian girl. So he helps Xuthus to prepare a great public feast as a token of gratitude to the god. The most splendid tapestries in Apollo's treasure house are borrowed to make the pavilion.

Euripides seems so far to be encouraging the weary Athenians attending their Dionysia to look in on the splendors and commotions of another festival in bygone times. The scenes which he brings into the theater might have been suggested by those bright flashes that occur at the end of the *Hymn* to the Delian Apollo; his main interest is in movement, vitality, humor. But beneath all that, there is a much more complex grade of action, still vital, still humorous, but involving the erratic actions of the gods and the narrow intentions of their mortal respondents. On this level Euripides begins making drama in the spirit of the Homeric *Hymn* to Hermes. He invents heavenly deceptions, ruses and counter ruses; he manufactures a visible sort of magic which compares with the devices employed by the infant Hermes in the theft of his brother Apollo's sacred cattle: driving the animals backwards, for instance, so that their tracks would be misread; or making the lygos withes with which Apollo tries to bind him take root and grow into a thicket covering up and concealing the whole herd. In fact *Ion* in scenic ways resembles the famous vase painting which illustrates the *Hymn;* there in one view the little Hermes is to be seen cuddled innocently in his cradle, Apollo is glowering over him, and the sequestered cattle are well concealed far back in the woods.

But now in this festival drama Hermes, grown up and reconciled with Apollo, has acted as prologue for the piece. From him we have learned that some years earlier Apollo had ravished the maiden Creusa in a cleft on the side of the Acropolis and that, at Apollo's request, Hermes had rescued the infant which Creusa had given birth to in secrecy and had left to die in its cradle on the very spot where it had been begotten, and that it was Hermes who had carried the child in its cradle to Delphi and put him where he was found on the temple steps. The child of course is Ion; the mother of course is Creusa the Queen; though neither knows that the other exists. The king-consort of course is not the father, except by a deceptive way of speaking often resorted to among the gods. Hermes, having delivered this preliminary account of lucid facts and ingenious concealments, retreats into the laurel at the side of the temple plaza. He intends to stand by and wait with understandable curiosity to see what will happen.

What happens is beyond divine foresight or reasonable prediction, so entangled is the course of the action in the opaque ways of human life. Xuthus knows that Creusa won't share his new-found happiness in his presumed parenthood; yet he can't contain himself in his feelings of good fortune; Creusa can't abide this sudden turn of events, believing that for Apollo to award a bastard son to her consort, after having forced her to bear and then to expose their own child, is the god's final betrayal of her.

In her fury Creusa sends an old manservant with a drop of Gorgon venom to the luxurious pavillion where the feast in Apollo's honor is about to begin. The old servant with a grand Homeric show of hospitality fills the wine cups, putting the poison into Ion's. As Ion lifts his arm to drink, something disturbs him and he calls for the wine to be poured onto the ground as a libation. Doves descending in the Greek heat drink the spilled wine; the bird drinking from what had been in Ion's cup suddenly shakes, falls and thrashes on the ground, and dies in agony. Ion seizes the old manservant, forces a confession from him, and leads the pack of Delphian guests off in pursuit of Creusa. They intend to pitch her from the crags overhanging the holy place. When Creusa, forewarned, takes sanctuary on Apollo's altar in front of his temple, Ion, rationalizing away her right to sanctuary, advances to seize her. At this point the prophetess foster mother of Ion comes from the temple. She is carrying a wicker-woven cradle in her hands.

By means of this instrument and the tokens within it, the mother and son discover one another. Each is overwhelmed by the thought of the narrow chances that saved the mother from killing her child, the child his mother (ll. 1516–18).

> Ah strange!
> Yet—midst the bright embraces of the sun
> Somewhere do such things day by day befall.

Though the winds of heaven have shifted to summer weather, the fact persists even into the closing lines of the play that both Ion and Creusa have reason to be discontented with Apollo; Xuthus too, but he is left in his fatuous ignorance. Creusa still finds Apollo's rape of her hard to forgive; Ion his deceits hard to reconcile. Both are aware of his present defection, in that he refuses to speak for himself in an epilogue. Their Ionian descendants will share now and again in their ancestors' bewilderment.

Yet it is to be noted, and Ionic wit will never forget, that neither a burning indignation such as Creusa's nor a wounded sense of integrity such as Ion's quite composes the essential dimension in a human being. More significant than his skepticism is Ion's many-sidedness. We saw him in the first place lightly and gracefully embattled with the birds that befoul the temple, and at the peak of the action furiously leaping a table at the feast to crush the poisoner. Creusa is as intricately presented; she is both the girl weaving a coverlet for her unborn child and the mutely resentful childless older woman.

Ion is more complex than any of its facets can possibly suggest. In it there is no single line of action that can be abstracted, no ethical argument or political message; there is only the total action, the total art. The plot does not reduce itself to a logical narrative but rather to a show, as Euripides says, of strange things happening amidst the embraces of the sun: human things, but as unexpected as if they were the product of the Heraclitean fire and as puzzling as the fossil impressions of fish which Xenophanes found in the rocks in the mountains of Syracuse.

The Athenians, on the verge of collapse as head of a proud empire and as a city of independent people, were treated to a view of a realm where issues were not razor sharp, where the middle was not rigorously excluded, where ideology was not supreme law; the gods therefore could be their despicable selves when they had to and could still be

honored from day to day. The descendants of Ion were not rigid. The
Persians with their ruthless enterprises had taught them flexibility. So
had the Athenians, when under Pericles in 439 B.C. they destroyed
Samos and transformed the Delian league of Ionic people into an imperialist Athenian monopoly from which there was no appeal.

Now, when *Ion* was being played in the Great Dionysia and the
Ionians were rebelling and the empire crumbling, one wonders what
the feelings out in the vast audience were. One wonders whether there
may not have been some envy of the Ionic attitudes which were en-
livening the stage. Or perhaps it was too late for envy. Perhaps the
irreversible heaviness of spirits was already upon them. We can hardly imagine their own Athena making herself heard and understood if
she were to say to them in cheerful Ionic tones what she had said to
Odysseus when he had complained about her hard dealings with him
(*Odyssey* 13. 320ff.):

> Always the same detachment! That is why
> I cannot fail you in your evil fortune,
> Coolheaded, quick, well-spoken as you are.
>   (trans. Fitzgerald)

XIV

The Ionic smile, however, could not in present circumstances have
always brightened the faces of the descendants of Ion during the last
quarter of the fifth century B.C., when they themselves were victims
of a war with which they had had nothing to do. No longer autonomous, deprived of the right to strike their silver coins, their famous
harbor taken from them as the last overseas prize which the Athenian
navy possessed, the Samians languished. Neither Samos nor its closest
Ionian neighbors ever fully recovered. The great days of the temple
builders were over.

And yet, as if in one of Euripides' "tyche-dramas," another strange,
bright thing was destined yet to befall in favor of the Ionians. On the
flat shore of the Aegean, in the center of the small town Yenihsar, a
dozen miles south of Miletus, stands Didyma, today the boldest monument of colossal Ionic architecture left over from antiquity. By the
rules of chronology the temple of the oracle Apollo Didymaeus which

Temple of Apollo Didymaeus, 1973:
a tall frontal fragment of the great Ionic structure at Didyma.

we see now is Hellenistic and therefore would seem to be of no great consequence in the study of the archaic period.

The case for its predecessor would have been otherwise. It had engraved its towering image on the imaginations of too many makers of poems and questioners of the quandaries of history ever to be forgotten. But that temple had stood as a broken wreck of itself from the time that Darius had departed after 494 B.C., leaving the ruins of Miletus and the despoiled sanctuary behind him.

Thus matters stood for nearly two centuries. Thereupon the unexpected happened. After Alexander the Great had come and gone in 334 B.C., on his way toward Halicarnassus and the East, everywhere declaiming his intention to Hellenize the world, he avowed it to be his particular purpose to effect a complete restoration of the precincts and temple of the Oracle at Didyma. The project waited, however, for the most enduring of the generals who survived Alexander, Seleucus I, to fight his way back to the Aegean seacoast, establish himself, and start to make good his young king's pledge. Seleucus pressed the rebuilding of Didyma on the Carian population. The new king, at long last, was fulfilling the theme of a young man's rhetoric: restore that which was Greek to the Greeks; impose that which was Greek upon the barbarians. The program, like Seleucus's coinage, could not do otherwise than to insure his popularity among Greek subjects. The restoration was taken up in earnest shortly after 300 B.C.

The effort was at least largely to duplicate the gigantic earlier building, to produce a facsimile which would be as nearly accurate as possible. The present foundations lie almost exactly on top of the former, exceeding the original dimensions by a slight margin. The colonnade is a multiunit dipteral enclosure, such as the former had been, with columns soaring to an unusual height and being unusually slender shafts: sixty-four feet tall with a lower diameter of one-tenth their height. The result was an orderly grove of slender tree trunks, in the Homeric metaphor, surrounding a sunken interior court with the traditional spring and growth of laurels, and toward the north end a secondary Ionic temple of no mean size, which housed a large, archaic, bronze statue of Apollo.

The Didymaion thus rebuilt ranks with the Heraion of Samos; and with the Artemision of Ephesus: which having also been rebuilt following the fire of 356 B.C. argues for the premise of the facsimile reconstruction. This structure unfortunately has disappeared into the marshes of Ephesus. In the reconstruction at Didyma, however, the architectural limits of the original colossal aspirations seem finally to have become clearly recognized: no roof apparently was ever contemplated as a cover for the temple. Such submission to practicalities must signify that the spirit of the Archaic Age had worn itself out.

Another peculiarity of the design is the presence of a lofty platform within the colonnade at the top of the entrance steps. This area, which overlooks the sunken inner court with its lesser Ionic temple at the farther end, may have functioned as a stage on which some part of the ceremonies of the Oracle was enacted. In fact oracular uses undoubtedly committed the housing of Apollo in this case to eccentricities which had long been established and were not necessarily later innovations.

In any event the temple even in its present lofty, fragmented but still coherent form, echoes in a shattered diapason something of what such sanctuaries once had been. The famous cult statue, a work in bronze by Canachus of Sikyon, and without a doubt the most valuable item of plunder which the Persians carried off after 494, gives the imagination a vivid hint of the magnificence which the giant structures once had sheltered. In one of the few triumphant passages in the tragic history of the Didymaion, we are told that after an absence of two hundred years the archaic bronze masterpiece was returned to its original site by Seleucus I, from Susa. This act of justice bespeaks the not always unworthy motives underlying the wholly confused moral pattern of the conquests.

The statue of Apollo, as reproduced on a much later Milesian coin, shows a certain likeness to the striding Apollo on the silver coins of Caulonia, though the pose on the bronze is one of quiet, unmoving contemplation. In the palm of the right hand the Ionian Apollo is holding a miniature stag which closely resembles the stag in the field of the Caulonian coin. The characteristic of the mobility of Apollo seems to have been reserved for this tiny animal, which, according to Pliny, the sculptor had attached to the hand in such a way that a thread could be passed alternately under each of the pairs of hooves.

On the whole the perplexity about Didyma, I think, is hardly the problem of what is Hellenistic and what is not, but rather the problem of the original total effect. The Temenos with its sacred approaches, its lesser temples and great altar, its sanded avenues (where Thales once traced the figures of geometry with his staff) have left no hint of their former existence. The traffic of the present shudders too continuously against the narrow circumference of the enclosure to suggest the processions on the Sacred Way which once proceeded among flanking statues from Miletus to the harbor at Panormus and on to the sanctuary. Nor is there a fresh spring or laurel anywhere about. But still the fluted marble leaps up into the glaring Mediterranean sky, and the cool Aegean blue lies at the foot of the slope, as must always have been the most striking of its ancient characteristics.

XV

And on the very day of the performance of *Ion* in Athens, a giant relic of this same heroic, fragmented past stood on the lowlands fully visible from the upper tiers of the theater. By one of the prettier casts of fortune a cluster of columns still flowers in what had once been the meadow on the banks of the river Ilissus, where Deucalion's flood is said to have subsided. Near this spot Socrates and Phaedrus had strolled while discussing the splendors and humiliations of—we might say—Beauty. And today in the twentieth century there are columns still there to behold, well below the looming masses of the Acropolis. The broken ranks of fifteen or sixteen enormously tall fluted shafts, most of them tied together at the top by sections of a clear-cut architrave, stand in a small artificial park, under which in dark conduits the sacred waters of the Ilissus may still be flowing. This is what is left of the temple of Olympian Zeus, begun under the Pisistratids, wholly Ionian in its conception, imitating Ephesus and Didyma and Samos. Work on the structure was broken off when the Pisistratids fell in 510 B.C., but was resumed from time to time, until Hadrian consecrated the new-old temple in A.D. 131–132. In the course of the centuries Pentalic marble replaced the original tufa; the Corinthian order took over from the Ionic, but nothing about the edifice ceased being colossal, and not quite manageable. What we see now at Didyma or here in Athens seems to exist like a great afterthought, trying to perpetuate a brilliance which people once found peculiarly enjoyable.

Opposite—A Beast that Haunts Men's Dreams. *Cyzicene silver tetradrachm, photo courtesy of Numismatic Fine Arts, Inc.*

3
A PORTRAIT OF AESOP

Scene: Hades. AESOP *and* HOMER.

AESOP.   You must have been very daring to leave your readers to put allegories into your poems! Where would you have been had they taken them in a flat literal sense?—The gods mangling each other, thundering Zeus in an assembly of divinities threatens Hera, the august, with a pummelling; Mars, wounded by Diomed, howls, as you say like nine or ten thousand men! . . .

HOMER.   Why not? You think the human mind seeks only truth: undeceive yourself. As a matter of fact, and one which you ought to know, my gods, such as they are, without mysteries, have not been considered ridiculous.

AESOP.   You shake me, I am terribly afraid that people will believe that beasts really talked as they do in my fables.

HOMER.   A not disagreeable fear!

AESOP.   What! if people believe that the gods held such conversations as you have ascribed to them, why shouldn't they believe that animals talked as I made them?

HOMER.   That is different. Men would like to think the gods as foolish as themselves; but never the beasts as wise.

—Fontenelle (trans. Ezra Pound)

A GOOD QUESTION is, Was Aesop an ugly man in his physical makeup? Tradition has pictured the teller of the jaunty fables as a small, misshapen human being, a wry-mannered entertainer who seduces the mind with his fantastic tales about men and beasts. The grotesque image pleased the Ancients. It persisted through the Middle Ages. But this idea of deformity has become repellent, apparently, to the modern, more scientific and scholarly age: so much so that Aesop's ugliness is dismissed by good authority as mere fiction, and along with it, often enough, the very existence of the man himself. Modern specialized scholarship, I think I can show, is too prim to deal effectively with Aesop.

At the same time modern readership is too snobbish to take much pleasure in the *Fables*. The catalogue of the central library serving my county in California relegates its large collection of Aesop to one simple category, Children's Books. To the shades of Aristophanes, Chaucer, Erasmus, La Fontaine (and Marianne Moore), Fontenelle and Ezra Pound, James Thurber . . . peace! And on top of all that, in a better library, the nearest thing to an attractive and reliable present-day edition of the Fables prints them with their morals lopped off, on the grounds that their sly, jesting didacticism is "an insult to our intelligence." The book is called *Aesop Without Morals*. To satirists, jesters, and stylists everywhere . . . peace!

It adds up obviously to a rather funny business. I propose to take a look back in order to see how the Aesopic tradition fitted into civilized activities in the past and to speculate a little on what has happened to it. The place to begin is on the island of Samos in the midst of a glittering archaic age, some six centuries before Christ, where the threads of an intelligible biography can be picked up.

II

Herodotus (2. 134) puts Aesop on the island at this time; and for the facts about any person living in the dawn of recorded Western history the *Histories* of Herodotus, needless to say, take precedence far and away above any other documents. So then, Aesop the fable maker was a slave, definitely a slave of a man named Iadmon in Samos. Nevertheless, he eventually landed in Delphi, a long way off on the upper side of the Greek world, where the priests of the oracle of Apollo put him to death. It was not just any slave's death, though, because after a period of time the Delphians sought out the grandson of Iadmon in an effort to make an atonement for their crime. It must have been a shocking and memorable event, this death; we will consider it more closely in a moment.

If Aesop was no beauty, he was, according to Herodotus, a fellow slave with one of the most famous of beauties, Rhodopis, whom Sappho's brother, Charaxus, eventually redeemed from her life as slave-courtesan at enormous expense. From the beginning, history seems to have contrived the pairing off of ugliness and beauty, the handsome body and the sprightly brain, Rhodopis and Aesop. The one, living in luxury in Egypt, became wealthy enough to send a valuable dedication of iron spits to Delphi, the other, acquiring somehow the prerogatives of the rich, made the journey himself to Delphi and died miserably.

"It was within the power of one and the same state, Delphi," Plutarch observes, "to provide Rhodopis with a place where she might dedicate the tithes of her earnings, and also to put to death Aesop, her fellow slave" (*Mor.* 400F).

Aesop has a fable which illuminates this aspect of the ancient juxtaposition: "A fox and a leopard got into an argument about beauty. The leopard boasted about the variety of his markings. The fox replied, 'Then how much handsomer I am than you! I have variety not on my hide but in my head.'"

The Delphians, I suppose, decided for the leopard, but lived to regret it.

Herodotus in any event is firm on the key points—slavery for Aesop in Samos, execution in Delphi—buts adds nothing in the way of comment or explanation.

But was Aesop really ugly? Are his blemishes a matter of historical fact? There exist several versions of a *Life of Aesop*, an uneven, compiled narrative, dating in its present form from toward the beginning of our era, though doubtless existing in other forms in earlier times. Among its most authentic chapters—there are 142 short chapters altogether—a large group centering on Aesop's career in Samos makes no bones about his physical defects; to the contrary, it exploits them. The

Aesop as he was Seen by English Eyes: *a copy of the woodcut portrait which William Caxton attached to the translation of the* Fables *in 1483. As a frontispiece, it is itself a copy of a frontispiece used in an earlier continental translation. Its novelty is the iconographic references to events in the light-hearted ancient biography which precedes the telling of the subtile histories, as Caxton calls them. See* Caxton's Aesop, *ed. R. T. Lenaghan (Harvard, 1967), from which I have taken the illustration used here.*

whole is a rollicking semiromance. It elaborates the ingenious sleights by which Aesop lived, telling for instance how as a slave he mastered his master, the philosopher Xanthos, apparently the predecessor of the man named Iadmon, in public debates, and mastered his master's wife in private amusements.

The quality of this helter-skelter *Life of Aesop* is discernible in its opening sentence, which Elizabethan printers adapted in this wise to form a title-page for their editions of the Fables:

The Fables of Aesop in English with all his life and fortune: how he was subtle, wise, and born in Greece not far from Troy the great in a town called Amonco: he was of all other men most deformed and evil shapen: for he had a great head, large visage, long jaws, sharp eyen, a short neck, crookbacked, great belly, great legs, large feet: and yet that which was worse, he was dumb and could not speak: but not withstanding this he had a singular wit and was greatly ingenious in cavilations and pleasant in words, after he came to his speech. London. Imprinted by W. Powell. 1551.

Except for a few details, this was the Aesop of tradition. Among the details, his portrait would have been more properly rounded out, not with those big feet and legs mentioned above but with undersized extremities. He was dwarfed, *kolobos*.

But on the grounds of the unreliability of the *Life* and the absence of any notice of Aesop's deformity in the earlier written references to him, Emile Chambry, most excellent of the modern editors, dismisses the whole thing as distasteful folklore, attributing to Himerius in the fourth century A.D. the first definite indication that Aesop may have been comical to look at.

Art historians have long known better. In the Vatican collection there is a red-figure cup with a scene painted in the bottom which has been uniformly (and inaccurately) described as "Aesop talking with his fox." The figure, though not specifically named so, is certainly Aesop; what the scene represents we will consider later; for the moment we note only this, that the figure is comical, caricaturish, grotesquely dwarfed. The picture has often been reproduced; it appeared, for instance, in Ernst Pfuhl's authoritative *Masterpieces* (1923), and as recently as 1965 in C. M. Bowra's and *Life Magazine*'s popularization called *Classical Greece*. But not until 1961 has any scholar dealing with Aesopic matters taken notice of it. Pfuhl dates the kylix at about

Figures in a Red Figure Kylix, c.
460 B.C. *Vatican Museum: E. Pfuhl,
bibliog. item 63, fig. 79.*

460 B.C. It is actually the earliest surviving item that presents Aesop to
us, predating even Herodotus.

Its peculiar significance is to authenticate, to some degree at least,
the madcap *Life of Aesop*. This is not to be interpreted as a proposal on
my part to take all of the *Life* literally or to conclude that Aesop was as
badly deformed as either the cup or the *Life* makes him out to be. But
I do say that behind the tomfoolery there must be biographical substance.

III

Our hardest task is to move Aesop from Samos to Delphi, and then to
get him killed off. The *Life*, in its wayward way, accounts for some of
the essentials, in that it sketches his rise to a position in Samos which
renders the rest of his story possible. His wise counsels to all and sun-
dry, decked out with his fables, eventually win him his freedom. His
subsequent prominence in the forums of the Samians puts him in the
middle of a potentially disastrous dispute between the Samians and the
Lydians and sends him on a diplomatic mission to Sardis, the Lydian
capital.

Now the curious fact about Aesop's activities in Samos, which read
like frivolous romance in the *Life*, is that they are also indicated in
general terms by sober authority. The scholiast to Aristophanes' *Birds*
(471) implies, for instance, that the half-mocking, lyrical praise which

Aristophanes gives Aesop was in fact justified by the fabulist's success in leading Samian debate. Aristotle, apparently on the authority of an early Samian historian named Eugeon, notices the strong impression which Aesop made by the judicious use of a fable now and then in his public speeches, and in the *Rhetoric* (2. 20), he records a vivid incident, probably extracted also from the Samian annals of Eugeon, which in the translation of S. A. Handford will tell its own story:

Aesop spoke in the public assembly at Samos when a demagogue was being tried for his life.

"A fox which was crossing a river," he said, "was carried into a deep gully, and all his efforts to get out were unavailing. Besides all the other suffering that he had to endure, he was tormented by a swarm of ticks which fastened on him. A hedgehog that was on his travels came up and was sorry for him and asked if he should pick off the ticks. 'No, please don't,' replied the fox. 'Why not?' said the hedgehog. 'Because these have already made a good meal on me, and don't suck much blood now. But if you take them away, another lot will come, all hungry, and drain every drop of blood I have left.' It is the same with you, men of Samos," said Aesop. "The man will do you no more harm, for he is rich. But if you kill him, others will come who are still hungry, and they will go on stealing until they have emptied your treasury."

This is the mentality of the Aesopic fable at its dryest, as we say of good wine. The argument in favor of the demagogue is free from demagogic appeal; it is disillusioned, wryly pragmatic, tolerant; it asks the court to forego cheap self-righteousness and to cast an objective vote. It disarms us of our clichés. It leaves us at once squirming and amused.

And so when the Samians found it necessary to answer the imperialist demands which Sardis was making on them, Aesop, as the *Life* says, could very reasonably have been sent to Lydia to plead their cause. It appears that he did go and that he succeeded, and that he thereby moved himself a long step forward toward his disaster in Delphi.

"Just Zeus acted unjustly," Callimachus writes in a fragmentary iambic poem, "when he deprived the animals of speech and turned all the talking over to men, because that only made men more garrulous and pedantic. . . . *Aesop of Sardis told this*," Callimachus adds, *"whom the Delphians did not receive well when he recited his tale."*

In asserting that Aesop was "of Sardis," and in foreshadowing the violence in Delphi, Callimachus relates in the third century B.C. the gist of what is contained in the romanticizing *Life:* namely, that Aesop persuaded the Lydians not to try to impose subjugation and tribute payments on Samos, and having enjoyed so much acceptance from them, he stayed on, writing out his fables and "putting them in the library," becoming, so to say, Aesop of Sardis.

For the interim anyhow. Regardless of his precise activities, he assumed the role in Sardis, if we are to believe Suidas, of court favorite. But then, after this period of prosperity, followed by another in Samos, the mischievous *Life* sends him off on a boisterous tour of Babylonia and Egypt, the account of which, fortunately for the zealous sifters of truth from fiction, turns out to be patently an interpolation of an oriental romance in which Aesop's name is substituted for that of the hero, Ahikar.

The Babylonian digression, however, does not invalidate the evidence for an interval, or more than one interval, in Sardis. Good authority supports the connections of Aesop with Lydia, though Croesus is the monarch named. Plutarch will go so far as to maintain that Aesop was employed as an emissary on missions abroad, including the ultimate one to Delphi; and though Plutarch is more or less fanciful in his treatment of Aesop in the "Symposium of the Seven Sages," his explanation at another place of what happened in Delphi merits closest attention. Practically all accounts agree that once in Delphi, Aesop lashed out at the priests of Apollo, and in reprisal they forced him over a cliff near the temple.

IV

Modern researchers reject the career of Aesop in Sardis because in surviving texts it is always tied in with the reign of Croesus. What upsets them is the fact that Croesus mounted the throne in 560 B.C., by which time Aesop, roughly a contemporary of Sappho's, would probably have been dead. This is prim reasoning and astonishingly inappropriate in view of the power of famous names to attract credit to themselves for the noteworthy deeds of others. Records assign to King Alfred, for instance, or Charlemagne many actions which must have belonged to less conspicuous heroes. In our case oral history has probably assigned to Croesus actions which properly belonged to his father, Alyattes. Croesus the magnificent, Croesus the golden, enjoyed a fame which tended to extinguish earlier brilliance and to draw all stories to the younger man: Chaucer's Monk counterfeits his downfall from Polycrates' murder. Aesop played much the same trick on other fabulists. The scholars who insist on the anachronism of pairing Aesop with Croesus, make a great point about Aesop's name being falsely attached to the bulk of ancient fables, many of which could not possibly be his.

The father of Croesus, Alyattes, in his time was no less brilliant than the son, and Alyattes fits the partly legendary narrative of hostilities against Ionia somewhat better than does Croesus. He began his career fifty-seven years before Croesus took over by persecuting the Milesians with year after year of warfare, until by a trick in which the priests of Delphi participated, he was switched into forming a strong alliance with Miletus. Since Miletus was both close neighbor and natural enemy of Samos, the alliance could hardly have spelled anything but trouble for the islanders. It was to Alyattes, too, that the three hundred Corcyrian boys were being transported, to be made eunuchs for the decoration of his court, when the Samians intercepted them and released them. His great tomb, which still looms on the sky, was financed chiefly by the earnings of prostitutes. He murdered the knights of Colophon when they were guests in his palace. He was the oriental monarch par excellence—and equally the head of the wealthiest, most adventurous, fashionable and resourceful capital of the times—a Paris for Sappho, a London for Alcman—its eminence being most clearly demonstrated by the invention in Lydia of coinage in gold and silver. Only when Alyattes pointed his ambitions for conquest eastward against the Medes, did the pattern of his hostilities turn away from the direction of Samos, where Aesop was a councilor.

On the other hand Croesus, before taking over from Alyattes, was no shrinking violet in his own right. The scraps of information that have survived show him involving himself as a young man in reckless entanglements in order to finance mercenary troops and establishing himself on the throne only after a furious struggle with his half-brother Pentaleon, whose chief partisan, a wealthy Lydian, Croesus put to

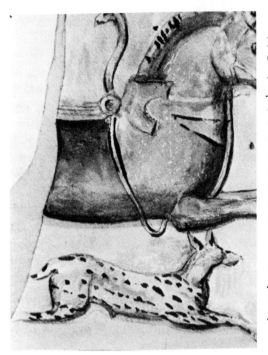

Man's Faithful Four-legged Counterpart: *one of Alyattes' dogs of war. The father of Croesus, seeing Lydia ravaged by hordes of Cimmerians, the wandering Sea People of the time, mounted his army in chariots and armed the drivers with wardogs. This strategy is remembered on a decorative cornice tile from Sardis, in the land of the animals of Cybele, where Aesop was born. Photo from a color restoration, bibliog. item 79, vol. 10, frontispiece.*

death, once the issue of the succession was settled, by having him dragged across the spikes of a carding machine. When Croesus did finally become king, he was thirty-five years old; Alexander the Great was dead at thirty-two; a lot could be said for the hypothesis that Aesop became attached to the party of Croesus before Alyattes died at what would have been an extremely old age.

Probably the best way of dating the context of events to which Aesop belonged is to rely on Suidas, who says that Pherecydes of Syros, a key figure in the period, "lived in the time of the Lydian king Alyattes and the Seven Sages," which is to say, in and around a year which can be dated with unique accuracy by Thales' famous "prediction" of the eclipse of the sun—585 B.C. This Pherecydes is said, too, to be the first to bring out a book of narrative material in prose, though prose annals, such as Eugeon's, may have been written earlier.

V

A telling instance of the aggressions of Alyattes and of the activities of the Seven Sages, the legendary associates of Aesop, is the siege which the oriental monarch laid on Priene, another close neighbor of Samos, when the strong little maritime city was under the leadership of Bias, one of the most pert of the Seven. In the midst of the privations which the Prieneans were suffering behind their walls, Bias contrived to send a pair of fat mules with well-fed drivers on an errand to Alyattes' camp, and Alyattes seeing that "the robust condition of his enemies seemed to extend to their very beasts of burden," concluded that he had better let the Prieneans off more cheaply than he had planned. He sent negotiators into the city. But Bias had prepared for them by piling heaps of sand in the market, which he had disguised with a covering of grain. When the negotiators went back and reported the great abundance of grain that they had seen in the city, Alyattes abandoned the siege. He was so impressed by his experience at Priene that he urged Bias to come and visit him in Sardis; but Bias told him "to chew on his onions," which is to say, to weep.

Bias and Aesop are of a family, even though the one rejected Eastern hospitality and the other accepted it. Over both of them, as over all seven of the Sages, there hangs, admittedly, a glow of folklore. The hoodwinking of Alyattes by a similar stratagem is said to have occurred at Miletus in an earlier period; the records may be only loosely factual. Nevertheless the story of Bias does document Ionian trouble with Alyattes, and it does illustrate how hot and cold oriental fervor could blow, while Ionian wit remained poised, shrewd and essentially disdainful. It was Bias who said, "Hoi pleistoi kakoi" ("Most men are bad"). But to Ionians the words probably meant nothing so black and white as that sounds, nothing so theological but rather something more humane, more *malin:* man on the whole is a pretty bad bargain. Who will deny the truth of such a statement? It's the sort of wisdom that the Sages relished, which will not be impeached by charges of folklore, and of which Aesop partook most generously.

It is possible that in the court of Alyattes, after Aesop had ingratiated himself and his fellow Samians with the impetuous king, the councilor fable-maker may have met the poet code-maker, Solon of Athens, as Plutarch says he did. He may have met Chilon, another of the Sages. For it is told that Chilon inquired of Aesop what Zeus was doing and received the answer: "Pulling down the high, and raising the low." This is the excellent Thomas Stanley's translation; the Loeb Library's Diogenes Laertius (1. 69) uses Biblical tones: "Humbling the proud and exalting the humble."

Again, I am not so much interested in whether or not these exchanges belong in the realm of actual happenings as I am in the quality of their content. They throw a sidelight on the tradition to which Aesop belonged. It was a gossipy, witty, ironical tradition, deeply all this in ways in which the more familiar fanatical Hebrew tradition, which somewhat resembles it in its pessimistic undertones, was not.

The first hint of how trouble started for Aesop in Delphi is to the effect that he was put to death for the sacrilege of stealing a holy object, a golden cup being found in a search of his baggage. The second adds that the cup had been planted among his belongings by the furious Delphians because he had scorned them for being parasites.

The anonymous, romancing *Life of Aesop* sketches out the sequence of events in a comprehensive fashion, which goes something like this in the abbreviated translation of La Fontaine:

On his return from Babylon, Aesop, still feeling the compulsion to go about the world, seeing and learning, left the court of Lycurgus, where he enjoyed all the benefits he could want, and departed to visit Greece once again.

Of the cities in which he made stops, Delphi was among the most noteworthy. The Delphians liked listening to him very well indeed, but they rewarded him with no honors or benefits whatsoever. Annoyed by being misprized, Aesop compared the Delphians with chunks of wood floating on the sea: from a distance they might look like something pretty considerable; but close up they turn out to be nothing. The comparison cost him dear. The Delphians conceived such hatred, such desire for vengeance, such fear of being derided far and wide, that they decided to dispose of him. They hid one of the temple cups in his baggage, meaning by means of it to convict him of theft and sacrilege, for which they would be able to condemn him to death.

When Aesop left Delphi and was on the road to Phocis, the Delphians came in a rush after him like people in pain. They accused him of stealing a cup; Aesop swore that he had not; his baggage was searched and the cup was found. All that Aesop could say couldn't stop them from treating him like the evilest of criminals. He was taken back to the city, put in irons, locked in a dungeon, and then condemned to be stoned from the cliff. Unable to defend himself with ordinary weapons, he tried fables, and was mocked for them.

"A frog," he told them, "had invited a mouse to come and see her. In order to ferry the mouse over the pond, the frog tied him to her foot. But once they were on the water, she tried to drag him to the bottom, meaning to drown him and make a meal of him afterwards. In his distress the mouse fought back as best he could. A bird of prey, seeing him thrashing the water, swooped down, and carried him off together with the frog, who couldn't get loose, and feasted on them, the one and the other.

"It's thus, filthy Delphians, that a greater power than we are will avenge me. I will perish, but you will perish too."

Then, when Aesop was being dragged to the cliff, he broke free and took sanctuary in a little chapel of Apollo. But he was torn from the altar. He told them then another fable, possibly his best, the one which is most elegantly his own, to which I shall want to return later, because Aristophanes made a great deal of it, and was perfectly aware that Aesop had defended himself by telling it when the Delphians were about to put him to death. It is the fable of the eagle and the dung beetle. Here it is in the version adopted by Emile Chambry:

An eagle was chasing a rabbit. The rabbit, finding himself without hope of escape, ran to the only living thing that happened to be in sight. It was a dung-beetle; he supplicated it to try to save his life. The dung-beetle reassured him; and seeing the eagle coming down, it conjured her not to seize its supplicant. But the eagle, disdaining so small a thing, devoured the rabbit before its eyes. So full of resentment was the beetle that from that time on it never stopped seeking out the places where the eagle built her nest and when she got ready to hatch her eggs, it would fly up and roll the eggs out and break them. Finally, the eagle, having been pursued everywhere, had recourse to Zeus, because it is to Zeus that this bird is sacred, and prayed him to give her a secure place where she could bring forth her young. Zeus permitted her to make her nest in his lap. But the dung-beetle was not caught defenseless by their new arrangement: it made a ball of dung, took flight with it upwards, and when it was just over Zeus's lap, it let it fall. Zeus, jumping up to rid himself of the dung-ball, shook the eggs out before he thought, and they plummeted down to earth. It's said that since then eagles will never try to nest in the season when dung-beetles are around.

Moral: Don't underestimate anyone. There isn't a being so weak that he may not be able some day to turn the tables on you.

That's practically the end of the earlier accounts of what happened in Delphi. Grimacing, likening himself to one of the lowest and ugliest of things, yet never ceasing to scorn the most honored establishment in the world, Aesop went headlong over the cliff.

VI

The weakness in these early accounts is the absence of convincing motivation for the Delphians' wrath. Aesop's invective, biting though it could easily have been, hardly constitutes cause enough for a public execution, which Herodotus took seriously, and for which the community itself had to make humiliating reparations later on.

Plutarch provides the way to make good this deficiency. Although he wrote some six centuries after the event, he was always effective in research and he was for many years one of the two priests of Apollo in Delphi. If there were documentation to be recovered anywhere, it would probably have been more available to Plutarch than to any other commentator. Here, in the Loeb translation of the "Divine Vengeance" essay (*Mor.* 556F), is what Plutarch has to say:

You will recall the story that Aesop came here with a sum of gold from Croesus, intending to offer a splendid sacrifice to the god and distribute four minas apiece to every Delphian; but falling into an angry dispute (the story goes) with the inhabitants of the place, he performed the sacrifice but sent the money back to Sardis, considering the people unworthy of the bounty. They therefore trumped up a charge of temple robbery and put him to death, casting him down from the cliff.

Since the name Croesus is hardly an obstacle, the one challenge in this passage is to account for the part that the Lydian gold plays in the story as Plutarch tells it. There can be no absolutely positive answer, of course. But the range of likelihoods is not wide. Either the gold was to pay for the oracle's support in a personal matter, something such as Croesus's claim to the throne, just as Croesus's great-grandfather, Gyges, had used Delphi to secure himself in the sovereignty after he had murdered his predecessor and married his wife; or it was to establish a political advantage for Sardis. Here too the range of possibilities would appear to be narrow. The largesse would either be aimed at the procuring of allies (normally in Lacedaemonia) or at softening up places for conquest (Asiatic or east Greek) or both objectives combined.

In any one of these projects poker-faced double-dealing on the part of the oracle might occur. In fact the likelihood is that if possible it would occur, as it had to Alyattes at Miletus. It follows that if the Delphians were caught red-handed in a fraud, the gifts that were intended for them would be withheld. Now these gifts were considerable, the money amounting to four hundred ancient drachmas apiece to every inhabitant of the place. The Delphians were not only venal, they were greedy. "Swarming like flies around a goatherd, or wasps from the ground, or Delphians from a sacrifice": Callimachus is only mentioning the sort of conduct that had become proverbial (Fr. 191).

Aesop withheld the Lydian gold and the community of the oracle was enraged. An emissary from a distant, barbaric kingdom had struck an ugly discord in their local orchestration. The Delphians therefore stoned him into silence. We can remember the plight of Creusa, the queen, in Euripides' play *Ion*. Those Delphians tore her also from the altar of Apollo and were about to drag her toward the cliff when the utterly unpredictable revelations of the Pythia changed the course of events. The ancients were prepared to believe that harsh and irrational happenings could occur in the holiest of places.

But I can't imagine that they would have had much credence in a quite recent theory that makes Aesop out to have been a scapegoat or *pharmakos,* that is to say, a victim of a ritual which is supposed to have been practiced in the Thargelia, a festival honoring Apollo. This celebration was agrarian in origin, an ancient annual offering of the first fruits of the harvest, and as such it was a happy event, a "good season," as Hesychius defines it, and as Archilochus implies in a fragment written in the century before the time of Aesop:

> Dawn breaks,
> Phesinos.
> . . . Now it's the Thargelia!

But there occurred in some past eras, at some places, a dark reverse of the happy aspect of the holiday: human sacrifice appears to have been an attendant rite, the purpose of which was to heap the ills of the community on a victim and by getting rid of him to get rid of all accumulated evils, like sweeping away the filth that has been gathering through the year. The victim chosen was required to be the worst, the poorest, the most criminal, repugnant and ugly individual that the place had produced.

The rite appears to have been abandoned in the Greek area before the keeping of records, even in the form of oral temple traditions, had begun. Symbolically it may have persisted as a kind of negative by-play, as in Athens, but not as the real thing. Gilbert Murray, in an appendix to *The Rise of the Greek Epic*, shows in detail how lacking in pertinence for historical times are the texts which hint at actual sacrifices of *pharmakoi*.

In 1961, however, a German folklorist, Anton Wiechers, published a dissertation proposing to demonstrate, with the aid of some dazzling pedantry, that Aesop was put through the ritual of the Thargelian sacrifice and died the death of the *pharmakos*. To support his argument Professor Wiechers noted that the place was a seat of Apollo; that the victim was the thief of a cup or the unwilling ritualistic recipient of a cup that had been rendered unholy; that he was therefore a criminal; that he was ugly; that he died in the appropriate way, at the foot of a cliff.

The argument is a series of puns. A shrine of Apollo is not per se a site of human sacrifice. The cup is not necessarily a folk-ritual element: planted evidence has often been used for nefarious purposes and I'm afraid will be used in the future. Aesop is not a criminal in the sense of being worthless to the community; he is the master of a Lydian fortune, for the moment anyhow; he is one of the eminent persons in the broad world of his day; otherwise he would not have been in Delphi. He is ugly, but that is an attraction, a part of his stock in trade as a speaker; he is not ugly in the ways that make a *pharmakos* ugly. He is put over the cliff. So was anyone suffering execution.

The whole hypothesis seems to me to be misconceived. A ritual death—the exercise of the rite of human sacrifice—must by definition follow prescribed forms which can only become ritual by systematic repetition, festival after festival. If such had been the case in Delphi, Herodotus and everybody else would have known about it, and would have talked about it, just as Herodotus does when he comes to his account of the wild Tauri (4. 103).

Professor Wiechers does come up, nevertheless, with the exciting discovery of the Vatican red figure kylix, which I have already mentioned, and the possibility that something new in the way of knowledge about Aesop may be derived from it. For the folklorist, though, the picture in the cup is no more than an argument for the contention that Aesop was ugly and therefore eligible to be a *pharmakos*. To my eye the picture is different. The quizzical looking fable maker with the big domed pate and the bright animal facing him, which Professor Wiechers calls a fox, are a sprightly pair. There must be a fine fable in the making here.

VII

The picture, as I said, has been reproduced in general art books, where too often one illustration fades into another and into an undistinguished text. Totally otherwise is its impact in a masterly study of the mechanical arts in Greece: A. Orlandos's *Les Matériaux de Construction*. In this context we observe that Aesop is holding a hammer in one hand (a *krotaphis* or metal worker's tool, according to Orlandos) with which he seems to be gesticulating for the edification or amusement of the animal seated upright on its haunches opposite him. It seems that the two of them are engaged in a dialogue, and the objects on which they are seated—Aesop looking perplexed, the animal gaily waving its forepaws—are anvils. Their seats are easily identified as anvils by comparing this picture with Orlandos's page 110, where a metal worker, depicted on an oenochoe in the British Museum, is resting his tongs on the raised lip of an anvil while another man is about to hammer the hot metal on its broad lower face. An object of this size and shape would serve well enough as a stool.

The scene is a smithy, a metal worker's establishment, and it does in truth have a fable to go with it: "A smith had a dog. While he was working, the dog always slept, but when he stopped to eat, the dog would hurry over to him. Once, having let him have a bone, the smith said to him, 'You poor tired old fellow, always sound asleep while I pound my anvil, but wide awake at the least click of my teeth.'" Lazy sleepers who live by the labor of others see themselves in this fable.

American editors have underrated the beauties of the fable in this version, which is included in good manuscripts and has often been published in the past. Editors in general, so far as I know, have overlooked the connection between the fable and the Vatican kylix, and art editors who have noticed the cup have misnamed the animal. It is curious that this should happen because foxes, though plentiful in fables, are scarce in paintings, and when they do appear, as on the Chigi vase, they are small, short-legged and bushy-tailed, looking nothing like the beggar on the cup, unless the rim of the anvil is mistaken for a brush. Aesop's dog looks just like later Greek dogs, limber-legged, skinny-waisted, prick-eared, sharp-nosed, thin-tailed—just like the animals attacking Actaeon in the Pan-painter's picture.

The Greeks apparently visualized a fox not as a sophisticated Reynard nor as a brazen sociable quadruped like the one on the cup, but as a furtive small beast; witness Aristophanes' calling the town-bred soldier, "a lion in the city, but only a fox in battle" (*Peace* 1189–90).

Not the least of the beauties of the scene in Aesop's smithy is its power to evoke the primeval world from which all fables seem to have come. Archaeologists have rescued enough pictorial material, small decorative mosaics and the like, to show that the very ancient peoples enjoyed the fantasy of animals playing the parts of men, rivaling men in sapience, outwitting men, outwitting one another, defrauding one another just as men do; born to be asses but still determined to play the harp. There's a certain asperity in these fantasies and also a great deal of kindliness toward the natural world.

On a tablet from Sumer a sort of narrative proverb was written down thirty-five hundred years ago, but was doubtless in common speech long before that. The little thing as translated by S. N. Kramer goes like this:

> The smith's dog could not overturn the anvil;
> He (therefore) overturned the waterpot instead.

The smith and his dog have already started the more or less affectionate contention among creatures which will become one of the primary stuffs in Aesopic fables. "While the ox pulls the plow, the dog spoils the deep furrow," is the gist of another Sumerian comment.

A phenomenon worth meditating is the fact that Sumerian civilization, though controlled at the top by the stiffest of religious hierarchies, should have through the middle a population of smiths and farmers blessed with an observant sense of the antics that go on in this world. This paradox holds for the other arts. The temple statue makers continued through a millennium and more to represent human beings

mostly as worshipers, in a kind of hypnotic trance, their hands clasped in prayer, their gaze directed heavenwards, but outside the temples, in mosaics, in seals and friezes, in jewelry and figurines, animals are formed with round imaginative vivacity. The formal literature also, the *Gilgamesh* sort of thing, is as far removed from the interests of the dawning Greek consciousness as the rudimentary proverb-fable is close to it. The Sumerian tablet which says, "Just as I was escaping the ox, the wild cow confronted me," would need no gloss for Greeks. Nor probably, in view of Anaximander's interest in the diffusion of

A Menagerie in the Phrygian Style: *A bull, a lion, and a goat. The animals depicted here have the abiding fantasy in their makeup which I imagine goes back to the beginnings of consciousness itself. The lion's head on the coin from Cyzicus (p. 257) suggests terrors remembered from the Ice Age. But so extravagant may be the terrors of the great predatory beasts, so enervating the struggle with them, so fortunate the escape, that deep recollections may seem unreal, even comical, like something half-recalled from a nightmare. Hence the second lion; hence the other fabulous creatures which were encountered in tales and seen on coins and visualized in the constellations. To call them "Phrygian" is a matter of convenience. Their Urartian, Hittite, and Syrian components are noticeable, but since these components were translated into the arts of Phrygia and then transplanted as great orientalizing elements into our own early Greek world, the band across Asia Minor which we associate with music and jewelry and heroic friezes, and with Aesop himself, Phrygia is apt enough as an identification of their source. These particular animals appeared on tiles. Their lavish floral and geometrical decorations seem particularly appropriate to the fabulous texture. The fact that the tiles, to the best of my knowledge, were found incorporated in Moorish architecture in Spain adds to their interest. Those civilizations which adopted the Arabic language have been most careful to preserve intact many documents which they inherited from the past.*

fluids, would this: "The fox having urinated into the sea said, 'Now the whole sea's my piss!' "

The scene in Aesop's smithy evokes likewise the Greek archaic age at its best, before the times when the specializations with their snobberies had taken over. It was a period which valued the universal man, much like the Italian Renaissance. Just as the Seven Sages were men of broad experience, worldly in their businesses, professional in their love of wisdom, in the same way a master metal worker was not either a craftsman or an artist; he was both. The most notable offering that he saw at Delphi, says Herodotus, was a welded iron stand for an enormous silver bowl. Glaukos the Chian is remembered as its creator, Alyattes the Lydian king as its donor. The workshop and farmstead and wild forest, far from dishonoring the fables with menial concerns, give them their marvelous homely concreteness.

VIII

The habit of fable making apparently traveled westward from the Mesopotamian valley into western Asia Minor, becoming exceedingly popular in Phrygia and regions somewhat to the south, where the Greeks picked it up. Phrygia, according to solid tradition as well as the skittish *Life of Aesop*, was Aesop's birthplace. Another tradition mentions Thrace; but Phrygia makes greater sense. In the times of Aesop, Phrygia had fallen under the sway of Lydia. As a center of slave markets, it could have been the most likely place where a not quite handsome boy would be bought at a slave dealer's price and shipped to Samos. As the scene of Marsyas's disastrous battle with Apollo and King Midas's outrageously profitable encounter with Silenus, it was the background for the kind of half-legendary, half-mythical event on which fable thrives. But most importantly for Aesop it was rich in artistic representations of the great beasts of the fables—the ox, the boar, the stag, the lion—most particularly the lion, which, as T. J. Dunbabin pointed out, emerged from the Near East to occupy first place among animals in seventh-century Greek art, replacing even the aristocratic skinny stallions of the Geometric period.

And with the lion, of course, the lioness: the lioness who, when the fox reproached her for giving birth to only one offspring at a time, could reply, according to Aesop, "Yes, one only at a time, but a lion."

Over the animals, Cybele, the Asiatic Mother-Goddess, was mistress. In the course of time she took up an abode in the Artemision of Ephesus. Her favorite creature, the lion, with his fierce Syro-Hittite mane, faces you from the earliest coins in the world, including the first silver coins of Samos, where a winged boar or the forepart of an ox was stamped on the obverse. As a matter of fact the willow-wound Hera of Samos had not a little of the Mother-Goddess's blood in her veins.

The resurgence of these graphic images of the old animals in the arts of the younger lands is accompanied by the practice of fabling about them, both in proverbs and at narrative length. In the orientalizing period, which produced the Chigi vase with its vivacious, richly colored foxes and lions and other animals, Greek literature had a great day of its own; but what was a vast literary output has survived only in scattered fragments. Enough remains, however, to show that Archilochus, in the seventh century, was Aesop's great predecessor in the fable and quite possibly the greater master in his own right.

Some of his work reads in its fragmentariness like the little parables on the Sumerian tablets. This justly famous sentence of his is an example:

> Fox knows many tricks;
> Hedgehog knows only one
> . . . but it's a beauty.

Or this, in J. M. Edmonds's text in the Loeb Library:

> We have an ox that's a handsome, high-headed devil!
> Knows how to plow too, but refuses to do it.

But Archilochus also created strong complex poems of some length, sardonic in tone, with which no doubt the Epodes of Horace are comparable in important respects. In composing them Archilochus often used a fable as a basic structural device; about a dozen fables, all recognizable as belonging to the present Aesopic canon, figure in what is left of these pieces, as the researches of André Bonnard, reported in the Budé edition of the Lasserre text, have brought out. It appears that Archilochus liked to surround a fable, which he narrated in dramatic detail, with verses of bitter invective, abusing certain persons whom he detested, particularly a woman, Neoboule, to whom he had been betrothed and who later became a courtesan, and her father, Lycombes, who had broken up the betrothal.

Not enough of any one of these fable-working poems has survived to support a clear-cut description of them, but by improvising very freely and following the hints assembled in the Budé edition we might come up with something like the following as a paraphrase of the Fourth Epode of Archilochus:

A lion had got old.
It could not prowl around
And take by force
The prey it wanted.
So it thought: How to beguile
The unwary?

It went to its cave
And lay there, pretending delicate health.
It called out from time to time,
Asking the animals of the forest
To come, out of pity, for a visit.

When one by one they came,
The lion dragged them one by one
Back to its bed in the cavern
And devoured them.

The passing fox,
Hearing the lion calling from the doorway,
Suspicious,
Standing apart,
Asked how the lion felt.

"Bad, my sweet creature, bad.
Come in and console me.
When I was happy and well,
You were pleasant to me.
Now for old times' sake
Come in and comfort me again."

The fox replied, "I would,
If it weren't for one thing.
I see animal tracks going in,
But none coming out."

And so, Neoboule, by pointed tracks
I'm warned. Once times were better, that's true.
But not now, never again: you cast loose my ship
Between the wind and wave, and yourself cast loose.
Sailing the tortuous alleys of the camp
At Hera's temple, you clung to men straining
Above you, like Odysseus to the stinking ram.
Then Xanthe steered you, lent her house and bed,

Brought guests, whom you devoured. Now you're old,
Flaccid and hollow under that golden cloak,
Mangy, with bad teeth, but still with strength to claw.
You're nothing now that's either male or female:
Don't put seductions in your voice for me.

The tellers of fables who succeeded Archilochus seem to have agreed that the very personal, moralizing application like that turned loose against Neoboule is not appropriate to the fable form. Horace felt good about bringing "the Parian iambics into Latium," and the verse patterns and intelligence of Archilochus into his own *Epodes;* but he rejected a program of pursuing a victim the way Neoboule is pursued above (*Epistle* I. 19). The application of the fable of the old lion to one decayed human female is too tight it seems, too special, too elaborate; sensational though it must have been in Archilochus's proper idiom, for he always used the realest words and in other contexts often the gentlest.

The true art of the fable, however, seems to be what Aesop made it, not Archilochus—a prose art, characterized by an absolutely uncluttered, clean narrative. Efforts to goose up the flow of the narrative with superfluous dramatic touches invariably fall flat. The soundest model for the strict Aesopic tradition I believe is the Samian parable about the Fox with the ticks and the Hedgehog. Of course a great poet with a disciplined meter can take a fable and make it his own pasture. But in my opinion, only La Fontaine merits really high praise for the departure from prose. Lessing, so far as I know, was the first to describe the unique effectiveness of the prose fable. It is uniquely effective. The art of Aesop is a mature art, entertaining to children though it is.

Appending a moral to the fable is fundamentally a matter of style, of sly prose style; but comparable with the couplets at the end of a Shakespearean sonnet, or the plaudite at the end of a comedy. The lessons are usually, and intentionally, twisting half-truths, which provoke reflection back over the narrative. La Fontaine called the moral the soul of the fable, but in practice he liked best to breathe it into the whole body of the apologue. I think the moral of the prose fable is more like the conscience, that poor worried thing, always rightly a little uneasy about its verdicts.

One fable in various forms has nagged the conscience of three or four civilizations. It's no ordinary fable; rather it's an orientalizing "Milesian" tale, originating on the coasts behind Samos, and told about a widow of Ephesus. I propose to retell it and to put its moral up for grabs.

In Ephesus a woman who was noted for her devotion to her husband, followed his body into the tomb when he died suddenly. In her grief she refused to return home, but instead set up to live in the chamber with her husband's sarcophagus and her little maidservant. This further proof of her capacity for womanly devotion made her now indeed the wonder of Ephesus. It happened, however, that the bodies of three temple robbers were hanging from crosses nearby, with sentinels posted to see that the relatives of the dead men would not come and take the bodies away for burial. A young soldier standing guard over these dismal trophies of justice became curious one night about a light in a tomb. Using thirst as his excuse, he crossed over and discovered the widow and the servant girl. With his own eyes he saw a beautiful grieving woman. With the help of the girl he persuaded her to break her fast and, in short, to accept those consolations which he could give her. In her grief she was grateful for his solicitude. The feelings of each prompted the act of love, which once begun continued night by night. Then a dawn came when the soldier saw an empty cross standing between the other two. Knowing that his defection could not be concealed, he sagged to the ground. The widow, recognizing the cause of his trouble, told him not to fear, the body of her husband was at hand, they would put it on the cross in place of the corpse which was missing. By her action she made it possible for the sentinel to escape disaster.

"Thus did vile infamy take the place of famous virtue," the Phaedrus version of the fable concludes, while the Petronius version ends with a raucous roar of laughter from the sailors who had been listening. Among modern scholars "The Widow of Ephesus" has been offered as an example of the kind of low fable which has crept uninvited into the texts of the great Homer. Well, in all conscience the Widow does provoke a laugh and is frailty, and yet quite possibly she is something else too, something like uncalculating selflessness, unreserved devotion. Her disposition, like the ugliness of Aesop, has more beauty to it than meets the eye. Or perhaps it does. There are stories, some most interesting stories, like Hera's seducing Zeus on top of Mount Ida, upon which it is folly to try to make a pronouncement.

IX

While in prison waiting out the festival which had delayed his execution, Socrates had visitors, one of whom questioned him about the rumor that he had been writing poetry. Yes, Socrates replied: he who had never written a line of verse, felt that he should try to comply with a recurring dream which urged him to make music. So he wrote a hymn to Apollo, whose festival had given him the respite, and then "considering that a poet ought to tell stories as well as make hymns," he undertook to versify the fables of Aesop, not having the gift for inventing stories of his own (*Phaedo* 60Dff.).

It was no accident that Socrates should have pitched onto the fables of Aesop for the narratives in his poetry, rather than, say, the famous myths, because he had affinities with Aesop which went deeper than we are in the habit of remembering. In Socrates' lifetime these affinities were well enough known; they are implicit in Alcibiades' description of Socrates in the *Symposium* (215A–216D): "He is exactly like the busts of Silenus, which are set up in the statuaries' shops, holding pipes and flutes in their mouths; and they are made to open in the middle, and have images of the gods inside them. And I also say that he is like Marsyas the satyr."

In other words, ugly on the outside, beautiful within—just as Aesop was known everywhere to be. Aesop, in the *Life,* is given his own specific likeness to Marsyas, the shaggy Phrygian satyr, "whom country people loved, and," according to Ovid, "for whom the shepherds wept," when he was felled by the malice of Apollo (Ovid *Met.* 6. 392ff.).

It was said that Socrates brought philosophy down from heaven to earth. It could be said that Aesop brought the mystery of Prometheus's handiwork—mankind—down to earth, and that both shared in a love of a peculiar kind of wisdom, along with a very low-heeled, if not a downright bare-footed, attitude toward it, which is put best by Erasmus, who speaks more or less for the whole Renaissance, in an Adage having to do with Socrates, the *Sileni Alcibiadis:*

Anyone who took him at face value, as they say, would not have offered a farthing for him. He had a yokel's face, with a bovine look about it, and a snub nose always running; you would have thought him some stupid, thick-headed clown. He took no care of his appearance, and his language was plain, unvarnished, and unpretentious, as befits a man who was always talking about charioteers, workmen, fullers, and blacksmiths. For it was usually from these that he took the terms with which he pressed his arguments home. . . . In short his eternal jesting gave him the air of a clown. In those days it was all the rage, among stupid people, to want to appear clever, and Gorgias was not the only one to declare there was nothing that he did not know; fusspots of that kind have always abounded! Socrates alone said that he was sure of one thing only, that he knew nothing.   (trans. M. M. Phillips)

Protesting one's ignorance so cheerfully as Socrates protested his, can be reckoned as the last act in the ancient comedy of the Seven Sages, in which each Sage disclaimed being the wisest and passed the prize for wisdom on to his neighbor.

The last act because, before Plato had finished his portrait of Socrates, a new philosophy had taken over. The new wisdom was austere, remote from fullers and blacksmiths, on its way back to heaven. With the aid of one of the fables of Aesop Socrates himself is maneuvered by Plato into foreshadowing the shape of the new ideas which were taking form. This is the fable; we will get to its moral in a moment:

An astronomer, who Socrates says was no other than Thales the Sage of Miletus, was in the habit of going out in the evenings to observe the stars. Once while he was strolling on the outskirts of the city with his eyes fixed on the heavens, he fell into a well. He howled, and a Thracian maidservant who came and helped him get out, said to him, "You're so eager to see what goes on among the stars that you don't see what's at your feet."

Socrates is inspired by this fable to make a resounding distinction in the *Theaetetus* (174ff.) between the philosopher and the vulgar crowd. "To the general herd, the philosopher's awkwardness is fearful, and gives the impression of imbecility. . . . Our philosopher is derided by the vulgar, partly because he is thought to despise them, and also he is ignorant of what is before him, and always at a loss." But about the philosopher: "The truth is, the outer form of him only is in the city; his mind, disdaining the littleness and nothingness of human things, is 'flying abroad' as Pindar says, measuring earth and heaven and the things which are under the earth and on the earth and above the heaven. . . . He hardly knows whether he is a man or an animal; he is searching into the essence of man" (trans. Jowett).

Two remarks are pertinent: one, this is not the Socrates of the Marsyas metaphor, but more nearly the Socrates of the *Clouds;* two, the opposites projected, of worldliness versus otherworldliness, will explode in the face of anybody who tries to cohabit with the one at the exclusion of the other. But here again, how literally should we read the *Theaetetus?* It may be nothing more serious than a sentimental farewell to the life of contemplation, which Plato was moved to write just before his enlistment in the tyranny at Syracuse.

In any event the fable of the Astronomer and the Thracian girl cannot be felt to be antiintellectual unless one is prepared to think of intelligence as a highly trained, carefully specialized, and sterilized power which cannot stand the contamination of everyday life.

As for the vexing question of ugliness, the emphasis which Erasmus puts on it in the passage above is obviously not meant to be derogatory, and the defects he stresses fit Aesop just about as well as Socrates. Plainly the looks of a man become better or worse at the pleasure of whoever does the reporting. So what after all is ugliness? Was Dr. Samuel Johnson ugly? was Cyrano de Bergerac? Whatever the answer, Lucian makes both Socrates and Aesop comedians in temperament and actions in his account of the immortals in Hades, over whose banquets Aesop presides as jester (*Ver. Hist.* 2. 18). In common to each of them is the willingness to jest about serious things, and jesting leads naturally to the funny facial expression and tone of voice, to the use finally of the personal eccentricity. Aristophanes, for another example, makes the most of his bald head. He complimented himself at length in the *Peace* as the baldheaded man who made the comedies which delighted Athens. And then, once the peculiarity is noticed, legend begins taking over with exaggerations which run in all directions. Aesop's humped back finds its counterbalance in Pythagoras's golden thigh.

X

The *Peace* of Aristophanes is the greatest existing memorial to Aesop. It is a heartbreaking comedy straight out of the lives of smiths, fullers, carpenters, farmers; it is a long clamorous musical appeal for peace, literally for putting a stop to the Peloponnesian War, then and there, in the year 421 B.C., unconditionally, with nothing demanded of the Spartans except the cessation of hostilities. With this urgent motivation, it rises to high fantasy and unfettered poetry. Aesop provides Aristophanes with the vehicle which carries the comedy and its hero, Trygaeus the Vinegrower, to heaven to solicit Zeus to bring peace to the Hellenes. The vehicle is the dung beetle of the fable.

The play unfolds in the vast, stone-benched open theater of Dionysus on a spring afternoon during the festival of 421 B.C. Stretched across a long low stone stage are the façades, the "flats," of three or four "houses." The one on the right is the modest dwelling of the pacifist vinegrower Trygaeus, a widower with servants and children. The one on the left is the abode of the gods (when they are at home) and is no more lofty, as is fitting in comedy, than the neighboring houses. Of these, one is the paddock of a giant dung beetle, whom Trygaeus, it is announced, intends to ride on the flight to heaven to ask Zeus to stop the war.

Everyone in the vast audience squeezed into the flank of the Acropolis has a painful, firsthand knowledge of the war. For years the Spartans had come during the growing seasons and had ravaged the farms and villages of Attica, forcing everyone to crowd into the city. They had been held back recently only by the threat of reprisal on the lives of three hundred Spartan prisoners—things had arrived at that stage of desperation. Meanwhile news from battles far afield was bad. The only good news was the announcement of the death of the Spartan commander in chief, Brasidas, and of the Athenian commander in chief, both by some miracle being killed in the same encounter. From these deaths sprang the strong new hope for peace. We must add that the dead Athenian was Cleon, the inflamer of the multitude, whom Aristophanes detested and pursued in comedy with all the rancor of an Archilochus.

The dung beetle is hidden from sight at first by the paddock wall, but the servants darting in and out, feeding him his ordure, make it quite clear that they've got a really remarkable bug penned up back there, one that their master has been at great pains to seek out for his trip. The dung beetle, the audience is reminded, is the only earthly creature that ever reached the gods, as they all should know from the fable of Aesop.

This species of beetle figures in other fables. Its fascination for the Greeks may be related to the fascination of the scarab to the Egyptians. The bug calls attention to itself by its fantastic habit of kicking a ball of dung up a sunny, dusty slope and letting it roll down again until the ball has become a good big round mass. This will house eggs and become a commissary for the younger generation, or for that matter, according to other fables, for any beetles who find themselves in need. This phenomenal activity, reduced to its essentials of the sun and the earth and the sphere, suggested, to the Egyptians anyhow, spontaneous creativity.

In the *Peace* creativity explodes after the introductory running and fetching, when up from behind the paddock wall, hoisted by the stage crane, comes Trygaeus, astride a six-legged, shiny-shelled enormous beetle, with wings outspread. The vinegrower's farewell to his family is touching; his takeoff is precarious; his flight is endangered by his steed's interest in the smells of the latrines of the Piraeus and the mechanic's carelessness in handling the levers that control the crane. But all ends well. Trygaeus is swung over to the abode of the gods.

Most of the gods, offended by the spectacle of what has been happening on earth, have gone away. But Hermes is left. Bribery makes him complaisant, and with his help and the aid of a chorus of country people, Trygaeus does get Peace—she is embodied in what appears to be a colossal archaic wooden statue—hauled up from the dungeon where War has buried her. With her come two living girls, the handsome attendants of Peace, Holiday and Harvest Home. Leaving his dung beetle in the service of Zeus, Trygaeus and the handmaidens of Peace start on foot to make the long descent to Athens.

The rest of the play is a celebration. A sacrifice is made to the goddess, in which a gluttonous sponging oracle is fought off. The beautiful Holiday, stripped naked by Trygaeus for the occasion, is presented to the Council sitting in their tall front-row seats. Trygaeus himself is married to Harvest Home. Just that; with much poetry, dancing, lighthearted obscenity, and joy in the workaday world.

There is toughness in these pastoral choric scenes. They reflect a countryside which properly complements the dung beetle. And Trygaeus remains the wry mocker who exploits the license of the fables. When he hobbles in after the long hike down from heaven, he looks out at the audience in amazement. "From up there," he says, "you looked awfully bad but so very small. Down here you look monstrously big and worse than ever."

Trygaeus's little daughter, with the sensitivity of the young, asked

An Immortal Pair: The Fox and the Hedgehog.
Figures from a sixth century B.C. vase in the Metropolitan Museum.

her father at the commencement of his enterprise, why, if he has to fly
off to visit the gods, why couldn't he at least arrange to ride up there
on Pegasus, like a hero, instead of on this ugly old dung beetle?

The answers which are insinuated in the ensuing dialogue seem to
me to speak from the point of view of a grimacing, baldheaded fabulist-
comedian, an Aesop metamorphosed into an Aristophanes. Pegasus
would never do; heroes have only had trouble with the likes of him;
once Bellerophon was on him on a hard gallop towards heaven when
he fell off and lamed himself for life: Euripides has told all about it.
And as for this famous Pegasus, we don't know anything about him,
we don't know at all what he really is; but this beetle is unmistakable,
he's a living creature; you can tell it by his unabashed interest in feeding. And if you'll come right down to it, you have no business looking
around for help from a pretty prancer like Pegasus when you've got an
ugly war on your hands. A dung beetle will serve you better.

Of course praising the dung beetle won't serve in itself as a suitable
epimythia for the *Peace,* helpful though it may be in explaining contemporary behavior among pacifists. Always in control of the ugly, in
comedy and fable alike, is the artistry, always the inside of the Silenus
figurine as well as the outside. The primly genteel is bad, the offensive-
ly ugly is bad. When Erasmus wrote a prose comedy of his own by
expanding this tale of Aesop's to put among his Adages, he ended by
saying that between the eagle and the beetle you face a dilemma.
Eagles are like contending generals—say, Cleon and Brasidas; beetles
are their humble but persistent opponents. Eagles may rend you limb
from limb, but beetles, once agitated, fly around and around and won't
be shaken off; you're ashamed to use force on them, if you crush them
you're defiled.

Fables bring up more dilemmas than they give back answers; that's part of their excitement. It's perhaps one reason too why they were favored in ancient times but have become relatively uninteresting in times which want answers, black and white, doctrinaire answers, right now.

But speaking of Aristophanes' *Peace,* I suppose we do look up sometimes from our ponderous global preoccupations and see ourselves from Aesop's point of view. I, at least, was amazed when in California, in a meeting of a Sunkist cooperative recently, I heard this fable recounted:

A hen and a pig were traveling along a freeway. The hen said, "I'm hungry." The pig said, "All right. Let's get off and find a place to eat." They took the first exit ramp and almost immediately saw a restaurant with a sign above it—Ham & Eggs. The hen said, "I'm willing to be committed to that!" The pig said, "I'm not. From you they ask a small contribution, but from me, total involvement."

4
PYTHAGORAS OF SAMOS

Scene: The Limbo of Festival and Plague. Time: in the reign of Queen Elizabeth I of England. Coming to Croydon in the time of the plague, Thomas Nashe reduced the history of poetry and philosophy into verse in Summer's Last Will and Testament, *sportively divulging shady practices and abstruse doctrines.*

WINTER

(castigating the misuse of Summer's treasures)

When Cerberus was headlong drawn from Hell,
He voided a black poison from his mouth,
Called Aconitum, whereof ink was made:
That ink, with reeds first laid on dried barks,
Served men to make rude works withal.
After each nation got these toys in use,
There grew up certain drunken parasites,
Termed Poets, which for a meal's meat or two
Would promise monarchs immortality.
They vomited in verse all that they knew,
Found causes and beginnings of the world,
Fetched pedigrees of mountains and of floods
From men and women whom the gods transformed.
If any town or city they passed by
Had in compassion (thinking them madmen)
Forborne to whip them or imprison them,
That city was not built by human hands,
'Twas raised by music, like Megara wells;
Apollo, poets' patron, founded it.
Next them, a company of ragged knaves,
Sun-bathing beggars, lazy hedge-creepers,
Sleeping face upwards in the fields at night,
Dreamed strange devices of the Sun and Moon;
And they, like Gypsies, wandering up and down,
Told fortunes, juggled, nicknamed all the stars,
And were of Idiots termed Philosophers:
Such was Pythagoras the Silencer;
Prometheus; Thales Milesius,
Who would all things of water should be made;
Anaximander; Anaximenes,
That positively said the Air was god.

THE FIRST PERSON ever to adopt the name philosopher comes down to us looking the most bizarre. An uncommonly big rosy man with an elegant cloak and a handsome beard, he is reported also to have had a golden leg, a flighty head for mathematics, an ingenuous belief in metempsychosis, and the power of working miracles. The guardians of the memory of Pythagoras have contrived a fantastic legend about him. It is just about as fantastic as the legend with which Aesop the fabulist was immortalized, only it goes toward the opposite extreme, Apollonian beauty rather than Satyric ugliness; and it has been even more puzzling to the keepers of old records than the Aesop legend.

Although traditional history gathers encrustments which can never be removed, I have hopes of restoring the outline of the person Pythagoras must have been by considering him very closely in the light of his Ionian origins. These origins are the primary fact about him; he was an Ionian of Samos, an Ionian who migrated westward, it is true, and settled in Italy in a strange intellectual climate; but he was "quite old enough," says W.K.C. Guthrie, "to have studied mathematics before he left the East, where a strong mathematical tradition continued." For Herodotus, and for his closest contemporaries, he was Pythagores of Samos, spelled out like that with the *e* in Ionic Greek. It follows that he was one of the close small family of the earliest Ionian philosophers —Thales, Anaximander, Anaximenes, Heraclitus. He was basically in agreement with them, and he was not by any means the least of them either, as Herodotus goes out of his way to remark (4. 95).

But he remained, like the other Ionians, more or less a stranger to what became the Athenian tradition in philosophy. Pythagoras's tradition was the tradition of Democritus, "who went to Athens and nobody knew him"; and I don't mean the Democritus of atomism so much as of the whole complex archaic inquiry which gave rise incidentally to the theory of the atom. The shape which this inquiry casts backwards onto the shadowy presence of Pythagoras is what this chapter is about.

My real concern of course is with something more than putting together a jigsaw puzzle portrait of an imposing personage with Samian features. In Pythagoras, possibly for the first time in history, a human mind attempted to achieve a wholly objective conquest of the many faceted structure which is our universe, and in the course of doing so, it discovered the mind's plight. Along with positive insight into things taken separately and individually, Pythagoras encountered an inherent principle of negativity, summed up in irrational numbers, which implied that things on the whole did not hang intelligibly together. To this day the problem in the form of many sorts of indeterminacy is still deeply troubling.

II

In view of the irregular presumptions which guide the present account, it won't be inappropriate to take our first look at Pythagoras through the eyes of Lucian of Samosata. For all of his glittering malice, the satirist Lucian has the solidist of merits, and I regard his entrance here at the outset of our affair as peculiarly suitable, because for Shakespeare, for Ben Jonson, for everybody in the bright days of the Renaissance, Pythagoras was known almost exclusively as the vaguely preposterous character in Lucian's sketches.

The philosopher whom Lucian writes about had arrived at midphase in the development of his legend; he is already much overblown but not yet divorced from his original humanity. The following is a sample of the sort of amiable caricature for which Lucian is responsible. It is an excerpt from "Philosophies on the Auction Block," in which the satirist imagines Zeus as putting various systems of philosophy up for sale for the benefit of mankind. The scene is a sales arena; the auctioneer is Hermes. Acting as impersonations of their doctrines, the founders of the philosophic schools come up one by one for auction, and while the buyers consider them, they expound their views and make what claims they can to recommend themselves and their doctrines. Here, in slightly condensed paraphrase, are the negotiations involving Pythagoras. The dialogue amounts to an epitome, a motley but sound epitome, of the Pythagorean creed in a second-century A.D. guise.

HERMES. Who shall we put up first?
ZEUS. The one with the long hair. The Ionian. He shows off pretty well.
HERMES (*to Pythagoras*). Come up here.
ZEUS. All right, sell him.

HERMES. Here, gentlemen, this one's tops! Who'll buy him? Who's for superman? Harmony of the universe? Music of the spheres? Who'll bid for the transmigration of souls?

BUYER. He looks all right, but what can he do?

HERMES. Arithmetic, astronomy, falsifications, geometry, folk-songs. . . . He's good at picking futures, and great at group therapy.

BUYER (to Pythagoras). Where are you from?

PYTHAG. Samos.

BUYER. Where did you go to school?

PYTHAG. To the Sages, in Egypt.

BUYER. If I'd buy you, what would you teach me?

PYTHAG. Nothing. But I'd help you get started remembering some things.

BUYER. How would you do that?

PYTHAG. First I'd make you freshen up your soul.

BUYER. How?

PYTHAG. By requiring you to keep silent. For five years you'd keep perfectly still.

BUYER. Look, maybe you'd better get yourself sold to Croesus, to teach that deaf and dumb son of his. But if I buy you, what after that?

PYTHAG. After that, music and geometry.

BUYER. That's better. I'll take up the guitar!

PYTHAG. All right; and then you'll learn to count.

BUYER. But I can count already!

PYTHAG. Let's hear you.

BUYER. One, two, three, four . . .

PYTHAG. Stop, that's enough! You're to ten right now. You'll learn that four is ten. It's the perfect triangle, the oath we swear by.

BUYER. Well, by Ten! that's the headiest idea I ever heard of. Four is ten! What a platform for a philosophy!

PYTHAG. Then you'll find out about earth, air, fire and water. . . . You'll learn that God is Number, and Intelligence and Harmony. And that you are not who you think you are.

BUYER. I'm not me?

PYTHAG. For the moment you are. But you were somebody else before you were born, and you'll be somebody else after you die.

BUYER. What you mean is, I won't die, I'll just turn over and become somebody else? Well, that wouldn't be so bad. But look here, if I take you, what would you want to eat?

PYTHAG. No meat. Everything else except beans. They are sacred. Besides, the Athenians use them to vote with.

BUYER. That suits me just fine. Now strip off and let me see what you look like. By Heracles! his thigh is solid gold! I'll take him! What do you want for him? Ten minas? He's mine!

ZEUS (*to Hermes*). Get the buyer's name.

HERMES. He seems to be an Italian, Zeus, from Croton . . . or Tarentum.

Just under the flamboyant surface of Lucian's dialogue, there is a straightforward review of Pythagorean topics. The translation of the long-haired Ionian to the rich, restless Greek cities at the bottom of Italy is basic history. As for the pack of doctrine which he took with him, the range of his teachings and the peculiar variety in its content are represented fairly enough, though the language is the language of clowning. But even so, according to the brilliant study of Lucian by J. Bompaire, the gaudiness of the expression derives in part from the professional rhetoricians, who loved to make lectures on Pythagoras, and in another part, from the shoddy teaching slogans resorted to by the Pythagoreans themselves. Either way the creed became a patchwork of inflated clichés, which Lucian is only too happy to put on display. He lets the crudest claims of the cult ridicule the cult itself, and that is a sound measure of his true genius.

Eventually the cult invented extravagances which must have exceeded anything that Lucian knew about. He does not mention, for instance, the late Neoplatonic claims that Pythagoras possessed some very picturesque divine powers. In regard to the supposed connection of the master with the supernatural, here is what Iamblicus says with a straight face about the later Pythagoreans:

They thought their opinions deserved to be believed, because he who first promulgated them was not any casual person but a God. For this was one of their questions: What was Pythagoras? For they say that he was the Hyperborean Apollo; of which this was an indication, that rising up in the Olympic games, he showed his golden thigh; and also that he received the Hyperborean Abaris as his guest, and was presented by him with the dart on which he rode through the air.   (V.P. chap. 28, trans. Taylor)

Et cetera, et cetera: he conversed with animals, handled snakes, appeared in more than one city at exactly the same hour of the same day.

Gods make all things possible, the Neoplatonists argued, and to top all potential absurdities in the argument, Suidas describes a late medieval rite called the Pythagus, in which words written in blood on a mirror are read in the reflected image of the full moon, with certain edifying results.

Obviously the stream of the legend has left its fountain sources so far behind that nothing pertaining to Ionian philosophy has come down in it. This is not surprising. If we are aware of the difficulty of expressing any distinct idea aptly, with no slanting at all, we certainly can't be blind to the difficulties of transmitting philosophical ideas from generation to generation. When the ideas take popular, activist forms, the difficulties are all but insurmountable. Think of what has happened to existentialism in the few decades between Sartre and the hippies. While the topics remain firm, the slogans and badges and anecdotes and lurid applications change with the weather.

But on the island of Samos the memory of Pythagoras bore a very different sort of fruit. In the third century A.D., some seven centuries after Pythagoras's death, a large imperial bronze coin was struck on which was depicted a seated man surrounded by the legend PYTHAGORES SAMION. The chair he sits in is a heavily carved massive stool, a throne by convention. A robe is wrapped around his lower body, with a corner hanging over his left shoulder. His hair is bound around with a circlet. Lodged in his left arm is a staff. He is leaning aggressively toward a sphere mounted on a pedestal, applying a flat object, perhaps a disc with its edge toward us, to the surface of the sphere. He appears to be in a deep study of the mathematical problem which Democritus stated in one of his titles, "On the Contact of Circle and Sphere," in which is formed a sort of irrational angle called the horn angle.

The man commemorated is the founder of systematic geometry. I suppose it is no accident that this portrait resembles copies of Pheidias's Zeus which were struck on many Imperial coins. The implications are self-evident. "He's also a god who first discovered Wisdom," as Lucretius said of Epicurus, a god of totally different powers, however, from him who soared around through the heavens on Apollo's golden arrow. The effect of the coin is to extricate Pythagoras from legend and Neoplatonism and to restore him to the beaches of Samos where, drawing geometric figures in the sand with his staff, he properly belongs.

III

He was born and raised in Samos in a period when the Sardis of Croe-sus dominated the Eastern world, and the Egypt of Amasis the south-ern Mediterranean. Samos had important ties in both directions, most conspicuously in Egypt, where in the Greek settlement of Naucratis the Samians were numerous enough to have a precinct of their own dedicated to Hera. Pythagoras, it is said repeatedly, undertook exten-sive travels in the pursuit of his early studies. Although similar excur-sions are attributed right and left to the Sages, there is no reason to think that a man as strongly attracted to a wide range of knowledge as Pythagoras was would be less mobile than the multitudinous visitors to oracles and games and festivals, or the innumerable merchants and colonizers and adventurers of the sixth century, of whom Sappho's brother, Charaxus, is only one interesting example.

Herodotus says very deliberately that when Sardis was in its heyday, "all of the learned men of Hellas" came together there, as the chances of life and opportunity permitted (1. 29). And many voyaged to Egypt; Solon, we believe, was one; Thales, another. But the surest instance of an inquiring traveler is Herodotus himself. So, most likely, Pythagoras did set off in his own time in his own way and, as Lucian says, went to school to the Sages, in Egypt. If so, he need not have been touched significantly by Egyptian religious practices, any more than Herodotus was or any more than Eudoxus of Cnidus was, despite insinuations to the contrary which seem to stem from the Athenian schools.

In Egypt he would have learned something a little more complicated however than "the art of measuring land" which is specified by He-rodotus, for along with the resurveys of the boundary lines that had been swept from the fields by the annual flooding of the Nile, went further geometrical and astronomical procedures on which could be founded an accurate calendar of the rise and the fall of the river, the phenomenon that controlled the whole flow of Egyptian life. Even the placing of the monster pyramids seems to be related to the problem of determining the solstices and equinoxes and the heliacal rising of cer-tain stars whose advent meant that this or that stage of the river was going to be now at hand.

In Sardis, with Mesopotamia looming large in the background, he would have found similar versions of the same sciences, and along with them apparently an even more brusque challenge in the form of star charts, coinage in precious metals, a wide variety of art works, a vivid mythology, bustling commercial enterprises, philosophic debates, and grandiose political intrigues.

But simply as a Samian Pythagoras must have had the advantage of being a combatant in the prolonged, jarring discussions which went on in his immediate corner of the world, where Miletus, just across a narrow blue strait and a barren rocky ridge, was the particularly famous theater of learning. In other words, he was one of the tribe fathered by Thales; it could not be otherwise. He was one of the new cosmologists who looked for instruction to the circling stars and circulating winds and spiraling eddies in the muddy currents of the Meander. They were sailor-farmers, warrior-merchants, these philosophers, enjoying a small respite from the furious exertions ordinarily required just to maintain life, and having the time to look around at things, they concentrated on natural things; they were not atheistic in their materialism, but not animistic either in their interest in nature, as has been supposed simply on the basis of their archaic language. They were witty pessimists, trying to understand life and to make the most of it. It was a rare interval in the world's history.

A man named Mnesarchus, gem engraver, was the father of Pythagoras according to a story which seems to originate in the Samian annals of Duris. Gem engraving, in any event, was a specialty of the high archaic period, when the artist-craftsman was held in particular esteem. Another engraver of gems, Theodorus of Samos, became renowned for a chariot and four which he carved on a tiny seal-stone, almost as renowned as for his Gargantuan labors in designing and building the colossal temple of Hera, about which he is said to have published a book, possibly the first treatise on architecture ever to be written.

On the whole the preclassical interval in Samos was illuminated by the poetry of Anacreon; by incredible feats of engineering; by scientific animal breeding; by an array of sculpture scattered over the island; by the systematic practice of medicine; by compilations of astronomical and mathematical data; in short, by the arts and works sponsored by Polycrates the Tyrant.

This brings us to the crux in our insubstantial biography of Pythag-

oras. At the height of Samos's glory, her greatest ornament left Samos
for Italy, because, it is said, of his hatred of tyranny. Coming from
Aristoxenus, this report could be taken as a doctrinaire condemnation
of a popular leader, such as Polycrates undeniably was; but what
makes skepticism a little awkward here is an incident which Athenaeus
recounts in his table topics. Once, Athenaeus says, Polycrates, thinking he had reason to fear a conspiracy, went so far as to burn down the
wrestling schools of Samos because he suspected them of being the
"counterwalls to his own citadel" (13. 602D). Since a wrestling
school was the equivalent of any school and Pythagoras was a teacher,
and since at some undetermined date after Polycrates had seized power
Pythagoras moved away to Italy and became a famous teacher in the

Challenging Art Works, Vivid Mythology, Sky-charts, Coinage, Commercial Enterprises: *triumphs of the sixth century B.C. Before moving from Samos to Croton, where the science of medicine would dominate other studies, Pythagoras profited by intellectual horizons that may have lain no farther away than Sardis in Asia Minor. Nor, as is suggested by this metrically decorated vase, may other regions have been more rewarding to a young mathematician. Admittedly Athenian black figure pottery, with its intensely dramatic scenes, outstripped rival achievements; nevertheless I offer here an example of a contrasting metrical art which was characteristic of the Phrygian belt on the continent opposite Samos. The difference between the two styles of vase-painting is significant, black figure running parallel with the drama enacted in the theater of Dionysus, metrical design suggesting science and the dance. The amphora illustrated here is Cypriot, originating where the Phrygian belt encountered the inflow of traffic from Egypt. It employs a metrical structure of encircling bands, which recalls Mycenean symmetries rather than the columns of stiff figures framed in swastica patterns on the Dipylon geometrical vases. The Cypriot amphora introduces floral patterns, in the form of lotus blossoms, along with freely improvised, very mobile linear sequences of a dancelike arrangement. Other orientalizing ceramic pieces utilized stylized decorative figures, beasts and birds in the main, which make a similar measured, wholly controlled impact on the senses. The present vase is ten inches high.*

politically oriented gymnasia of Croton, it does seem possible that in Samos he may have got mixed up with the wrong party and ended by exiling himself from his native island.

In Samos Pythagoras was beyond all doubt the natural philosopher, "investigating the laws," in the words of Vitruvius, "and the working of the laws by which nature governs"; and not overly concerning himself apparently with the edicts of mortal rulers (9. 6. 3).

Regardless of his place of residence, he continued to be at home, in my opinion, in a well-defined intellectual setting, the boundaries of which were strictly Ionian. Vitruvius, the Latin writer on architecture (whose credentials as an authority on archaic Greek matters I will come to in a moment), puts Pythagoras in a group with Thales, Xenophanes,

Anaxagoras, and Democritus, naming the five of them as the first who studied among other phenomena the motions of the stars, not like the Chaldeans to cast nativities, but to know the seasons better and the patterns of the weather. Vitruvius, loyal Roman that he is, shows respect for astrology; but for calendars and meteorological matters he has an enthusiasm born of close acquaintance with life in the seagirt settlements of the ancient Mediterranean world: witness his anxiety about the way in which the long-prevailing seasonal winds can funnel dust and debris through the streets of a city. He has exactly this sort of concrete appreciation of the Pythagorean triangle and even of irrational numbers; of the use of the compass and plumb bob and gnomon; of the curvature of the earth and the march of the constellations through the heavens—and he is the first I think to try to translate into writing the whole glorious panoply of the early sciences.

With a sturdy but graceless art Vitruvius reveals a tactile sense of the things with which Pythagoras was concerned. For us this is all the more informative because it is not colored by any doctrine or any of the partisanships of the schools, or any astonishing individual genius of his own. Nevertheless his errors have been underscored while his good sense on most topics has been overlooked, as on occasion it seems to be in Jean Soubitan's finely elaborated new Budé edition of Book 9 of the famous *Ten Books on Architecture*. Vitruvius's point of view, at the worst, is unconventional. The early investigations of nature had slashed a road open, he seems to believe, that led to Democritus and Eudoxus, and from them to Archimedes; a route that for all practical purposes bypasses the metaphysical bailiwicks of Plato and Aristotle and the dialectical preserves of the Eleatics as well. Therein, I am convinced, lies both the distinction and the disrepute of Vitruvius.

But what we are finally interested in is the evidence for the persistence of Ionian thinking in Pythagoras himself and in his closest followers, despite the deviations which many of the Italians pursued so ardently. Vitruvius assumes the fundamentally Ionian position as a matter of course. Other evidence is not wanting. The Samian historian of the end of the fourth century B.C., Duris, is quoted in Porphyry to the effect that the son of Pythagoras, Arimnestus, maintained Samian connections and was besides the teacher of Democritus. Duris documents his statement by describing an imposing bronze tablet in the

Samian Heraion which bore a formal epigram in which the monument speaks as follows:

> Me Arimnestus, who much learning traced,
> Pythagoras' beloved son, here placed,
> (Trans. T. Stanley)

To the information that this man Arimnestus was tutor to Democritus, possibly during a period of Arimnestus's exile in Abdera, Duris adds a fascinating footnote. Someone named Simos, Duris says, was guilty of the theft of one of the seven Pythagorean arts—the stolen one being the art of music—which had been inscribed in canonic form on the bronze tablet erected in the temple, and by publishing the theft as his own work, he had destroyed the harmony of the whole.

Or something very much of that purport: the passage is difficult and I've fallen back on Thomas Stanley's old interpretation of it. However fanciful Duris may sound, the record of a bronze monument of this sort in Samos substantiates the theory of a continuing existence of an east Greek intellectual discipline, to which Democritus obviously adhered. And Duris's epilogue has what seems to me to be a wholly unexpected value. It tells us exactly what the final intent of Pythagoras was. The great Samian aspired to nothing less than the accumulation and perfect harmonization of all knowledge, of all seven branches of what can be known.

That, of course, is just what Heraclitus held against him: the fact that he was a confirmed polymath, an inquirer—his Ephesian neighbor contended—who outstripped all men, who grasped at all learning, but got nothing better in return than a handful of frivolous results. Clearly the fierce concentration of Heraclitus's mind would automatically reject the ambition of a Pythagoras to attain universal knowledge. But in an archaic age, when it was presumed that the comprehension of all things was within reach of the human intellect, that ambition, though continually falling short of confident fulfillment, was nevertheless the begetter of spectacular results; and with the eventual realization that its ultimate failure was inevitable, there came a sense of betrayal, like death.

At first, though, it appeared to be otherwise. At first all branches of science seemed to flourish together, like an espalier on an arbor.

IV

An early document dealing with Pythagoras, and in my opinion one of the most genuinely instructive, is certainly one of the most dazzling. This is hardly surprising since it is a page which has survived from the work of the poet Callimachus, a favorite model for the poets of Roman Italy, and in brilliant, scholarly, third-century B.C. Alexandria, a fastidious authority on the books and the arts of the past. The fragment I have in mind occurs in the first of the *Iambi;* its facts, it is said, were taken from the Ionian historian Maeandrius of Miletus. It recounts a version of the ancient story in which someone travels the world over, hoping to discover the wisest of the Sages in order to honor him with a splendid award, in this case a golden cup. Each Sage however modestly disclaims his own preeminence, so that eventually the prize is set up as a dedication in a temple of Apollo.

In Callimachus's surviving verses Thales of Miletus is proposed as the leading candidate for the prize. But such are the involutions of Callimachus's artistry that it is not Thales so much as Pythagoras who turns out to be the wise man par excellence. Thales is granted a share of Pythagoras's glories: he is pictured as being a studious follower of Pythagoras. The chronological absurdity of this sequence is overcome by making Pythagoras and Euphorbus, a Phrygian of Trojan times, one and the same person under a poetic license derived from the doctrine of the transmigration of souls. What Callimachus seems to suggest is the fact that Pythagoras soon became the great master of the arts with which Thales had been preoccupied: which is an entirely legitimate proposition.

Callimachus puts a special emphasis on a coterie of studies—astronomy, geometry, ethics. His mosaic of semitechnical terms and imagery is appropriate in a scene invoking archaic intellectual concerns, the legendary Sage and the mythical Arcadian ambassador, and it describes impeccably both the problems and procedures, the reach and the grasp, of science in the act of getting onto its feet. The passage follows. In my effort to imitate the way in which Callimachus contrives the scene, I have taken chances with some evasive words and flickering innuendos:

To the Milesian Thales went first choice.
Gnomon-like his mind: he chalk-lined out
That glittering asterisk, the Lesser Wain,
By which Phoenician sailors steer their ships.

Him the prelunar scout from Arcady
Spotted in Didyma, with elegant stick
Graving on sanded walks the bold designs
Shaped by Euphorbus, Phrygian redivivus,
Who first inscribed the arches of the spheres,
First fitted right triangles to the arch.
. . . .

First taught the abstinence from living things,
Although but few complied: some did, but few. . . .
. . . .

"Since to the wisest Sage belongs this cup,
Accept it. . . ."
                Eying the drawings, Thales said:
"Not I, it's not for me. Perhaps for Bias. . . ."

As for Thales, Callimachus epitomizes the historical activities of the
man. His addiction to star gazing is confirmed by sources as varied as
Herodotus's *Histories* and Aesop's *Fables*. The Ionian poet Phoenix
of Colophon is eloquent about the usefulness—presumably nautical
usefulness—of his star knowledge; and in a metrical version of the
Phaenomena of Eudoxus of Cnidus, who was not many generations
removed from Thales and Pythagoras, the poet Aratus explains the
Phoenician preference for the Lesser Wain, or Bear, or Dipper (the
name has varied) as the constellation marking true north: its orbit had
the advantage of being smaller than that of the sprawling Great Bear,
or Wain, or Dipper, by which the Greeks sailed. The choice was not
exactly simple, of course, in an age in which the precession of the
equinoxes had not as yet fixed a Pole Star as a recognizable center of
the northern skies.

While Thales' astronomy seems to have been limited to just such
large-scale applications, the inquiries of Pythagoras-Euphorbus are
obviously probing deeper, moving through applications toward general
laws. Not only that: they are discovering the grounds for the kinship
among disciplines. Astronomy and geometry emerge like twin Miner-

vas from the designs taking shape under Thales' staff. And along with them by a fragmentary connection which will become clearer later on, there is concern with a peculiar ethical premise, having to do with the eating of meat.

These are facets, I believe, of a unified archaic consciousness. They reflect an interplay among older topics—astronomical, meteorological, mythological topics, such as those appearing in Hesiod's *Works and Days*—together with the newfound ability to diagram these ancient stuffs along lines which defined their intellectual significance. So we begin with the stars. We begin with star myths and Hesiod, and we will let the intellectual refinements which Pythagoras introduced come out as they will in the course of the narrative. Although it may seem prodigal to stop to look for Pythagoras among the constellations, I think that that is where his trail can best be picked up.

V

Orion and his dog Sirius, Boötes and the Great Bear, the Pleiades and Hyades, with whom Homer is well acquainted, take on highly schematic positions in Hesiod's account of the annual rotation of the heavens. The astronomical knowledge of the misplaced Boeotian farmer whose family origins lay in the East is in no way inferior to that of the metropolitan Babylonians; and, somewhat inexplicably, it does not differ in essentials from a body of observations in which all western Asiatics and the Egyptians as well seem to have shared. Perhaps the one great difference is this, that in the fastnesses of oriental ziggurats political omens were sifted from the stars; whereas for Hesiod, in spite of his brooding pessimism, nothing more sinister is to be watched for in the heavens than the sunrise setting of the Pleiades, which only meant that the season was approaching when it would be prudent to bring the ships up from the sparkling sea, to pull out the bilge plugs, brace the hulls with stones, and hang sails and rudders indoors for the winter.

Only in the Hellenistic age did astronomy become learned enough, and ingenious enough, to perfect orthodox astrology and Ptolemaic celestial mechanics. Only in the fourth century B.C., according to Otto Neugebauer, did the Zodiac, with its very ancient constellations, reach

To the Stone-buck, Aesop's Wolf Said: *"Come down from that high cliff before you fall and break your neck!"* But the wild ram was Capricorn, fixed in the sky and in no danger of falling. —An ibex from the same series of terracotta tiles.

that state of organization which it displays in our morning newspapers. Pythagoras, thus, is backwards by two good centuries from a peak of folly in astronomical thinking, and is by the same token just so much a closer relative of Copernicus's than the run of sky readers—Aristarchus of Samos always excepted—during twenty intervening centuries. This is no vain boast. Pythagoras's system in all likelihood was not geocentric. If the earth did not move in more complicated ways, it appears, according to the theory published by Philolaus, to have revolved around the true center of the universe, a Central Fire which lay always out of sight behind it and in which the sun may have had replenishment in its nightly journey back to the eastern horizon.

Although cosmic questions remained unsettled, the skies themselves had exhibited in the constellations an array of designs which made indelible impressions on generations of wakeful human beings. They were geometric impressions, geometric in a special but exact sense of the word. Unfortunately for us the sky charts which have been preserved are not ancient, and consequently they have pictured, not the old archaic images, but the ponderous beasts and heavily attired human personages of Renaissance scientific art. We will do well to try to revisualize the constellations. When we look for the Lion, the Ram, the Bull, the Swan, or for Orion or the Virgin, what we should expect to see are figures resembling those which in pre-preclassical times were sketched in paint on vases, engraved on seal stones, drawn with a minimum of strokes on a thousand different sorts of surfaces. After all, the constellations mainly are the creatures of geometric art in its early orientalizing phase. And they are, equally, the beasts and birds and heroes of the earliest myths and the earliest fables.

To the trained archaic eye the things looked like what they were called. The serpent constellations, for instance, are sinuously extended star meanders, of which Draco for us in the north is a vivid example. In Scorpio we still can see the likeness of a scorpion such as might have been scratched on an island gem; and in the Bird, which was later arbitrarily translated into the Cygnus of the story of Leda and the Swan, we are reminded of what it probably was at the start, a simple crosshatch of the wings and body of a large bird in flight, a crane as likely as not.

The lion which dominated the early outburst of oriental stylization in Greek vase painting is always drawn as a formidably arch-necked beast, maned or unmaned, with compact forequarters and a lolling tongue: what better than the tense sickle of bright stars—the sickle is the oldest of mutilating weapons—to show the King of Beasts in summary fashion, as it does in the constellation which we still call Leo?

Some of the animals, on the evidence of Aratus, seem to be visualized in a recumbent position, with the head turned round backwards above the body, pointing toward the hindquarters. The pose transfers itself into a compact composition suitable for filling a small area, such as the shoulder of a Wild Goat style vase or the surface of a seal stone, or a patch of black sky, or a sandbox abacus. This is the coherence apparently of the Ram and the Bull, possibly even the Lion.

In contrast with the compressed menagerie, there are figures that spread out, of which Orion is doubtless the most resplendent. It is his belt, of course, the tightly cinched band of three stars, which for millennia has been the unmistakable mark of the gigantic hunter. But a narrow belt, noticeably cinched in, has the closest of associations with heroic naked men, warriors or worshippers or inscrutable adventurers, in large reliefs and small bronze statues from Minoan times down to the end of the archaic age. Seeing the belt, the knowing eye would supply the whole figure.

"How many pebbles are required," asked Eurytus the Pythagorean, "to imitate a man? How many for a horse?" What he is apparently thinking, as Aristotle suggests, is that figures of all sorts may be visualized as sketched out on a framework of points, which could be indi-

Hunter or Handsome Adorer? *In mythology Orion pursues a course in swift strides which brings him quickly to a dangerous peak in manly ambition. He becomes the first of the hunters of savage beasts, the first of the conquerors of lovely women. As a constellation his belt is the brightest star-group in our skies. It suggests a broad-shouldered naked giant of a man, a concentration of physical power, with which our bronze statuette will stand in a certain comparison. The figure is of a not uncommon type. Among small bronzes from Minoan Crete the right hand is raised in this fashion in what is thought to be a religious salute; such figures have been referred to as* adorants. *In some bronze works of the archaic period the hand reveals an opening which indicates a lifted spear: the man is taken to be a hunter or a warrior. The old Minoan figures are normally thick in the waist and wear loin-cloths; this kouros is wearing the cinched, multiple-stranded Phrygian belt which bespeaks his origin. We are probably looking at a Phrygian bronze figurine, probably manufactured for the Phoenician trade in dedicatory objects at temples. Although the representation of an* adorant *would hardly be possible a half-dozen centuries after the fall of Crete, the image obviously had a power in its general form to last and to reproduce itself after its early meaning had been forgotten. These peculiar, unintelligible persistencies make me think that familiar dedicatory objects such as this may be remarkably good reflections of the ancient constellation imagery.*

cated by pebbles arranged on a patch of hard sand, just as are the figures of geometry; just as are, on a larger scale, the surveyor's boundary stones on an odd-shaped farm; and just as are the star pictures in the sky. Archaic art, in fact, achieves what we regard as its admirable style because it is willing to move in summary fashion from point to point. The story is told that two sculptors, the famous Theodorus of Samos, already alluded to, and his brother Telecles, collaborating on an archaic wooden statue of Apollo, worked one on one half of the statue in Samos, the other on the other half in Ephesus, and yet when the two halves were brought together the whole had the appearance of being the work of one man. We may presume that they were not bound to a rigid "canon" or pattern of art, but that after agreeing on a model, they could translate it into whatever number of points it would take to make a layout of the figure they had in mind, transfer the points to the rough wood and start carving.

What I am saying is, of course, that the archaic image is a creation of Democritus's much-disputed convention, as also of Anaxagoras's celebrated *Nous:* an act of the archaic mind supported by the imaginative trick of being able to see that which is suggested, though for inexperienced eyes nothing of the sort appears to be really there. The evasive shape of a constellation, however, often seems to become somehow solidified by the mythology which surrounds it. At this point symbolism, along with a sense of the myth behind the symbol, comes to the aid of us who are only casual astronomers. The circlet of brilliant stars which is called Corona, for example, "is Ariadne," according to Vitruvius: in this case only the symbol not the woman herself is to be seen. But Corona, so described, brings up the whole tragic narrative of Ariadne, the recipient of Amphitrite's crown, her suffering at Theseus's hands and her marriage finally to Dionysus. If along with this, one has in mind the Ionian dances that were danced in her honor in Delos, and the festive rites in Naxos, she becomes all that Walter Otto has claimed for her; and as the fairest and saddest of women, she can properly disappear in the symbol which is her crown.

One of the better known eccentricities of Pythagoreanism is to claim symbolic meanings for geometric figures, for numbers themselves, and for many haphazard objects. The relish for symbols was indulged in with increasing abandon as a cult grew up, until in the course of the centuries the irrationality of the whole procedure becomes astonishing.

But there are several levels of irrationality, some of which undoubtedly attach themselves in no trivial way to the earliest investigations of Pythagoras, as well as to most all serious inquiry. The original seat of the trouble may have lain in the stars. I want to look at two possibilities. One, the fables associated with the polar constellations; the other, the role of Heracles in connection with the configuration which bears his name.

The wheeling motion of the northern stars, "which never drown in the sea," is the key to ancient speculation, be it mythologically high flown or coldly scientific. One way, it ends in geometrical projections; the other way, it produces a pursuit fable of not too mystic a psychoanalytic impact, which Jung calls "the negative supraordinate personality." The basic fable, which is referred back to Hesiod, tells us that in life the Great Bear was a young huntress named Callisto who hunted wild beasts on the mountain in company with Artemis. One day she chanced to arouse the desire of all-seeing Zeus, who did what Zeus does on such occasions. Some time afterwards, Artemis, noticing the mark of Callisto's ensuing pregnancy while she was bathing, turned her into a bear, to be herself hunted, until Zeus out of pity put her among the stars. But even there her suffering continued: "Behind the Bear," Aratus says, "like one who drives her, comes the Bear Warden, who is also called Boötes." Boötes had been in life the child which Callisto conceived in her mishap with Zeus, a boy that Callisto's vengeful father had butchered and served up to Zeus at table.

And so together they go round and round forever. The story has the elegance, as geometers like to say, of the most rarefied of Olympian myths. It is also properly troubling. And when that happens, people usually look around for a substitute myth which is more tolerable; after the Apollonian assertion comes the Dionysiac escape; after the cosmic oracle, the homely fable. In the case of Boötes and his mother, people early decided against the very premise of the Great Bear; they chose to believe that the constellation looked more like an oversized cart, a wagon or wain of some sort. (To us, since it has changed its shape a little, it looks like a dilapidated dipper.) In any event Boötes, in this alternative, could be taken as the driver of the ox pulling the Wain. Which could inspire fables of a different order:

An ox driver was driving his wain along the track, Aesop said, when he let it slip sidewise into a deep ravine. Seeing the trouble he'd got himself into, he started praying to Heracles at the top of his voice. Suddenly Heracles appeared in the track beside him. ''Get down there and put your shoulder against a wheel and lay on with your whip,'' Heracles said. ''The gods will hear your prayers better when they hear you bellowing at your ox.'' (Babrius 20)

The myth of Callisto has a logical circularity, a final indeterminacy, which is as old as anything that can be thought of; the myth of Heracles, whose constellation dominates the summer skies, is exactly the opposite, in that it does not represent the workings of the prehistoric mind, but rather the exploitation of pseudorational possibilities which developed later on. Heracles, though a popular figure in very ancient art, is by no means an early comer to the heavens. For Eudoxus-Aratus, even for Vitruvius, the man imagined to be seen in his stars was a nameless phantom Kneeler, a care-worn, toil-worn, pain-worn shadow of someone who could have been anyone, perhaps any of us. But just as Heracles gradually acquired a twelve-chaptered story relating and systematizing his labors, so the Kneeler became the Heracles whose labors were superimposed upon the twelve signs of the Zodiac. According to Plutarch, he became a sun god, a variant on the Egyptian god Set.

From this there resulted some foolishness in later antiquity which is most pertinent to our story. Another passage in Plutarch, which in my opinion displays how complete was the collapse of the Pythagorean tradition, asserts that adherents of the cult believed this sun god to be a demonic power; that whereas the triangle belongs symbolically to certain deities (Hades, Dionysus, and Ares), the quadrilateral to others (Rhea, Aphrodite, Demeter, Hestia, and Hera), the dodecagon to Zeus, the polygon of fifty-six sides belongs to Heracles-Set, ''as Eudoxus has recorded.'' All of which must be construed as utter confusion.

Poets have made Heracles the butt of comedy; and sometimes again the subject of great poetry, from Panyassis, the uncle of Herodotus, to Yvor Winters. Nevertheless, the demonic powers with which he was mantled, together with the loss of meaning in the geometrical properties assigned to him as presider over the visible heavens, are evidence of the calamity which overtook the Pythagoreans. Mystical geometry attracted them in much the same way as did the murky ritual of the blood and the mirror and the moon which is recounted in Suidas. We should be able in a moment to deal constructively with the geometrical confusion. Meanwhile, in view of the sequence of the events we have noticed, we must suspect that doctrinaire mysticism, such as the Orphism sometimes associated with the earliest Pythagoreans, is probably much more a late miscarriage of Pythagorean philosophy than it is, as has sometimes been argued, an instrument of its inception.

The fabric of geometry, as I think we shall see, was originally a well-woven, very firm stuff.

VI

Once when the philosopher Aristippus was shipwrecked, he struggled up out of the sea onto a sandy beach with some companions, and then, discovering geometrical designs drawn in the sand, he cried out, according to Vitruvius: "We can be of good cheer! I see the traces of man!" He had every reason to feel cheerful. The story goes on to say that the castaways and the natives of the place, Rhodes, embraced one another, each cherishing the other because of their mutual ability to converse in the language of geometry. Back at home in Cyrene, Aristippus got into the habit of saying: "Young people should be provided above all with the sort of wealth that can swim with them, even from a sinking ship."

We can reconstruct how the initial discussions of geometry went. Out of all of the shining indelible star figures in the sky, and all of the parallel circling motions which the constellations traced, the underlying simplicity of some aspects of astronomy suggested a sort of thinking in which there was, not so much the wonder and sorrow of myth, as a sudden, crystal-clear recognition of a starkly familiar landscape, a landscape of surveying and navigation and mechanical constructions. One constellation, the Triangle (Deltoton for the Greeks, Triangulum for the Latins) seems to have provoked exclusively geometrical associations; Aratus's short sentence about it describes it as an isosceles triangle. The inference to be drawn is that sky imagery is the key to the archaic intuition of what a point and line, a triangle and other several-sided figures, fundamentally are.

"A simple line," says Sextus Empiricus in a clear-cut reference to the earliest geometers, "is conceived as drawn from a point to a point." It is, as it were, the illusionary tie between two stars, the "lines of light" which Aratus saw in Cassiopea, or in much the same

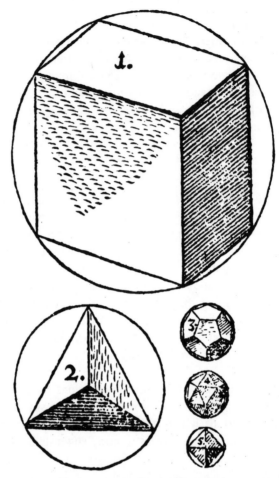

"We can be of Good Cheer!" Said Aristippus. "I See Graved here the Traces of Man!" *The cube, tetrahedron, dodecahedron, icosahedron, and octohedron as drawn in Johann Kepler's* Harmonice mundi libri V. *Kepler nominated the cube as the figure for earth or for the earth, the tetrahedron for fire or the fiery part of the universe, the icosahedron for water or the watery part, the octohedron for air, and the dodecahedron for the cosmos as a whole. What Kepler, good astronomer that he was, was looking for was a set, a* set *in the mathematical sense of the term, of interrelated figures to apply to the planetary system. When he finally found his ellipses they did not resemble the figures illustrated here, but the lessons learned from the study of the regular solids led to the isolation of concrete relationships which eventually bore fruit.*

way the fading impression in the dust made by a cord stretched between two stakes. Similarly, as Sextus adds, lines drawn from one point to another to a third point and back to the first enclose a plane which is triangular in shape, and if lines from the three points are connected with a fourth point lying above the triangle, the result is a solid figure, a pyramid on a triangular base. And so on for other figures, for a cube for example.

So then, if a straight line can be evoked in the mind's eye by a cord stretched from a point to a point, a curved line can be as easily projected by the swing of the tip of a stick at the end of a tether fixed to a pivot or looped around several pivots. Geometry in practice was at first an art of cord stretching, as Democritus himself describes it, a landscaping art which was useful to builders and fascinating to study on an improvised abacus on a seashore.

But while the stretched cord could be converted into the ruler and compass and plumb line of a Pythagoras, or a Vitruvius, the similarity of earth-based constructions with astronomy would have been missed by no one, and we do know definitely that the likeness of earth figures and sky figures had impressed another polymath, Archytus, a contemporary of Democritus's, whom Horace celebrates in a moving ode: "Measurer of the sea and land, / And unnumbered grains of sand."

The eye of Archytus had caught the perfectly curving orbits which a sort of toy, a whirler, produced when boys swung it around at the end of a string at certain festivals, and his ear had caught the change in pitch in the whistling sound which the toy emitted as it traveled faster and faster. The curve of its flight, he implies, is related to that of each of the heavenly bodies: he had already noted the mathematicians' discernment of the speeds of the constellations, rising and setting. The sounds which the whirlers made moreover, in addition to being steadier than ordinary sounds, resolved themselves into ratios which reflected systematically the speeds at which the whirlers were moving. Here was an interplay of curved flight lines and speeds and sounds and forces, with a mathematics of its own, yet obviously reflecting the new realization of the definite arithmetic ratios in the attunement of a lyre. For Archytus, or someone a little later than he, or a little earlier, perhaps the stars were whirlers afar off, sounding tones of their own, which might be called the music of the spheres, with no primary aesthetic meaning intended.

In the beginning geometry went back and forth to and from the stars. But before long, Sextus Empiricus goes on to say, busy minds began playing with the idea that a simple line should be more fully rationalized than these first archaic intuitions had provided for. A line must be created, the Eleatics began to think, by points lying side by side, shoulder to shoulder; and a plane would be a whole field of points. But what then was a point? An imponderable abstraction, it seemed, which could be pursued only into the absurdities of the paradoxes of Zeno or the rigorous atomism of Democritus, or resigned to the supernatural where disembodied forms replaced simple stars.

But before that impasse loomed ahead, a triangle, the triangle, was simply a Deltoton constructed out of the imaginary—the Anaxagorean lines—that flew "straight and swift between the stars," in the phrase of Wallace Stevens, whose point in the poem is to praise the imaginative Anaxagorean concept. Furthermore, it was the right triangle in a semicircle, isosceles or scalene, which revealed itself, according to Callimachus, most delicately in the sand under the nub of the Sage's staff, which is to say, the triangle of the Great Theorem.

I abstain from discussion of the Pythagorean Theorem. Its place in history is familiar and clear. One of its beauties is that, like the equivalence of the angles of any triangle to two right angles, the proof is self-evident. At least, in several elementary constructions, I think it is, and even the classic windmill construction of Euclid (1. 47) seems to have a transparency of its own, or perhaps compelling interest as a suspense thriller. Be that as it may, Thomas Hobbes, having reached age forty with no knowledge of geometry, happened to notice this proposition on the page of an open book while he was waiting in a gentleman's library. "By God," said he, as John Aubrey tells us, adding that Hobbes would swear now and then by way of emphasis, "this is impossible!" So he read the page again, checked back to some earlier propositions, and ended "in love with geometry."

Like the right triangle the pentagon is a potent ancient symbol for Pythagores of Samos. Lucian's gibe to the effect that "four is ten" evokes the wonder that can be worked with pebbles and a staff on a patch of sand beside the sea. It meant something that looked innocent enough when the sun-and-wind–burned philosopher put his markers down like this: ($\cdot$ + $\cdot$ $\cdot$ + $\cdot$ $\cdot$ $\cdot$ + $\cdot$ $\cdot$ $\cdot$ $\cdot$) equals ten. But when he arranged the pebbles another way they represented a triangle which began to hint at a mathematical chasm. Then, on top of that came a second design, equally powerful, equally disconcerting, which Lucian describes in a short fantasia called "Slip of the Tongue." The first was a triangle of indeterminable dimensions. The second was the star pentagon:

Of each it might be said that *this is Pythagoras,* in the sense in which it was said that Corona is Ariadne, and just as the crown signified all womanly beauty and sadness to the knowing, so appropriately enough the star pentagon came down to the more knowing Pythagoreans signifying manly health.

The special power of the pentagon lay in its ability to function as one of the twelve surfaces of a regular solid called a dodecahedron, which acquired a dazzling reputation as the "cosmic figure" that was thought best to picture the geometric structure of the universe. To any eye, not the archaic eye alone, the dodecahedron can suggest a cosmos, on the sagging facets of which the constellations (or galaxies) are spun precariously, as I hope my flat little supplementary sketch will suggest.

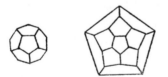

The twelve-sided globule, though, is not exclusively a creation of the geometer's art. This particular solid, like the cube and the single and double pyramids, existed as an archaeological fact, according to many discoveries, including a decorative Etruscan dodecahedron dating from before the day of Pythagorean geometry. And it continues to exist at the present time in the form of decorative, star-pointed, glass-and-tin, suspended lamps, coming apparently from Arabic sources, through Spain, to the artisans of contemporary Mexico.

The cosmic import of the pentagon rises to its true height, however, when it is combined with an equilateral triangle and inscribed in a circle, yielding an equal-angled, fifteen-sided figure. And this wondrous thing, though its significance seems to have faded early in the annals of the Pythagorean cult, is nevertheless the mainstay in the *analemma*, Vitruvius's (and antiquity's) complex sundial, which recorded not just trivialities like the hour of the day, but the day of the year, the number of days back to the solstice and ahead to the equinox. The analemma diagramed the morning on which Sirius could be expected to make its heliacal rising, an event of great significance in Egypt, for instance, because of the agriculture bordering the majestically fluctuating Nile, and in Samos somewhat similarly, because of certain ancient vegetation festivals. It could do this, and more, because the base where the shadow which the sun cast from the tip of the gnomon was circumscribed in a way which corresponded in its fifteen divisions to the tilt of the ecliptic. The angle of the ecliptic was taken in other words to be one-fifteenth part of a circle, or as we started saying some centuries later, twenty-four degrees. By reading the position of the sun according to a shadow on a scale of this range, the observer of the analemma had a well-wrought almanac spread out at his feet.

"With regard to the last proposition," writes Proclus at the conclusion of *Euclid,* Book 4, "in which he inscribes the side of the fifteen-angled figure in a circle, for what object does anyone assert that he propounds it except for the reference of the problem to astronomy? For, when we have inscribed the fifteen-angled figure in the circle through the poles, we have the distance from the poles both of the equator and the zodiac, since they are distant from one another by the side of the fifteen-angled figure." (Heath, *Eu.* 2, 111)

Probably no one person "discovered" the angle of the ecliptic, since it was a phenomenon which would have been observed intensively all over the world in connection with the study of the solstices. But the sun's slow teetering path through the celestial sphere, as stimulating as it was to the seasonal awarenesses of people in Yucatan, at Stonehenge, on the islands of Syros and Tenedos, in the Nile valley and the Euphrates, could not have come in for close description, let alone a measurement of the inclination to the celestial equator, until some way of diagraming earth-sky relations came into being. The solution of this problem I think can reasonably be attributed to Pythagoras himself.

Official Clock and Calendar for a Great City. *The sundial at Cnidus stood toward the center of a loose group of public buildings, in a plaza between two harbors, where crowds may be visualized as gathering to exchange the news of the day. Long Island University expedition photo in* American Journal of Archaeology.

The fifteen-sided figure is geometry and astronomy simultaneously: it transposes one thing into another, triangles and pentagons into the circle of the zodiac, in accordance with the well-known belief of the Master in the interrelatedness of all parts of the cosmos.

In analyzing the geometry of the ecliptic angle, Pythagoras would have had a good amount of crude data at hand. Hesiod, for instance, who is detailed and sufficiently precise in charting the course of the sun from solstice to solstice, introduces the word *tropic* as the technical term for its turning points in summer and winter, with full implications as to the zones and the curvature of the earth; while the measure of the angle is attributed in the Aëtius summary to Pythagoras himself, though this claim did not go unchallenged. The real difficulty, of course, was to find a way to speak of the angle or even to think precisely about it. If the mere size of the sun gave so much trouble to the pre-Socratics—"bigger than the Peloponnesus"; "28 times the size of the earth"; "broad like a leaf"; "no larger than a man's foot"—in comparison with these dimensions, the fifteen-angled figure in a circle is a marvel of precision.

Unfortunately it is more accurate as geometry than as astronomy, although the small error of a fraction of a degree went undetected until the time of Eratosthenes. The fifteen-angled grid served well enough for the analemma; and maybe that is as much as should be required of it. It was accurate "for all practical purposes," which is a standard hard to improve on, since no unchanging, absolutely accurate value could ever have been stated for it. Here again, Pythagoras's postulate that all of the gears of the universe meshed smoothly together seemed to show under further testing some wheels that were seriously mis-shapen.

VII

But before the evidence of the fallibility of the system turned up, Py-thagoras had tried to bring all facets of the archaic consciousness into harmony, one program with another. To be a cosmologist, which Py-thagoras eminently was, meant just that: a *kosmos* being that which held all things in due order, mind and matter. And so, to the drawings on the paths of the sanctuary at Didyma, there is to be added an ethical structure which Callimachus also is mindful of.

The connection of the stars with human conduct is ancient, and not necessarily so frivolous as astrology would like to have us believe. The author of the *Titanomachia* made the centaur Chiron, in his role as teacher of mankind, bring to the human race a knowledge of "oaths, holy sacrifices and the patterns of Olympus." These most important "schematics of Olympos" are the constellations, "the identification and mythology of which," says G. L. Huxley, "formed a substantial part of early Greek hexametric poetry." Substantially the same threads of ethics and astronomy are interwoven in Hesiod's *Works and Days*.

In the sum and substance of his teaching, Pythagoras, like Hesiod advising his brother Perses, censured the use of violence. For Hesiod the doctrine of moderation springs from a haunting recollection of the ages and races of men: in a good age, a golden age, men did not act to-ward one another like wild beasts and birds of prey, not like the hawk toward the nightingale in the fable. Men lived happily together on the grain-giving earth until the earth covered them and they were succeeded by another race. A virgin daughter of Zeus, Justice, moved among them. The story of the successive ages of men is retold as a constellation myth in the Eudoxus-Aratus shorter variant of the Hesiodic poem, where the application has become clearly Pythagorean: as in the *Metamorphoses,* Ovid's sacrificial ox with gilded horns eloquently protests.

The maiden, Justice, in this version is the constellation Virgo. She is "set among the stars not far from far-seen Boötes," says Aratus, because when the race of bronze came along in its unhappy time and gave swords to highwaymen and began devouring its ploughing oxen, she could no longer abide mankind. She fled to the starry heavens, where embodying *dike* she represents cosmic balance, or, in ethical terms, disciplined self-restraint and peaceableness.

Thinking of this kind is transparently the basis for Pythagoras's injunction against eating meat. As an article in the poetic archaic code, the prohibition is a figurative way of condemning disorder and of dramatizing cruel and reckless conduct by making the act of a man butchering his ploughing ox a symbol of self-destruction. It bears no resemblance to a taboo. There are archaic fantasies and digressions and folk platitudes in Hesiodic poetry, to be sure, but no stress on ritual as such.

Our problem hardly consists in trying to evaluate the abstract virtue of eating or not eating meat. All that is bad about killing amiable beasts is abstractly as self-evident to any sensitive person as the angle of the semicircle; our problem is to inquire into the extent to which the prohibition was literal or symbolic. For Ovid, Pythagoras and this counsel supply the substance of the greatest poetry in a great poem. The Pythagorean ethic in effect motivates a backwards gentle glance over intense ages and intense lives lived briefly and then metamorphosed. This is the important matter. On the whole I think it is irrelevant to speculate seriously on Ovid's or Pythagoras's personal dietary habits. But I defend the symbolism in its entirety.

The rule holds good: things are one, living things are one. We do not eat ourselves. (Consequently it could follow that beans, because they resemble testicles, were habitually pronounced unacceptable as diet; and wool, as a product of life, unsuitable for shrouds.) Under the rule of oneness, we undergo only a transmigration from ourselves upon our deaths. Nothing is created or destroyed. This root principle, often reiterated among the archaic philosophers, states as much as needs to be stated about the doctrine of the transmigration of souls. The problem again is the degree to which it is symbolic. Certainly, I venture to say, it is not to be taken literally, though modern scholars from Zeller to Guthrie have tended to do so. As a doctrine of Pythagoras's, it is voiced first in a satiric context by a great Ionian, Xenophanes: "When that puppy cries when somebody beats him, I hear the voice of my dear dead friend." How better to gibe at one who believes explicitly, as Pythagoras obviously did, in the oneness of life! But gibing is a sport which is pleasant enough in Xenophanes, and in Lucian and in Ben Jonson. Metempsychosis, somewhat similarly, offers the poet an aesthetic device, as in Callimachus—or exaggeratedly in Empedocles; or in Shakespeare when he wants a character to brood on Shylock's apparently wolfish appetites; or in Joyce in the act of creating an Irish Ulysses. Metempsychosis besides seems to have been the dull-witted teacher's rhetorical substitute for the true concept. In any event, one of the best of the Renaissance Neoplatonists, John Reuchlin, in his study of Pythagoras rejected literal transmigration, as do most close readers of the ancients, Albin Lesky, for instance. Specialist scholars have a bent for delving so deeply into a question of this kind that they find it difficult to straighten up and look around.

Because of this seemingly austere and impersonal ethic, it has been supposed that the Pythagorean community, when it comes dimly into view in Italy after Pythagoras's migration, must naturally have been a fraternity of Spartans. If being Spartan means being hardy and disciplined, the citizens of Croton, Pythagoras's adopted city, appear to have qualified for the honor, which nevertheless remains dubious. When they managed to destroy the Sybarites, those special fondlings of luxury, they were led against them by Milon, the famous wrestler, reputedly a follower of Pythagoras's. Now this Milon, whether or not because of the training his master had given him, was six times a victor in the Olympic games, six in the Pythian, ten in the Isthmian, nine in the Nemean, when previously the Crotonites had become inured to winning none at all. He is moreover the most renowned glutton in history. He ate twenty pounds of meat, twenty of bread, and drank eight and one-half quarts of wine a day; he carried a sacrificial ox the length of the Olympic stadium, slaughtered it, roasted it, and devoured it all by himself in one afternoon. His ethic can't be described as austere or impersonal; the ways of gladiators seldom are, whether they are Crotonites or New York Jets. It is ironical, too, that Milon's triumphs, in the earnest judgment of Vitruvius, were worthless in comparison with the humane achievements of Pythagoras and the philosophers.

And as it happens Milon was not the only Crotonite champion who appeared at this time. Since on one occasion some six or eight teammates of his won first places at Olympia, something more than an ethic must have been at work among the young men of the city. A science of physical conditioning had quite certainly been built up among the Crotonite physicians, among whom was the much sought after Democedes, who later migrated to Samos. According to Athenaeus, athletes were taught to eat with more than normal heartiness while undergoing intensive gymnastic exercises. The result speaks for itself. In Pythagoras's time the development of pragmatic sciences in civic life was a lot more impressive, I would say, than the practice of asceticism.

Nor is austerity apparent in the Pythagorean tradition. Ionian enjoyments, Ionian excitements, Ionian intellectual poise, continued evidently to govern the lives of the successors of the transplanted Samian. Eudoxus of Cnidus and Archytus of Tarentum were worldly men, polymaths, and ruling powers in their cities. Eudoxus, for whatever it is worth, is reported by Aristotle to have been a hedonist; and indeed the seat of hedonism, the Cyrene of Aristippus, produced more than its share of the later Alexandrian masters of the old Ionian arts. But if the pleasure principle was adhered to, it was adhered to (theoretically anyhow) with reserve, with common sense, with a sort of gallantry, because after all, the real heirs of Pythagoras—ignoring most of the chattering cult—were Democritus, Epicurus, Lucretius, and a multitude of gifted, peaceable men in later times, including Gassendi and Thomas Hobbes.

But Pythagoras undoubtedly did found a school in Croton in which membership entailed closer adherence to a code than is expected of an audience attending lectures. The evidence for a brotherhood is as overwhelming in its gross weight as it is a hodgepodge of hearsay. We may suppose, as T. J. Dunbabin did, that the Samian exerted a personal magnetism which drew a tight band of followers around him. Such a group wouldn't be likely to be either democratic or aristocratic, since there wasn't a popular tyrant at work in Croton, nor an ambitious landed gentry. It could have been a more or less exclusive club which engaged, in the manner of the age, in philosophic inquiry, sports, and broad political action. Since we assume that Pythagoras was uniquely responsible for it, it follows that he imported the seeds for founding a society of this sort from Samos; and in that event we can hardly suppose that the habit of pursuing free inquiry which he had formed in Ionia would suddenly give place in Italy to the cultivation of mystic or fraternalistic rituals. There must be a middle ground which is still to be explained.

Up to this point we have been saying of the archaic cosmologist, How grand the aspiration to combine all of the arts and sciences: arithmetic, astronomy, music, geometry, physiology! and how sad to discover that they don't always combine smoothly. In this predicament the cosmologist may suspect that in the end they won't combine in any ordinary way at all. He will tell himself at first that this is the fault of his pebbles, they are too coarse; his compass-dividers are not sensitive enough to make fine discriminations. But at some point he will begin to realize that the grand scheme he is in search of probably cannot be laid out on a beach, that it can only be defined, through a laborious personal effort, within the mind itself. "Every art is a system of apprehensions," says Sextus about Pythagorean thinking. This conviction is what the later Ionian, Anaxagoras of Clazomenae, pushed through to one logical conclusion. From such a principle it follows that to communicate a carefully ordered system to another person, the other person must submit to its slow unfolding within his own intelligence. The seven canonic branches of knowledge are not meaningful as external objects, but they become meaningful in the acts of patient explication and patient reconstruction within the recipient's mind. Hence, I believe, the Pythagorean motto, Silence; and the quasi-religious temper of the brotherhood. A doctrine of the memory of forms (which Lucian played with) is far beside the point, in my opinion. But it does seem to add up to this, that the more nearly coherent the system envisioned, the more evasive its final description, the more difficult the act of communication, and the greater the need for the concentration of the faculties, as within a Pythagorean society. Or, for that matter, within a cloister; or for the matter of all that, within the tower of the Château de Montaigne, where the books spoke and the mind worked.

For Pythagoras there came at some now-forgotten moment the public exhibition of the inner mechanism of his system, along with its troubles. An early follower named Hippasus is famous for having disclosed the secret of the dodecahedron, or, if not that, for having revealed the discovery of irrationals. Whichever it was makes but little difference. Pythagoras, according to one good reading of the Proclus "Summary," had discovered both already, and either disclosure has the reversion to Hesiodic chaos implicit in it. Since the dodecahedron is built of pentagons and pentagons of irrational numbers, the same mathematical evils came flying out no matter which of Pandora's boxes Hippasus chanced to open.

The axiom that Pythagoras had lived by was that differentiation within the cosmic unity could be expressed in intimately related number patterns. In saying this, I do not mean to repeat the perverse Aristotelean formula, "Things *are* number"; nor even the alternative, "Things *imitate* number"; but to go back to the verse phrase preserved in Sextus Empiricus, "Things resemble number" ("Arithmo de te pant' epoiken") or in deference to the antiquity of the language: "Within arithmetic all things find fitting place." There is no mystery about what Pythagoras had in mind. His crowning theorem, in one form at least, could be converted easily into the numbers $3:4:5$ for the sides of the Pythagorean triangle; music into the ratios $4:3$; $3:2$; $2:1$ for the fourth, fifth, and octave; the circle of the celestial poles into the fifteen-angled figure; the excess of darkness over daylight always equalizing eventually with the excess of daylight over darkness; the justice of the Virgin and her Balances ruling the creation, pound for pound, ounce for ounce. How far could these number systems be extended? Why not throughout the universe?

The answer turned out to be this: they could not be extended, they would not fit together even within their own immediate provinces. The secret of the collapse of the Pythagorean concept—Hippasus's infamous revelation—lies in the indeterminable nature, the "irrationality," of the diagonals of the three simplest geometric figures, which corresponds with a menacing consistency to the square roots of the first primary numbers. It began with $\sqrt{2}$, the diagonal of the square of unit value, it continued with $\sqrt{3}$, the perpendicular of the equilateral triangle which divides it into the most beautiful of Pythagorean triangles according to the ancient Platonists, the most useful according to modern engineers. The only problem with $\sqrt{4}$ of course is that it takes us back to our first problem; but as for $\sqrt{5}$, the diagonal of two squares

In Number All Things Find Fitting Place: *Sextus Empiricus. Here with tablets
in hand noble Arithmetica presents Boethius and Pythagoras, the new and the
old among mathematicians, to show us the difference between the use of Arabic numeration and the manipulation of an abacus. This illustration is from an
early, learned encyclopedia, the* Margaritam Philosophicam *by Gregorius
Reisch, 1512, a book which remains one of the superb ornaments of the Renaissance. I have used the microfilm in the Yale library, but this photo is reproduced from S. K. Heninger,* Touches of Sweet Harmony: Pythagorean
Cosmology and Renaissance Poetics *(Huntington Library, 1974), as is also
the figure on p. 136. The actual numbers recorded in this figure and the
assumptions in regard to the Platonic solids in the previous figure are acutely
Pythagorean in character.*

lying side by side, it is the basis for constructing the pentagon and is as irrational as they come. All of which left the tenets of Pythagoras in a bad way.

The full realization of this must have sunk in very slowly. That there could exist no number, regardless of how small the pebbles or how large the beach, which would correspond with the square root of two must have been ununderstandable at first. Archimedes explains that geometers attacked their problems initially by using mechanical methods—arrangements of pebbles, for instance—in order to study them, and only later adduced formal demonstrations of the proof. Working from the notes of Proclus, we are able to see geometrically that a continuing development of the exact length of the diagonal of a square leads no farther than into refinement on refinement of inexactitudes, ending nowhere. Whereas, on the other hand, as Archimedes observes, determining the volume of a pyramid comes to the opposite issue. By considering the pyramid as a stack of laminations, Democritus could see his mechanical models converging on the proposition that the volume of the pyramid was one-third of the equivalent solid, such as a prism, which Eudoxus was able to prove a little later with an elegant new method. So that was the problem: why should Psyche find the seeds in one bin uncountable, while those in another were grouping themselves of their own accord into natural measures?

VIII

I doubt whether all of the centuries since the sixth century B.C. have produced more cogent answers than the ones that Pythagoras found suggesting themselves to him. The cosmos ought to fit together, true; it must be subject finally to quantitative description, true; but irrationalities as we know them now or as any age knows them, hold the ordered system out there, always just beyond reach. Some of our own best efforts are spent in inventing rational sets of symbols which we hope may lay a cover over the chasm. Symbolic logic is the most ambitious example of latter-day strategy. Meanwhile the forthright mathematician is willing to take comfort in the very look of $\sqrt{2}$, regarding it as something perfectly precise, which in its way it is, not just 1.414214 . . . etc.; and yet if questioned closely, he can only say that he is able to extend the string of numbers in the fraction as far as is necessary for all practical purposes. If that isn't quite what we wanted to know, it will have to do.

Ettore Carruccio, who has looked acutely into contemporary logic and mathematics in the light of Pythagorean history, emphasizes the dimension which has been implicit in it from the first, the Anaxagorean twist that I have been referring to. If a rational system can be defined nowhere except in somebody's mind, then on the outskirts of the mind there must be frontiers of unknown boundaries. The boundaries of irrational numbers seem now to be fairly clearly surveyed. But the mistiness in the general area has not greatly dissipated. For one distressing example: a system can never contain some secret within it to prove its own consistency. Golden thighs must be ruled out.

Nevertheless, we have the not unpleasant obligation to persist in our old Ionian habit of tackling the mysteries of nature in the style of Pythagoras, as they come up, one and all. There is an encouraging fable which Lucian remembered: to the man who had been trying to tally up the waves rolling in upon a beach and had started to weep when he lost count, the fox said, according to Aesop, "Don't weep. Just start counting all over again."

Opposite—Persephone Sotira: *Cyzicene silver tetradrachm. See p. 257.*

5
PYTHAGORAS OF CROTON

Scene: Hades. SOCRATES *and* PHAEDRUS.

SOC.   Beauty! I think you must have met Plato somewhere hereabouts.

PHDR.   I speak against him.

SOC.   All right! Speak!

PHDR.   In my sense of things, the *idea* of the Ideas of which our marvelous Plato is father, is infinitely too simple, too pure, you might say, to explain the diversity of beauties, or the changing preferences of people, or the disappearance of many works into thin air, while others are created totally afresh: all this along with recurrences that are impossible to foresee. I could say more.

SOC.   But what do you think for yourself?

PHDR.   (*quoting Eupalinus*).   "I must come then to masterpieces which are the work of a particular person, and of which, as you said a moment ago, they seem to sing of their own accord. Now, I ask you, is that a worthless claim? Do those words sound irresponsible, invented only to sound well but not to be taken seriously? No, no, I hope not. When you said, Phaedrus, that my little temple made music, that it seemed to sing, your lips and a thought combined while you were speaking, to form a marvelous union. . . . Just imagine what monuments, very great and very small, can be conceived as drawing their sustenance from the purity of musical sound! The masterworks are as a well-tuned string is to a string that is slack and sagging."

—Paul Valéry

ON THE HIPPODAMEAN GRID PLAN of an ancient Greek city stands the present day city of Naples. In it there is a web of grimy streets which I remember with a bewildering nostalgia. High up on the house walls, strings of limp laundry festoon the window ledges; down at street level, dusty, bright-jacketed books lie in mosaics in shop windows. A pair of churches hangs like swallow nests on one stretch of this street. The University of Naples, like older universities everywhere, sits nearby on stiff haunches behind iron gates above flat steps. Inside, there are— how well I know this!—dusky corridors with stiffly varnished doors opening upon pale lecture halls. Inside the churches—how well I know this too!—varnished paintings merge into faded giltwork and nobly darkened bronze sarcophagi. In one gallery, one gallery only, are bright, often renewed rainbow patches of velvet coverings on the coffins of long-dead Christian knights. In these shadows one stops to think about Saint Thomas Aquinas and the *Summa Theologica*.

In Germany, too, there are university centers like this, though the staining of age has not penetrated quite so deep, and these centers, too, have put forth their share of the Summas of modern times. Walter Burkert's treatise on Pythagorean history, *Lore and Science in Ancient Pythagoreanism,* may be characterized as a summa philologica, and as such it is an exemplary work, a microcosm of traditional scholarship. And as such, in my opinion, it is also a remote work, one which, unfortunately, does not any longer lead the mind into the large cosmos that antiquity really was and still is.

Professor Burkert's slowly and carefully elaborated dissertation proposes a definitive answer to the "Pythagorean question," a question which we are told at the outset has its parallel in the "Homeric question." "The attempts of scholarship to grasp the underlying reality" of a Homer or a Pythagoras, the author continues, have turned up nothing more tangible than "the shadow of a great historical name." For this name one school of philologists had visualized "a figure of world historical genius" presiding over the beginnings of Greek literature— Homer—and another presiding over science and philosophy—Pythagoras. A more modern school however is inclined to assert that instead of any such persons there is to be seen in that distant past "little more than empty nothingness.'' To quiet a long-standing uproar of claims and counterclaims Professor Burkert resorts to a device which has been popular in modern intellectual circles. He pictures Pythagoras as someone who existed in a world of magic and ritual. In short, Pythagoras was a shaman, a fascinating historical shaman perhaps, but one who is encrusted in legend so deep as to defy identification.

A moment's reflection should remind readers of this treatise that the blaze of disintegrative scholarship dealing with the Homeric question, which Friedrich August Wolf sparked shortly before 1880, died down considerably when the winds shifted from philology narrowly conceived to archaeology and comparative literature, numismatics and epigraphy. Before Heinrich Schliemann, Milman Parry, and Michael Ventris got through with their work they had pulled down the sails of a whole Homeric industry. Some similar deflation is probably in store for the philology we are about to consider. The varnish on many a famous lectern has been darkening and fading into the shadows in halls that have been much closer to us than those of the medieval University of Naples.

Not that philology has not been adding a generous dimension to the life of the modern educated man, but the science of reading texts is at its best only when it is cultivating its own proper gardens, which can hardly include the phenomena of anthropology, certainly not the ways of religion. The archaic civilization of the sixth century B.C. was not likely to have been so befuddled with medicine men as the befrocked academicians have wished it to seem to be. The grotesque portrait of Pythagoras which emerges from *Lore and Science* is negligible; Professor Burkert himself has announced rather significantly in the preface to the new translation that his own enthusiasm for the concept of shamanism has slackened off considerably since the publication of the original text. And so, putting that formula aside for the moment, I wish to acknowledge my admiration for the author's astute evaluation of the composition of the Pythagorean written documents. No less, even more, is my admiration for linguists who have collected and put in order many chaotic fragments of early Greek prose that found their way into the books of somewhat later writers. The Diels-Kranz *Fragmente der Vorsokratiker* is an example almost too obvious to mention; *Die Fragmente des Eudoxos von Knidos,* edited by François Lasserre, though newer on the scene, is not a whit less valuable.

In the study of the lore and science of the ancient world, the recovery from the blur of a palimpsest in Istanbul of Archimedes' letter on mathematical method, which J. L. Heiberg accomplished, which he very literally brought up from oblivion, is in my mind a very great event. The accidental discovery of the Dead Sea Scrolls four decades later is no more poignantly wonder-provoking.

The murky portrait of Pythagoras is one thing; the account of a mushrooming Pythagorean doctrine is quite another. The account of the impact of this other thing on the mind of Plato is in itself enough to make the book singularly informative. Before considering Pythagoras, we will turn to what is relevant to our purpose in the Pythagoreanism which becomes visible in the work of its best known advocate, Plato.

II

From childhood Plato had been the admirer and young friend of Socrates, if not directly his pupil; and so at about forty Plato bethought himself seriously of an opener world than that which the Athenian agora had become with Socrates gone. Those were the days of the political brutalities that followed upon the overthrow of the Thirty. But the cruel and irresponsible Thirty Tyrants, among whom Plato numbered some close relatives, had been hardly less violently fanatical than their democratic successors. These latter, moreover, were the ones who had sentenced Socrates to death in 399 B.C., for, of all things, impiety; and that action from Plato's point of view had been the blackest event in the history of his native polis.

Having carefully written out the dialogues which depicted the political and social philosophy of Socrates, Plato saw nothing ahead for him in Athens except frustration in his avowed intent to translate the principles of the Socratic dialogues into an active public life. And so, in about 388 B.C., being well informed about the long-established vigor of the Greek cities in Italy and Sicily, and the richness of the scientific and philosophic schools which were a legacy inherited from Pythagoras, he made his way to Corinth, possibly alone, probably accompanied by his adherents, Xenocrates and his nephew Speusippus, and sailed on one of the hundreds of nameless trading vessels out through the Delphian Gulf, crossed over by way of Corcyra to the Heel of the Misty Boot, and arrived at the first of the Italiote settlements.

This would have been Tarentum (Taras to the ancient Greeks), now the crowded small city and naval base of Taranto. In the time of Plato Tarentum was the metropolis of Archytas, the mathematician-philosopher whose imperishable epitaph still lives in the verses of Horace. In his own time, in his own day-to-day life, Archytas was the head of his city-state, which in turn headed the phenomenal grouping of states constituting the Italiote League. For all ends and purposes Archytas was the embodiment of Plato's ideal, the Philosopher-King, though as is evident to anyone who reads the *Seventh Letter,* the Tarentine was a worldlier philosopher and more an empiricist than Plato liked. Still Archytas was famous as a Pythagorean and geometer. His political power in Magna Graecia was conclusive; once in a later decade he dispatched a naval unit to extricate Plato from some serious trouble the Athenian philosopher had got himself into in the court of Dionysius II in Syracuse. Repeated dialogue with such a man as Archytas naturally left an imprint on the studies which were Plato's preoccupation and the substance of the curriculum of the Academy, which he founded on his return to Athens and presided over until his death in 347 B.C.

The beaches of Archytas's populous Taras were grooved with slots for the disembarkation of painted pottery and items of personal importance brought from Asia and the cities of the islands and mainland Greece and for the dispatch in return of raw materials, grain and dried fish, to the older centers. Taras was wealthy. But it was only the first of a string of provincial capitals which extended along the coast of the Tarantine Gulf and the Ionian Sea, between the easternmost cape of Italy and the Straits of Sicily.

Cities such as Archytas's Taras and the others must be reckoned with individually. Against a backdrop of forested ridges and long blocks of foothill farmlands, they had become the features of a unique civilization based on Pythagorean precepts. In them the vicissitudes of growth and the hazards of maturity were constantly interplaying, one against the other. Since the culture of these Greek settlements is our principal concern, we will name the array of small capitals one by one.

After TARAS (or SARAT as master coin makers liked to spell it in retrograde) came META-pontum, the city of horse ranges and fisheries and long, square-cut terraces of barley. A head of barley, the wholesome grain in the medicinal art of Hippocrates, was the insignia on the coinage of the city, and a golden sheaf of the fabulous corn was a noted

Sacred to Persephone: *the city badge of Metapontum. The barley ear is displayed on a silver stater of incuse fabric, 30 mm. in diameter, c. 520 B.C.*

dedication at Delphi. It is here at Metapontum that Pythagoras is reported to have spent the declining years of his life. Then came two illusive foundations, I-ERAKLEA and MSRS——, Heraclea and Siris, each a buffer apparently, marking frontiers between Greek places and the fastness of the native tribes. Both soon disappeared, but Siris only after a short period of great brilliance like that of a nova star. Next, not far along the coast to the south, came the site where the wealthiest of all of the abodes of men had flaunted shaded rooftops toward the Mediterranean sun, SY-baris: Sybaris, byword for luxury and dubious moral standards. It had disappeared in Plato's time, and its approximate situation was occupied by an Athenian experimental colony, THOY——, Thurii, with a theta on the coins, which despite its illustrious beginnings failed to survive for long the raids of the natives.

Then Croton. On the coins the name is abbreviated with the archaic koppa: QRO——, which is reminiscent of Corinthian usage and ancient ties. This had been the destination of Pythagoras, emigrating from

Tripod of Hail-healer Apollo: *badge of Croton. This silver stater is of the incuse type, but not of the earlier fabric. Although retaining the same weight, it is only 20 mm. in diameter and was probably struck at c. 480 B.C. As the knobs on the crane's neck suggest, a running drill, rather than an engraver's point, was the tool used in fashioning the die.*

Samos a century and a half, 142 or 143 years earlier. Whatever the exact figure, it had been continuously a substantial participant in the sea commerce of the west, receiving and dispatching cargoes and transshipping some of them to dependent cities on the Tyrrhenian side of the peninsula. It was the definite center of scientific studies, a home base for physicians, the seat in fact of the northern choir, as Galen called it, of the professors of medicine, the other two being located at Cnidus and Cos. The philosopher Philolaus called it his home, though as Plato was aware Pythagoreanism in Thebes was tied to the teachings of Philolaus in Boeotia, during an interval when he resided there.

Next, KAYL-onia, a foundation of Croton's, short-lived in its exquisite existence on a windy sea-bluff; then LO——, Lokroi Epizephrioi, Locri of the western zephyrs. This is the Locri of Plato's *Timaeus,* the most extended, out-and-out Pythagorean treatise in the Dialogues. Philistion the physician, whom Plato admired and Eudoxus of Cnidus sought out for a master-class, was a Locrian; so was Zaleucus the first creator of a code of written laws, which defined the crime and described the penalty beforehand, so that anyone standing trial was neither favored or disfavored because of his personal influence in the community. The code was said to be severe, but since power seems to have been in the hands of "the hundred families" rather than in an assembly of the "selected thousand" as elsewhere, the rule of the Locrian aristocracy was held effectively under restraint.

Dark Persephone Wreathed in Light: *plaque by D. K. Fry, based on the figure of the enthroned Kore in Hades as pictured on one of the Locrian terracotta reliefs, in the Museo Nazionale, Reggio. A Pythagorean cock, the bird of the dawning whom Lucian makes many pleasantries about, stands under the throne, while another rests in the Queen's hand beneath a sheaf of barley heads.*

A curious complement to the legal orderliness is the formally organized enterprise of temple prostitutes among the daughters of the
city. Since the coastal plain was neither deep nor fertile here, other
expedients could bolster the economy. If, as seems probable, the cult
of Aphrodite enriched itself by offering temple prostitution to the passing sailor, that fact only serves to underscore the complexity of these
nervously active cities. In Locri there has been found a store of votive
tablets, terracotta plaques the size of a folio page in an illustrated art
book, which were hung on the walls of a shrine, particularly a temple
dedicated to Persephone. These well-formed, brightly colored reliefs
bring together dramatic scenes from an interwoven mythology, centering simultaneously on the brightness of life and the black light of the
underworld. Hermes is in the act of mounting behind Aphrodite (or
perhaps Persephone) on a car drawn by Eros and Psyche; Persephone
and Hades sit nobly enthroned with a sacred cock resting under the
throne-seat and another on the throne-arm. Other plaques add to the
collection; some combine Aphrodite and Kore in remarkable ways,
and sometimes, as in the cock, the symbolism overlaps with the symbolism taken up by Pythagorean cults. This lengthy terracotta album
seems intent on turning familiar life-death mythology into single astonishing episodes. Dionysus is discovered, for instance, with a towering
vine of grapes and an enormous wine cup, standing before Demeter
who is seated loftily, as if in Hades, among a spray of barley heads.
Fine bronze mirrors and household utensils may be shown decorating
the chthonic scenes. There is vigor, originality, a studied abruptness.
By comparison the art of the homeland is usually neither so perplexing
nor so challenging as this.

And not more beautiful. As Pindar suggests (fragment 140B):

> Proud Ionians, there is a sort of song
> With flute-play, that may outreach your sweetest hymns.
> It is the artful fabric of a Locrian
> Of those Locrians who dwell beside Zephyrium,
> The white-crested hill, in their gleaming city
> Beyond th'Ausonian headland. Its music surges forth
> Like a bright chariot, singing, "Hail Apollo Healer,
> Hail the Muses." —And I, who babble along,
> Hear it as a dolphin hears it, playing
> On the waters of the waveless deep.

As Professor Burkert has rightly said, Pythagoras—and after fifteen decades, Plato—"entered a religious world of a peculiar character, in which Mediterranean, Italic, and pre-Doric, Achaean elements were amalgamated," a world in which, as I am convinced, Greek archaic leanness was filled out with borrowings from the fulsome Ionian arts and conscientiously empirical sciences, and was subject to a contagious native restlessness which was always in search of better pastures and better household furnishings. It was a world which happened to be unpredictably congenial to new intellectual adventures: for Plato obviously, so why not for Pythagoras?

III •

After Locri, the counter-Locri: Rhegium does not look up over its shoulder onto the Italian mountain but across the Straits at Sicily; and all of Sicily—that swollen, embattled island—looked from every direction toward Syracuse. The amassed fortifications which the first Dionysius had reared for protection against the Carthaginians and the encirclement of aroused native tribes, was probably not exactly what Plato had come so far to see; but whatever had been the attractions for him of Tarentum or Croton or Locri, Syracuse figured unmistakably as the climax of his western tour. It offered nothing in the way of philosophy and but little in other expressions of civilization; misfortune had ruined the necklace of brilliant Sicilian cities. For that reason, for that very reason—the want of refinement in Syracuse and the possession of crude physical dominance over a large quarter of the world—the city spread out, rich and beautiful and submissive, before the eyes of a philosopher with passionate political ambitions. To top off his vision of its potentialities, Plato met a youth named Dion.

Dion was, as it were, the regent apparent of Syracuse. Coming to maturity while the first Dionysius was aging and the second Dionysius was still a boy, Dion was almost incestuously implanted in the family of the tyranny. His opportunities to sway political events in Sicily promised to be so great that Plato lavished his wisdom on him, both as the youth he was at this time, and afterwards during his years of manhood. Dion was conspicuously, perhaps suspiciously, docile as a pupil, certainly conspicuously reckless later, when he took Sicilian af-

Goddess with Hermes Departing in her Chariot: *a photographic copy, courtesy of Guy Davenport, of his drawing based on a Locrian terracotta relief in the Museo Nazionale, Taranto. This goddess is usually identified as Aphrodite, and the team of children as Cupid and Psyche; see, e.g., Langlotz, bibliog. item 74, p. 246. Although I do not discuss this identification in the present account of Locrian culture, it seems necessary now to notice that the girl who is helping to draw the biga is carrying a Pythagorean bird on her arm, and the winged boy, a funerary lekythos. Consequently the goddess must be Persephone, the boy Thanatos, and the girl Psyche, all of which is agreeable to the Homeric Hymn to Demeter; and it makes Pindar's metaphor for Persephone—"her with the white horses" (Ol. 6, 95)—particularly powerful. Pindar is explicit in pitting death against soul-bearing life in Fr. 131. His words are a fanciful application of the basic myth of Kore's annual appearance above the earth and her autumnal disappearance beneath it; the passage also seems to propose that the soul has a power of survival in at least certain limited ways. As in Homer and Hesiod,* bios, *life, possesses superbiological attributes, including the* psyche, *which is a repository for such phenomena as dreams, intuitions, and recollections which are hard for us to explain away into nothingness. The merging of Persephone with Aphrodite, however, is in accord with Democritus's dictum, "Coition is a small apoplexy" (Frag. 32), and also with what we know about Locrian temple practices.*

fairs into his own hands. Plato failed as a mentor. Probably Plato died without ever recognizing the extravagance of his early hopes for Dion.

The substance of the nurturing with which Plato sought to prepare Dion for public authority was philosophical, but philosophical only in an elementary way, such as explaining the distinction between an abstractly perfect circle in the Pythagorean sense and a circle drawn by the legs of a compass. The emphasis, rather, was on moral education, and on a rather abstractly moral version of it at that.

The shape of Plato's earliest lessons to Dion is suggested by a sentence in *Seventh Letter,* in regard to the impressions he had gathered initially upon arriving on the coasts of Italy and Sicily: "I was not at all pleased with 'their blissful life,' as they called it, in which they gorged food twice a day and never went to sleep without fondling someone in their arms." Clearly, when Plato had landed finally in Syracuse, he was in a disappointed and critical mood. Knowing that governments are not at their best when the governing citizenry is bred up in licentious ways, he expounded a philosophy in which ethical virtue is the necessary condition for attaining spiritual freedom, and therefore the serene wisdom which characterizes every good head of state.

As distasteful as he had found the pastimes of the Italian Greeks, Plato thrived on their spirited exposition of Pythagorean precepts; so much so that he appropriated a selection of them for his own purposes. We stress his selection and reorganization of the precepts which eventually found their way into the doctrine of the Academy because among Pythagoreans themselves there could not have been a unified body of teachings; as to what the gist of the teachings may have been, there is wide disagreement among the authors, sympathetic or unsympathetic, who wrote the accounts which Professor Burkert pledged himself to set in order.

We can feel for Walter Burkert: coming face to face with the writings of blurred shades still huckstering their versions of who the master himself was; and what he himself taught, is as unnerving as Odysseus's encounter with the street mobs of Hades. Nevertheless from the hullabaloo of competing vendors of the creed, which became only more confusing as it reechoed through Platonism into Neoplatonism, Professor Burkert maps out some happily convincing patterns. Fortunately these account for most of the essentials in the mainstream of what we all recognize as a predominant philosophy in the Western tradition.

The key to the complexity of Pythagoreanism is the existence of a divergence which goes back to its very beginnings and which by Plato's time had become an out-and-out schism. The fundamental rivalry between Pythagorean sects makes its appearance in a number of passages in Iamblichus's commentaries on Pythagorean activities. Although much in the commentaries of a scholarly mystic writing in the time of Constantine the Great is inevitably suspect, Professor Burkert assures us of the authenticity of one summarizing statement.

There were, Iamblicus says, two kinds of Pythagoreans, one of which we may call the auditors who wore the habit and walked abroad, and the other the scholars who stayed behind and worked in the cloister: the *acusmatici* and the *mathematici:* "Of these the *acusmatici* are recognized by the others as Pythagoreans, but they do not recognize the *mathematici,* saying their philosophic activity stems not from Pythagoras, but from Hippasus. . . . But those Pythagoreans whose concern is with the mathematic life recognize that the others are Pythagoreans, and say that they themselves are even more so, and what *they* say is true." Here the issue is obviously the issue which has split men's minds and souls through the ages, the conflict between the outward and the inward, the active and the contemplative, life. It takes many forms. It was restated in the time of the Reformation, often again in rancorous terms. Should mind or morality have the priority? Should an elevated mental discipline, a theology, or good day-by-day conduct be the seat of saving grace? It becomes a maelstrom in which men like Erasmus of Rotterdam get caught and from which Plato is careful to back away.

If one takes the *Timaeus* as representative of the active Pythagoreanism of Italiote thinking at Locri, it seems evident that Plato was deeply responsive to both sides of the traditional quarrel. He is eloquently devoted to the habit, the symbol, the suggestive rather than the explicit, the mystical, even to metempsychosis though this must not be taken too literally, and above all, to the moral. His admonishments to Dion are weighted on this side of the balance. But over and against the limits of wholesome admonitions, he is able personally to read the divine order of the cosmos in certain scientific projections, such as the geometry of the regular solids, the pyramid, the cube, the dodecahedron, and the others. He is willing now to venture out on purely mathematical flights; and for once, in this dialogue, he shows his underlying respect for the evidence of the senses. He responds positively and imaginatively to *motion,* a phenomenon which had been usually repugnant to his longing for eternal stability; for once, he is able to picture a medium surrounding us which is a vast container for matter, for a structure which approaches being Democritean in its nature.

In these moments Plato is suddenly reflecting, unpredictably and as if by chance, the complex mode of thought of that particular individual named Pythagoras, who first prepared the way for his line of pugnacious successors: the polymath, the mathematic moralist and politician, the long-haired Samian, himself.

At such times Plato's esteem of himself as a mathematician, as a hardnosed geometer, is justified, the loftiness of his discourse notwithstanding. In this context he is closely related to Archytas and most nearly a true predecessor of Eudoxus of Cnidus. His respect for motion, the configurations of which are mathematically definable in musical pitch for example, or in the procession of the heavenly bodies; *motion* is the shaping hand which spins the thread that ties Tarentum and Croton and Locri to Athens, and to Cnidus, and back later to the Syracuse of Archimedes and thence to the upper reaches of the continent of Europe. It leaves somewhat in the background the original *arche* attributed to Pythagoras: "All things are like unto Number," or in the jargonish popular way of speaking, "Things *are* Number." In any event the way is opened for the escape from the irrational in numbers into the asylum of Eudoxan doctrines of supranumerical proportions and of infinitesimals.

Similar in effect is Professor Burkert's discussion of the problem of number itself, a word which has set off innumerable uproars in Pythagorean circles; and no wonder, since it has every right to stand for that evasive linchpin which is hidden at the center of the universe. The problem here is how to shake off the delusion that numbering cannot exist without discrete things being counted, a misconception which cuts the root out from under the Pythagorean system; namely, that there are linear numbers, triangular numbers, and pyramidal numbers, corresponding to line, plane, and solid; and that so far as counting goes, there must come after one, not a particular two, etc., but an "Indefinite Dyad" embracing all numbers relevant to the One nominated at the beginning.

In order to make the crooked straight in this case Professor Burkert credits the exposition set forth in Sextus Empiricus's summaries, particularly in *Against the Mathematicians* (2. 4), with as much genuineness as any record can possibly hold for us at this late date. The documentation supporting Sextus's record is brilliant. Sextus retrieved his material from the pages of the Stoic Posidonius, who in turn had it from Speusippus, Plato's nephew and successor in the Academy; and Speusippus had had ample opportunity to gather his information directly from the Pythagoreans while he was in Magna Graecia with Plato.

The first result of this reading of Speusippus as recorded by Sextus is to demolish the sort of thinking that led to the famous paradoxes of Zeno. Reliance is once more on motion: a moving point produces a line; a line moving to one side makes a plane; a plane lifting up or falling downward creates a solid. Thus a line is *not* a static, one-by-one rank of points, nor a plane an array of them, nor a solid layers or laminations of fields of them. This must be so because a point is not a possible subject for space-occupying predications.

At the same time these considerations deflate considerably the force of the equally famous Table of the Ten Pythagorean Opposites, which Aristotle must have garnered from the ubiquitous, plodding sort of auditor who prides himself on something he has been able to learn by rote. The opposites, beginning with Limit–Unlimited, Odd–Even, and ending with Good–Evil, Square–Oblong, are a silly and disorderly bombast composed of mere scraps of Pythagorean concepts. At this time Aristotle is no friend of the Pythagoreans. After all, when he was writing his critique of them, things had come to such a pass that Pythagoreans numbered among themselves many whom the comedians used as burlesque figures on the stage.

A philosopher, even if he is a good philosopher and not a proper butt of comedy, leads a precarious existence. At best, he is hard to understand. His words are often misconstrued, and in ancient times usually badly transmitted. Besides all that, if he is a pre-Platonic or a pre-Aristotelean, he has had, in our age of peculiar skepticism, a court of vehement, skeptical philologists sitting in judgment over him. Consequently it is greatly to Walter Burkert's credit, and a boon to serious study, that not only is Sextus Empiricus reinstated as a respectable historian, but a great philosopher, Philolaus, is deemed worthy to be studied once again. Philolaus in fact has been practically resurrected from temporary nonexistence. Professor Burkert is modest about his personal accomplishments; but the truth is that his own immediate forerunners and colleagues, whom he obviously reveres—Eva Sachs, Erich Frank, B. L. van der Waerden—would be better read if their own influential works were opened with the skepticism they themselves commend and with the steadier pages of Walter Burkert at hand.

IV

But who was Pythagoras? What can we do to penetrate the misty swampland of shamanism into which he seems to have led the professors in their ponderous pursuit? I would like to begin with a hypothetical case. Let us each suppose that we know no more about Albert Einstein than our recollections of newspaper stories that were published in the mid-decades of the twentieth century. We would recall a Nobel Prize awarded for achievements which, however they may have been comprehended at the time, developed, as it came out later, into a new comprehensive sort of mathematical physics. We realize now that what were once apparently absurd propositions, such as a fourth dimension which is required to give a quantitative account of a moving object, are rules that we turn to naturally in certain situations. A universe described in distances of light-years does not embarrass us, nor does the cosmic aberration of light rays; nor that most formidable of all laws, the universal constant of 186,000 miles a second as the top limit, the unbreakable ceiling, for the speed of any moving physical thing. Knowing so much, there can be no surprise in Albert Einstein's authoritative assertion, when a certain year came round, that atoms could be induced to rupture in gigantic explosions; nor, given a sense of a background of critical war years, that he might convey such information to a commander in chief of armies, Franklin Delano Roosevelt.

What followed will always be common knowledge, though the dimensions of the aftermath remain, will always remain, to be seen. Along with this no one would be ignorant of the fact that Albert Einstein was a Jew, politically a fervent Zionist, a gentle person, a musician devoted to the violin, that he groped tirelessly for an ideal which embraced an ultimate orderliness in Nature and worldwide magnanimity on the part of the political human being.

That is a roughly factual outline of a biography which you would probably find incredible if your life had not been in close touch with it. Assume a gap of twenty-five hundred years between the twentieth century and any other century and the outline would become exceedingly difficult to transpose into a coherent story, and its content beyond our capacities for confident evaluation. Just so the life of Pythagoras. The known facts, or at least the consensus of ancient clippings, call up a figure much like Einstein, perhaps in a wild metaphor which the General Theory of Relativity will excuse, an earlier incarnation of him.

The analogy suggests a new approach: Why did Einstein leave his homeland and come to America? Why did Pythagoras leave Samos and go to Croton? The answer must be, not for political reasons alone, if at all, because more fundamentally each man had matured in a fairly open, international world, and had followed pursuits which led to traveling and relocating as occasion arose. Einstein's life at Princeton fitted his studies; Pythagoras's at Croton fitted his.

The residence of Calliphon the physician, father of Democedes the physician, in Croton is answer enough to the question, why Croton? Democedes had been brought to Samos by Polycrates at the beginning of the tyranny along with other very able persons, Eupalinus, Anacreon, and Ibycus, for example; this would have been at about 535 B.C. Democedes as an interim Samian physician became the most celebrated physician of antiquity, thanks to Herodotus's detailed account of the man's skill, his later adventures in Persia, and his unswerving devotion to his native home in Croton. So this young physician, arriving in Samos, would have had a tale to tell Pythagoras about Greek works of all kinds in the West. Ibycus was in a position to add to the tale, rising even to a versified allusion to deep-sea moles like the cyclopean stonework at Samos and the celebrated causeway at Syracuse.

The key figure, however, must have been Calliphon, the father of Democedes, because with Calliphon in mind we reenter the world of scientific learning in archaic times. Most readers and the run of authors have failed to notice that the only institutions approaching the definition of a university in the several centuries before Plato pioneered an academy and Aristotle followed it up with his peripatetic formal lectures, were the well-established training schools for physicians, at Cnidus and Cos, as we said, and at Croton. They are often described by the esoteric term "cult-sites of the Asclepiadae"; or more realistically in reference to these three centers as medical guild schools. They taught a range of subject matter, the objectivity of which is suggested in the Hippocratic title: *Airs Waters Places*. The diversion of physical studies into metaphysical speculation was not encouraged, though many a well-trained resident in the community of physicians did become a philosopher. Alcmaeon, Empedocles, and Democritus are early, middle, and late examples. Aristotle's early experience was shaped by the guild regimen. Pythagoras, all things considered, must necessarily have found the medical school of Croton a congenial location in which to pursue his own advanced studies.

In this period the physician occupied a select position in society. The likeness of physicians alone was translated by devoted admirers into sculptured marble. It was not in honor of the local tyrant, or a priest, or an athlete, that the first identifiable portrait sculpture was made, but of "Somrotidas the Physician, son of Mandrocles," as the inscription on the right thigh proudly asserts. The statue represents in the style of the archaic kouroi of the day, a nude life-size man; it was found in Magna Graecia at Megara Hyblaea, and is headless. One wonders whether the head of the otherwise conventional, heroically youthful figure, was given the pointed beard which was the badge of the profession. If so, the effect would have been startling, but I dare say it would not have suggested a nude shaman.

A painted marble disc found at the Peiraeus is further support for the premise: medical schools were unique as institutions where that which was acknowledged as wisdom might be acquired. The marker, which was probably made for a tomb, is a portrait of a bearded man seated in a chair, fully clothed and attended by a boy. An encircling inscription identifies it as a likeness of Aeneias: "Aineiou sophias, iatrou aristou," the English for which I think, following Paul Friedländer, may appropriately be set down in archaic form: "This is a memorial to Aeneias his wisdom, of the best of physicians." The disc is about a foot in diameter. Like the statue of Somrotidas it dates from the mid-sixth century, a few decades before Pythagoras's arrival in Croton,

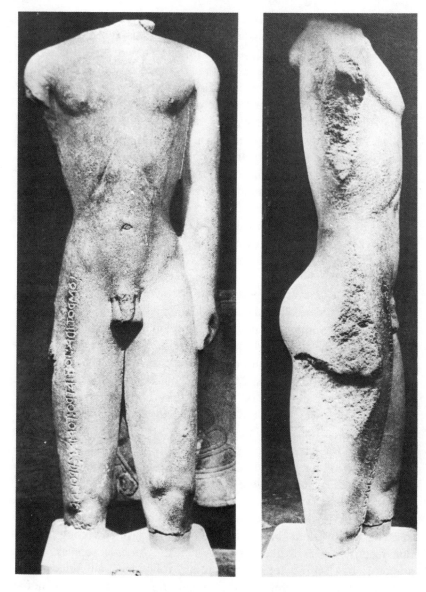

and it seems almost certain to be a portrait intended to represent that Aeneias who was the great uncle of Hippocrates (on his mother's side).

The only possible likelihood is that, for Pythagoras, Croton was a

Sambrotidas the Physician, Son of Mandrocles: *a sixth-century life-size marble statue from Megera Hyblaea in Sicily (Museo Nazionale Archaeologica, Syracuse). The photographs used here are from Holloway, bibliog. item 75, figs. 197 and 198. The conventions in which this nude figure originated are close to those which prevailed in mainland Greece, and the material is Naxian marble. Nevertheless this particular kouros is exceptional in that his is not the figure of an athlete or of some other anonymous youth. The body is smoothly plastic; the inscription on the thigh insists on the identity of the man rather than his being a dedication to the gods. These characteristics are eastern, though they became acclimated early, it appears, to the taste and the materials of the Italiote Greeks. The statues of Ionia, like those of Magna Graecia, are fuller bodied than those of Attica. Early serious portraiture, archaic though it may look, is also an Asiatic experiment: witness the portrait of "Darius, the great king" with bow and arrow, standing crowned in mule drawn chariot while attacking a lion (Cylinder Seal, B. M. 891032). The physical conformations of Sambrotidas, it is worth noting, resemble those of the kouros from Cyzicus which is preserved in the village school yard in Asağiyarici, Turkey: see the picture on p. 254.*

most favorable seat of learning. In contrast with Samos, it was a thriving intellectual center. Not that Samos was not in those particular decades probably the greatest city in the Greek world. But it had become

Memorial to Aeneias Physician of Cos: *sixth-century B.C. marble medallion found in the Peiraeus. From E. Berger,* Das Basler Arzt-relief *(Basel, 1970), p. 165.*

a thalassocracy, specializing in the practical and fine arts as well as commerce. Its poetry and pottery, its temples and triremes were incomparable. But intellectual life in these brilliant Ionian coastlands had gone slack. The Miletus of Thales and his celebrated successors was staggered by dread of the Persians, as were the neighbors of Miletus; Xenophanes had already emigrated to Magna Graecia when Pythagoras got around to doing so. While the scene for the practice of strenuous philosophy was brightening in the West, the stage for utterly hazardous military intrigue was fatally set in the East.

As for the fact of Croton's being a medical center, it is fundamental to Pythagoreanism. Schisms in later developments seem never to have subverted the first principle in its creed, the belief in health. As addled as the accumulation of symbols became, the pentagon, that irrational figure from the point of view of the numerical length of its sides but its perfect symmetry in spite of this, held steadfast to its place as the symbol of health.

V

Pythagoras disembarked on a coast where political accommodations were resolving themselves, not in hostile intrigues as in the Aegean area, but in a blanket of alliances among city-states. Compacts such as these required firm political coherence on the part of the inhabitants of each settlement. Pythagoras, according to every record and rumor, took over leadership of the strongest political configuration in Croton, which it is customary to describe as a political brotherhood or club. But to gather the slightest plausible notion of what a brotherhood really was like, we must find ways and means of filling the gaps in the scant written chronicles of Magna Graecia. In the long run coinage will come forth with the richest additional documentation. Coinage in and for itself, however, remains mysterious until its own general background is brought to light. Fortunately, the revealing context for coinage becomes fairly visible in the not too plentiful displays in museums, including collections such as that of the terracottas of Locri. In addition, and more comprehensive, are the remnants of architecture still standing on archaeological sites. And as of the past few years there have been published many skeletal, graphic, black-and-white archaeological photographs taken from airplanes, photographs which add an entirely new dimension to our story.

These photographs show that the cities which Plato went coasting by, and many others farther west on the shores of Sicily, were laid out early, at dates well antecedent to Pythagoras's arrival, and they show an astonishing unanimity in adopting a grid plan for the arrangement of their avenues and streets. This is indeed surprising. Orthagonal city planning has been named Hippodamean. But the Milesian, Hippodamus, who is presumed to have instigated the practice in the Greek world lived nearly a century after the founding of most of these cities. This fact brings up a totally new set of historical considerations. Colonists, of course, arrive together, roughly speaking; consequently from the beginning they have internal, mutually agreeable arrangements to make. Fundamental among arrangements would be planning fortifications and temple sites, selecting a central location for the marketplace with easy access to the harbor, assigning town lots and agricultural allotments in the country. It follows that settlers are in a position to exploit all forms of civic harmony, ranging from the most reasonable alignment of streets to eventually the adoption of something as complex as a coinage.

But in order to look a little further into the initial ground plan of a settlement, let us take Metapontum as an example. The colony was firmly established, it appears, when in the seventh century the Syba-

rites asked their Achaean connections to take over the harbor and fertile
plain of Metapontum both for the newcomers' benefit and for the sake
of the combined strength the two places would possess in confronta-
tions with Siris and Tarentum, whose borders joined theirs, and with
the often hostile native people living in the hills above the coast. This
is an early instance of the formation of an alliance. The foresight and
benefits it brought about were admirable, though, as is the way with
alliances, not without failure on occasion. Though its intention was defensive, it responded to some crisis that is now forgotten and destroyed
Siris utterly.

Metapontum prospered steadily. The aerial photographs show the
elegant geometrical shape of the city surrounding its ancient, silted
harbor, the checkered suburban plots, and above them the enormous
warp and woof of the fields farmed by the city. Parallel, equally spaced
drainage ditches divide forty square miles of land on the eastern slope
into thirty-eight strips, each of which is cross-divided into units for
cultivation. In the photographs the linear drainage boundaries are
prominent and appear to be very old; excavation shows them to have
been laid out on orthagonal boundary tracks which were already in
place early in the sixth century, several decades at least before Pythagoras's arrival in the West.

Pythagoras, in other words, immigrated into what was already a
sophisticated civilization. Consequently a characterization of him as a
shaman strikes me as being incredible.

Although Croton itself lies buried under an overlay of alluvial soil
and modern dwellings, the level of its civilization may be read in the
awesome, enormous, fractured temples which dominate the landscape
at other places, at Paestum, for instance, and Selinus, and hardly less
so in the Tavole Paladine on the outskirts of Metapontum; and equally
on the precincts of Acragas, Agrigentum, with its string of old temples.
Built of heavy stone, ponderous and powerful, only an atomic fission
lasting through the twenty-five hundred years between then and now,
which is after all only a wink in the eye of time, could account for the
gnarled debris which resembles what Hiroshima looked like before it
was rebuilt. Earthquakes of course have leveled cities. But most cities
have mostly been built of mud and rubble.

Many votive objects rich with allusions to the Delphian Apollo have been retrieved from underground at the temple sites. They include humble statues made of pottery and a small masterpiece cast in bronze, which represents a nude, striding Apollo and may have come from the workshop of another Pythagoras, the sculptor, also of Samos. That Apollo should have figured prominently in the imagery of Magna Graecia and predominantly in the legends of the Pythagoreans, came about inevitably because the settlement of the area was largely the work of migrants who had come by way of Delphi and whose former homes had been in its environs, from Locris to the east to Locris to the west. In fact one of the most famous of early Italiote traditions tells how the oracle instructed the colonists to choose wisely, to accept the health of Croton, for example, rather than the wealth of the Syracusan coast. In the same vein of folklore, health and wealth were the theme of an ironic comparison of Croton with Sybaris.

Apollo in his many guises was a god who, though capable of dealing harshly with mankind, had a generous, unmatched power to bring them relief. In Metapontum he was Apollo Lyceus, Apollo of light, of the lyceum, Apollo of peaceable discourse. Elsewhere in settlements under Rhodian influence, he was the deity of the life-giving radiant sun. At other places he seems to have borrowed his titles as the mood struck him, but they all verged on the concept of his arts as preserver of life.

In Croton he was directly the healer, Doctor Apollo, as Aristophanes calls him, the slayer at Delphi of "the monstrous black dragon, foster-mother of Python, Death" and hence the symbol of the medical schools of the West. One of Homer's titles for Apollo, Smintheus, mouse killer, is preserved in the coins of Metapontum, on one of which a mouse is depicted gnawing on a kernel of barley, the life-giving grain, which in the form of the spreading ripe head is the badge of the city. The reference to the mouse killing goes back to the plague which is in progress at the beginning of the *Iliad* and which Apollo, having brought it about, brings to its terminus in due course. The allusion is especially interesting in an expanded context, for if any one health-restoring practice is axiomatic in the Hippocratic treatises it is the administration of a mild diet of barley gruel to the patient stricken with illness. But impressive above all other symbols, I think, is the image of the striding Apollo of Caulonia, whose delight is in wholesome Airs Waters Places, as the Hippocratic canon puts it.

VI

We arrive face to face with the silver stater coins which have survived in good number from Pythagoras's adopted communities. In fact some may have survived from his own house and hand, perhaps even from dies which he himself fashioned. The coinage which concerns us is a very thin, very broad disc of silver, a silver wafer, characteristically nearly thirty millimeters in diameter and weighing the normal weight of a double drachm, a little over eight grammes. It represents the city badges we have been referring to, all of them carrying allusions to the Hail-Apollo Healer of the springs of Telphusa in the Homeric Hymn or of a river god represented as a bull, sometimes endowed, or burdened, with a man's face.

Broad petals of silver so slight as these would not have been strong enough to withstand handling in the marketplace, were it not for a system of struts which is built into each design. Inside a strong exterior ring, a convex relief forming the image on the coin is counter-indented on the other side by a concave, negative or "incuse" impression of the image, which exactly matches the structural lines of the positive, nesting into it, in fact. Now since these coins have these strong interlinked diagonal features, like any corrugated sheet they are practically rigid, not easily bendable in spite of their lightness, hardly breakable.

The Apollo of Caulonia, for instance, is pictured in mid-stride, one leg kicked forward, the other still extended behind him; one arm is thrust backwards swinging a lustral branch, the other leveled out and up in front, supporting a miniature human figure, who appears to be Boreas, also waving a lustral branch; while at the center of these extremities are the deep corrugations of the torso, upper thighs, and square archaic shoulders, the head and hanging hair of the nude figure of the Hail-Healer. Everything about this work of rarest art bespeaks motion, lightness with great strength, wholesome winds. The little running figure is usually identified as being itself a personification of the living sea breezes for which Caulonia on its coastal bluff was famous. Mechanically the coin matches its message. Mechanically it is the expression of a sophisticated, not shamanistic, civilization.

Skilled numismatists, with Charles Seltman as their chief spokes-

Coins from Pythagoras's Adopted Communities: *above, the early incuse Apollo stater from Caulonia; below, the later SYN Apollo coin from Croton (for reverse, see p. 199). The coin announcing Croton's alliance with the east Greek cities in the war against Athens was provoked, it seems, by a treaty formed between Athens and Dionysius I of Syracuse in 367 B.C., in which both parties agreed to support the other in the existing hostilities. Thus the Athenians made common cause with Syracuse against Croton, and the Italiote independent cities aligned their activities overseas with those of their Aegean cousins. A marble stele recording the Athenian accord with Dionysius is preserved in remarkably good script in the Epigraphical Museum in Athens: see Woodhead, bibliog. item 23, pl. 45. For the unfolding of events in the SYN wars in the east, see the following chapter on Eudoxus of Cnidus.*

man, are persuaded that only Pythagoras of Samos could have brought to the Italiote settlements the artistry necessary for the production of this unique fabric. Pythagoras's father had been a cutter of gems in

Samos. Since the dies of hard metal from which excellent Samian coins had been struck were carved with all of the finesse of a gem engraving—in fact the two arts are practically inseparable—it follows that the son of the Samian craftsman would be conversant with the methodology of seal making. The incuse, flakelike coins of Caulonia or Croton however are of too delicate a fabric to suggest the ordinary gem cutter's technique in the making of dies; the experts propose therefore the use of the *cire-perdue* process, in which engraved wax is lost in casting and the metal replacing it retains the features, down to the smallest engraved detail, which are required of the die to be used in the stamping of coins. The die is thus formed indirectly by casting rather than by working the die material itself, and the matching die is molded by pressing the wax for the second side into the form of the first. In both cases the firm wax on which the design has been fixed is painted again and again with coats of fine potter's clay. Then with the wax and its thick crust of clay standing on edge, the caster fires it like any pottery object, simultaneously pouring molten metal into an aperture at the top, so that the wax is burned away in the heat, and the metal replacing it copies it out feature by feature. The clay is then broken away, and with a finishing touch here and there the die is ready for use.

The *cire-perdue* or lost-wax process in casting was introduced to the Greeks, according to Pliny, by Theodorus of Samos and put to use there not long before Pythagoras's departure for the West. But the art had been relied on in Persia during earlier centuries, as studies of the Ashmolean collection confirm, for the reproduction of fine detail in bronze pinheads and other decorative objects. The formation of the iconography in wax as a preliminary to making an incuse coin die appears to me to be a certainty because every slip of the etcher's knife moving briskly has left a telltale track which shows up on the thin early coins: the back of the E in META (for Metapontum) is badly split, as are several other legs in the lettering; and similarly in my Caulonian coin, the terminations of the linear members in the letters KAY are fuzzy; they had never been cut off at the end in the original engraving. Wax though sufficiently substantial lets the tool run away from the engraver's eye, as it does not run away when he is working with a more resistant stuff such as annealed die metal or the gemstones from which seals were cut. The wax betrays its original presence too in the frequent shadowy echoes of details selected for excision on the reverse

Tracks of a Runaway Etcher's Point: *in META, standing for Metapontum, the tracery of broken lines is evidence of the use of a sharp point on a moderately resistant substance: the wax, in all likelihood, that is used in the* cire-perdue *method of casting bronze. Detail from the incuse stater illustrated on p. 157.*

surfaces of the incuse dies, for example, the minor figures, the city's name, and other symbols.

But *cire-perdue* is obviously a tedious process, and judging by the painstaking care that goes into the triumphs and the not unoccasional failures of the art which I have seen in its present day use in Malaysia and Thailand, I am certain that the casting of coin dies exacted a high tariff in terms of the die maker's time. In any event, before long the dies were being engraved directly, usually with the aid of a running wheel and drill, and lines did not wander, nor did they terminate in any other shape than large round dots. The Athena coins of the fifth century are distinguished quite pleasantly by this feature. It is to be noted too that in the Italian cities, when the transition to direct engraving came into use, there came with it a regression to the lumpy coinage which had always been normal in the rest of the world.

One asks, why the broad, thin flan, and the incuse design in the first place? Pythagoras, as Charles Seltman has also deduced, being eccentrically many-sided according to Heraclitus, may have had a good deal to do with this peculiarity. At least this much can be said with certainty: the geometrical elegance of the coins, the mechanical strength inherent in their design, and the consistent symbolism referring to health in one way or another, are all Pythagorean. As for the dates of the innovation, despite errors which appear in the footnotes of *Lore and Science* and elsewhere, no one familiar with the reexamination of the evidence relating to the earliest coinage of Ephesus will be convinced that incuse was necessarily in use in Italy before Pythagoras's arrival there.

The original incuse style is Eastern, taking the form of deep indentations stamped in the reverse of a coin apparently as a countermeasure to the habit in Asia Minor of punching the fairly thick primitive coins to see whether under the gleaming surface there was an interior of lead. Darius the Great King minted the coins with which to pay his mercenaries with deep punch marks already in them, so that no recruit would imagine doubting their value, though his imagination of course might play him false. Polycrates is known to have paid off some slow-witted Spartans with electrum plated lead coins, some of which still exist with handsome, beguiling punch marks the feature of their reverses. Pythagoras would not have been ignorant of the practice. In a world where commercial mistrust went without saying, the absolute, unmistakable value of the thin, outspread Italiote coins revealed itself at once to the eye and the touch.

We need not assert that Pythagoras invented this attractive, ingenious form of money. Few things are invented by one man working alone. Einstein did not invent the ways of amassing and using atomic forces. But we can feel assured that without Pythagoras the medium of exchange in the west Greek cities would not have been what it was.

VII

Pythagoras must have considered the question—who wouldn't?—of precisely what sort of currency on these coasts would be most useful; what shape should it take? Obviously, unlike the mercenary sigloi of the Great King, this money would not be spread about all over the world. Overseas commerce operated on the basis of direct exchange. A ship came into the port of Taras, or Metapontum, or Sybaris, or Croton with a cargo of this or that, which it exchanged for a cargo of something else, and sailed off again. In these circumstances, so far as I have been able to see, the chief place for the use of currency was in settling accounts with the city and harbor officials who worked out the details of distributing the imported goods and collecting goods to be exported. Eventually the man who bred and trained the horses to be shipped to Athens would receive payment to cover himself and his dependents in their work as horse breeders; eventually the cargo of pottery, some raw silver, and finished armor from Attica would be distributed and the money collected to pay the horse breeder. In all of these transactions, of which a harbor sales tax must come first, currency would be the most convenient means of moving things from hand to hand. But this currency would stay at home. Fees charged to merchant ships, even in the form of harbor or passage tolls, would be paid in goods. After all, when Rhegium, for instance, permits a Cnidian ship to pass through the straits, Rhegium would probably have its eye on some immediately useful goods, not on Aphrodite drachmas.

Coinage as uniform and as instantly recognizable as the incuse staters of the Italiote cities could, in time of trouble, be brought out of hiding, dumped into a leather bag and carried to a safer city. Hoards have been dug up where they were buried, not at home, but on the approaches to a sister city. The very uniformity of these pieces bespeaks the ease of their acceptance anywhere within the Greek area. Disaster might strike any place at any time. A sackful of distinctive coins made a pleasant baggage to tote along in the event of a need for flight.

Incuse currency is implicitly a badge of an alliance among the cities using it. And the remarkable twist in this generalization is that fact that, although the alliance could suddenly be interrupted by devastating warfare between neighbors, peace regularly brought a return to interchangeable money and the understandings that went with its use. I take the instance of the great war between Croton and Sybaris in 510 B.C. as an example of the finally unshakable entente that existed among cities. The military violence which ended in the destruction of Sybaris, if not a scandal in the history of Croton and Pythagoras, remains more than a little puzzling. However, I doubt whether it was quite the mad overthrow of civilized values that storytellers have made it out to be. The gist of the matter is simply that once upon a time there was a blissful, Dionysiac place, a Babylon in full bloom. The next day there was nothing left of it, and Croton its sister city, strengthened by the discipline of Pythagoras, was its destroyer.

More soberly put, the downfall of Sybaris followed systematically upon the violation of every principle which allows an association of independent communities to live and breathe. The Italian cities normally enjoyed stable governments under the rule of councils and assemblies, which of course could be more or less representative of the inhabitants as a whole. However representative the government of Sybaris may or may not have been, there appeared on the scene a certain Telys, a demagogue who acquired a disorderly following, and Telys and his partisans set upon the men who legally constituted the government, with the result that a company of surviving opponents of Telys, five hundred of the most prominent men whose farms had been confiscated, set out, according to Diodorus, with other refugees to seek asylum in Croton.

Telys demanded their return. After debate the Crotoniates, on the advice of Pythagoras, rejected the demand and sent thirty envoys to Sybaris to try to negotiate a settlement of the differences between the two cities. In the midst of nightmarish portents, the story of which delighted ancient historians, the Sybarites slaughtered the envoys. For politically minded Greeks such a crime was unendurable. War followed immediately. When the army from Croton was approaching, hosts of Sybarite defenders billowed out from their walls to meet the attack and were cut down by many fewer Crotoniates. The well-shaded, teeming metropolis was battered apart and the river Crati diverted so that it and its sediments engulfed, as they still engulf, its ruins.

Large portions of the Sybarite population remained in the new homes which they had found elsewhere. Many of the refugees must have been granted joint citizenship with the people of Croton, because at this period there begins to appear a series of stater coins with the Crotoniate tripod and the letters QPO on one side and on the reverse the Sybarite bull with the initials SY; another newly combined city issued coins with the Sybarite bull and the trident-wielding god Poseidon as respective reverses and obverses, but with the initials of one city in this case underscoring the other city's badge. The blending of populations in Posidonia (Paestum) is significant even though this city had started out as a colony of Sybaris; the quick manifestation of unity between Croton and Sybaris, since it could hardly have been expected, signals the overruling force of the basic alliance.

The way in which Sybaris was blotted out has been variously interpreted. Under the sway of Pythagoras, the expert on health and politics as well as mathematics, Croton underwent reforms which lifted it suddenly to a position of great power; its ruthlessness against its neighbor

A Noble Dedication to Hera at the Mouth of the Sele: *"The Temple of Neptune"* at Paestum.
Photograph from a tourist postcard.

The Fleeing Maidens: *a metope from the Heraion at Paestum (Museo Nazionale, Paestum: Max Hirmer photograph, bibliog. item 74, pl. 9). This sandstone relief is of compelling interest because it shows that in the archaic period, toward the mid–sixth century B.C., Greek sculpture in Italy found a secure footing for the shaping of soft stones by referring back to the "coroplastic" models which had been developed in pottery. The result was a peculiarly active representation of the chosen subjects, an underscoring of values as had also happened in Ionia: see Holloway, bibliog. item 74. In this metope the energy of the striding girls, along with the backward glance of one of them, probably springs from a collective mythology, a sky mythology, like the Pleiades with Orion in pursuit, in which the pursued are forever pursued and the pursuers never quite catch up, no matter how fearsome their approach may seem to be. The noticeably Ionian features of western art may have been enhanced by the material needs that led to generous modeling rather than restrained chiseling to attain the desired shapes. Such a point of view explains the cultivation of the effects of weight and massiveness and geometry in the architectural as well as the plastic arts of Magna Graecia, here at Paestum as well as elsewhere; and, together with these properties, the achievement of a dancelike flow of particulars, which is displayed in the motions of the girls represented here.*

however has seemed to be a betrayal of Pythagorean principles. Perhaps the ambiguity here is the same ambiguity as that which permeates many an event in history, not overlooking the bombing of Hiroshima. I am skeptical, however. The burying of Sybaris under the Crati river-bed is sensational; its permanent abandonment on the part of its former occupants is dramatic but not in the least sensational. Rich though it was, the valley of the Crati was malarial and notoriously unhealthy. In view of the laws of nature as set forth in *Airs Waters Places,* and in view of actual demolitions at other ancient places, reaching from Selinus to Cnidus, the likelihood is that Sybaris, once it had been blasted by warfare, was deliberately flooded, and by the motion of its former inhabitants was left unrebuilt.

Whatever the answer to a calculus of this sort, the advent of Pythag-oreanism in Magna Graecia coincides with an upsurge in the value of the currency of civilization. Professor Walter Burkert was wrong in his initial premise. As for Pythagoras himself, the inference that must be derived from the shallow litanies of his followers and their suscep-tibility to magic and ritual is not that Pythagoras but his followers were the shamans, village shamans, who became worse and worse, with marvelous individual exceptions, as the tradition degenerated into Neoplatonism and beyond. The true premise is that more often than not a downward road has been followed by succeeding generations of any extraordinary teacher: Lao-tzu and Taoism, Confucius and Con-fucianism, Buddha and Buddhism, Jesus of Nazareth. But always, with brilliant exceptions, including the Saint Thomas Aquinas with whom we began.

Pythagoras stands out more clearly on the horizon of our percep-tions than any of the others. His principles are easier to grasp. Health: "mens sana in corpore sano"; after the rule of the body, then the rule of the mind. When the brute incapacities are mended, then is the time for contemplation; not in a medical school; but afterwards, philosophy. The record is clear enough to satisfy any philologist who examines the indisputable fragments of Alcmaeon. Perhaps Pythagoras left no written axioms behind him, not a word which is incontrovertibly his, still his unwritten pages live in the early masteries that have emanated from that old world of his. First, to each and everyone, good health and a generous share in a congenial social currency; then to all, the joys of contemplating nature. If for the oriental philosopher, the most

Geometrical Preoccupations and an Italiote Vase. *The expressiveness of the iconography on this olpe comes from its insistence on a metrically harmonious decoration. In this respect the pitcher is comparable with the Cypriot amphora, p. 122; and it too stands in contrast with the dramatic masterpieces of the Athenian black-figure style. Although the vivid pottery imported from Attica found great favor in the west, particularly it seems among the Etruscans, its imitation elsewhere is not conspicuous. The local product tends, as it develops toward red figure, to emphasize burlesque scenes with satyrs, plastic youths in choreographic groups, and architectural settings that are noticeably mathematical in their treatment of perspective. Our vase is relaxed in its metrical style. Its interlocking circles fail to meet properly where they come together on the far side; and its shape seems to be voluminous rather than slender. These are interesting characteristics, with an architectural flair to them. They are just about what we would expect, a relaxed, contemplative product of what Plato scornfully called the blissful way—rather than the passionate way—of life. Private collection.*

joyous reward for labor was the contemplation of the gentle arch of a waterfall in a misty valley, for Pythagoras it was likely to have been the equally timeless interplay of a straight line like the horizon with the circle of the heavens. Geometry.

Opposite—A Cosmography of Rotating Cubes.
Photo courtesy of Jeff Edwards. See p. 222 infra.

6 · EUDOXUS OF CNIDUS:
A PROTO-CLASSICAL LIFE

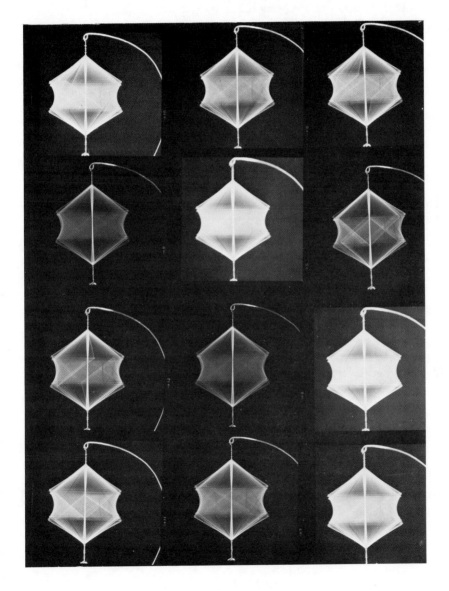

Scene: Hades. ARISTOTLE *and* ANACREON.

ANAC.   You did very well for the name of philosopher, yet I, with my "ditties," did not escape being called the wise Anacreon. . . .

ARIST.   Those who gave you that title took no great care what they said. What had you done, at any time, to deserve it?

ANAC.   I had done nothing but drink, sing, and wax amorous. . . . You pretend to laugh at it, but I maintain that it is more difficult to drink and sing as I have, than to philosophize as you have philosophized. To sing and drink, as I did, required that one should have disentangled one's soul from violent passions; that we should not aspire to things not dependent upon us, that we be ready always to take time as we find it. In short, to begin with, one must arrange a number of little affairs in oneself; and although this need small dialectic, it is, for all that, not so very easy to manage. But one may at smaller expense philosophize as you have philosophized. One need not cure oneself of either ambition or avarice; one has an agreeable welcome at the court of Alexander the Great; one draws half a million crowns' worth of presents, and they are not all used in physical experiments though such was the donor's intention; in a word, this sort of philosophy drags in things rather opposed to philosophy.

ARIST.   You have heard much scandal about me down here, but after all, man is man solely on account of his reason, and nothing is finer than to teach men how they ought to use it. . : . If you wish to limit philosophy to the questions of ethics you will find things in my moral works worth quite as much as your verses: the obscurity for which I am blamed, and which is present perhaps in certain parts of my work, is not to be found in what I have said on this subject, and everyone has admitted that there is nothing in them more clear or more beautiful than what I have said of the passions.

ANAC.   What an error! It is not a matter of defining the passions by rule, as I hear you have done, but of keeping them under!

—Fontenelle (trans. Ezra Pound)

ONE OF THE SEVEN WONDERS of the World, the enormous temple of Artemis at Ephesus, was burned down by a certain fanatic named Herostratus, because, according to his confession when he was put to the torture, he had hoped by an act of unparalleled violence to make himself immortal. Alexander the Great, in a related tradition, was born on the exact day, in the course of the same autumn afternoon in 356 B.C., on which the monstrous blaze occurred in Asia Minor. The motive which has led to perpetuating this page of legendary history is a strong suspicion that the son of a hot-blooded, superstitious Macedonian monarch and a frenzied Epirot Queen had also reduced untold quantities of the fine marble of civilization to common lime in the course of his brief but fiery conquest of the world.

And certain it is at least, that in spite of everything said in praise of the tinge of Hellenism which trailed behind Alexander on his rampant marches into three continents, his onslaughts destroyed forever several rare, and completely new flowerings of the Greek spirit which were taking place on the coastlands of the Aegean Sea. Among the casualties was the work, with its unique possibilities of contributing lasting benefits, of Eudoxus of Cnidus.

"If it had been revealed to men in that autumn," J. B. Bury wrote, "that a power had started up which was to guide history into new paths, they would have turned their eyes not to Pella but to Halicarnassus," that is to say, not to the birthplace of Alexander, but to the court of the Carian dynast, Mausolus, whose lavish purposes imposed a not disadvantageous discipline on every Greek city below and above the Straits of Samos, from Cnidus to Cyzicus, the two principal places where Eudoxus lived and taught and where he took the lead during his lifetime in revitalizing the earlier Ionian triumphs which had figured prominently in the forming of Western civilization.

My purpose is to try to set forth, along with some notes on the league of splendid eastern Greek cities, now mostly forgotten, a summary of the life of their most brilliant citizen.

Mausolus, Dynast of Caria: *a portrait abstracted from the Max Hirmer photograph of the colossal statue in the British Museum.*

II

Whoever attempts this sort of portraiture sits, as it were, under Montaigne's ceiling with some choice fragments of Eudoxus painted on the beams, wondering where in the thousand white vellum-bound volumes to begin his research, and where in the current archaeological journals, the mathematical, historical and philological studies, to find an excuse to stop. No one can be halfway fair to Eudoxus without being conscious of the extent of the materials that must certainly apply to him; and nobody can hope to deal confidently with all of them. The arts required would be too long; the life allowed, too short.

Nevertheless I am confident that two inscriptions on the beams take precedence over the others. Eudoxus of Cnidus was a physician and a son of a physician, a geometer, an astronomer, and a legislator. Such in essence is Diogenes Laertius's first sentence in book 8, chapter 8, of his *Lives of the Philosophers*. In his final sentence he observes that with his short dissertation on Eudoxus he has brought his account of the line of famous Pythagoreans to a close.

This, then, is the man we are looking for: a Pythagorean polymath; a member of the older school, probably the last of the precursors of the generations of specialists; a man something like Archytas, the mathematical philosopher and popular military commander of Tarentum; an adventurer in many fields and indubitably a master in each.

One additional fragment from Diogenes anchors the career of Eudoxus to later dates in the fourth century B.C. than have been conventionally accepted. Early in his life he traveled to the Italiote settlements. After short periods of apprenticeship with Philistion the physician of Locri and with Archytas himself, and a very brief stopover in Athens, he returned to Cnidus, and almost immediately he "proceeded to Egypt with Chryssipus the physician, bearing with him letters of introduction from Agesilaus to Nectanabis, who recommended him to the priests." The inferences to be drawn are decisive. As worked out by Giorgio de Santillana in the obscure wartime issue of *Isis,* the intervention of Agesilaus favoring Eudoxus could not have taken place before 364 B.C., when the former, after being cooped up in Sparta for years, visited the court of Mausolus in Halicarnassus in search, as may be expected, of Persian gold. Eudoxus was also there, or if his return from his travels took him first to Cnidus, he was within easy reach of potential patrons in the new Carian capital. He was still a young man in his twenties.

With François Lasserre, who at present can justly claim to be the leading authority on Eudoxus, we are compelled, in view of these key dates, to visualize the Cnidian, not as a contemporary and intimate of Plato but as a successor who was removed from the Athenian by the passage of time, by in fact a difference of some four decades in their birth dates, and as well by formidable political and geographical barriers. We should expect to discern certain differences between the aging philosopher and the physician with mathematical leanings. In contrast stand the richly intuitive, spacious and inspirational style of the Academy, where Socrates set the initial tone of immortal conversation, and the more rigorous, coherent, and often empirical preoccupations of Eudoxus's schools in Cyzicus and Cnidus, where the dominant train of mind seems often to anticipate the investigations of Archimedes. But on the other hand the concern which the new schools showed for humanity and mythology—for the arts of living, in other words—reveals the strength of the kinship with Plato and Socrates and the earlier Ionians.

The difference comes to this: Eudoxus was renowned for an observatory which he built in order to plot accurate star charts, Plato for his poetic record of the Daedalian glitter of the heavens at night. And the likeness to this: Eudoxus refers the constellations to the myths which remain to this day our oldest memories; Plato reduces again and again the stubborn thickets in the mind to some form of myth, leaving a sense of light where only darkness had been. Perhaps the difference is between Egyptian mental gymnastics and the Italiote love of the paradoxical.

In any event, for sixteen months, with his head and eyebrows shaven in the fashion of the place, Eudoxus worked with the keepers of the libraries and the observatories of Heliopolis, his concentration having turned obviously from medicine to astronomy and mathematics.

From Egypt he returned to the eastern Greek coasts, to start giving his own lectures, at first in Cyzicus, a very prosperous city on the island-studded south shore of the Propontis, famous for its beautiful coinage in electrum.

Here, in Professor Lasserre's convincing reconstruction of events, Eudoxus assembled the detailed astronomical data which he had collected in Egypt, and by combining it with new observations, and the fund of earlier Greek knowledge such as that which had figured in Homer and Hesiod, he produced his *Phaenomena*. His masterly description of the forms and the ancient associations of star groups in the heavens, was republished early in the next century in the astronomical didactic epic of Aratus of Soli, which has justly been famous through all history; and is the most eloquent, almost solitary facsimile of Eudoxus's own writings that we possess. From the same years in Cyzicus may have come a technical treatise on the motions of the heavenly bodies, which in its extant form is so abstract and overly simplified, that it may or may not fairly represent Eudoxus's original document called *On Speeds*. This study is assumed to have led directly or indirectly to Aristotle's inassimilable doctrine of interfitted crystalline stellar spheres. Much more interesting is the likelihood that *On Speeds*, with its emphasis on motion, on the speed of a figure turning within a sphere, led to Euclid's *Elements* Book 13, and through Euclid and recognizable byways to Kepler's *Mysterium Cosmographicum* (1596) and the founding of modern astronomy. Kepler explored theory, as did Eudoxus, and not, at first, any mechanical applications to the solar system.

Before midcentury Eudoxus left Cyzicus with some students or associates who later became famous (Menaechmus, Callipus, Dionastratus, Polemarchus, probably Helicon) and went to Athens. Why he did so has never been made clear, and ancient conjectures are utterly trivial. Though his interests had diverged from those of Plato, no doubt the new science of Eudoxus was a subject of exchanges between him and younger members of the Academy, including Aristotle. As Werner Jaeger and Erich Frank see it, the effect of Eudoxus was to have stimulated and irritated but not to have inspired revisions in the thinking of the Academy.

The magnetism of Athens for this prominent Cyzicene at this time was likely, I believe, to have been more political than philosophical. In the midst of existing turbulence along the east Greek seaboard, a crisis had arisen over the possession of Daskylion, an important Hellenized Persian city twenty miles inland from Cyzicus. In 355 B.C. Artabasus started a war with Persia because he had been ousted from Daskylion, his hereditary seat, by the Great King's favorite satrap, Ariobarzanes. There followed an explosive campaign in which an Athenian alliance led by Chares took to the field and presented Artabasus with a stunning victory over the royal Persian army. The victory, which Chares was so foolish as to refer to as "a second Marathon," had immediate repercussions, including ominous threats against Cyzicus itself.

The episode brought the existing Social War between Athens and the eastern Greek allies of Cyzicus to a showdown. We read that a "sudden inflow of threatening intelligence," which only Eudoxus, or a few others like him, could have brought to Athens, revealed the extent of the king's anger and his intention to retaliate forthwith against all of Greece. The Athenians, aware of their weakness, submitted to a second King's Peace later in 355 B.C.

Eudoxus's was probably the persuasive voice in the negotiations preceding the pact. In fact we may presume that he left the imprint of his own thinking on Demosthenes' famous first political oration, *On the Symmories*, delivered in 354 B.C. in the period of demoralization accompanying the Athenian surrender. Demosthenes' brilliant analysis of the purposes of an Athenian navy and the economics involved is factual and geometrical in its clarity, and it shows sympathetic insights into the eastern maritime accommodation. Only a year or so later, with Eudoxus no longer in Athens to advise him, the young political orator, pleading on behalf of "The Liberty of the Rhodians," delivered an address which contrasts with his first in that it is badly informed, doctrinaire, and sentimental; and evidently made no political impact.

The political role of Eudoxus in Athens is indicated conclusively by the fact that within a short time he was called down to Cnidus, a close ally of Cyzicus, to undertake certain legislative assignments. He was received on his return to his birthplace with public honors, and he made Cnidus his home for the rest of his life. Public demands upon him explain clearly his appearance with representatives of his school in Athens and just as clearly his return not to Cyzicus but to Cnidus.

In Cnidus, besides engaging in civic affairs, the nature of which will come out in a moment, he continued his astronomical studies, making observations from a special building which he designed for the purpose. The observatory of Eudoxus, like the Aphrodite of Praxiteles, attracted sightseers to Cnidus for several centuries. Lasserre believes that Eudoxus, after gathering new data, felt constrained to publish a revised, more empirically exact version of the *Phaenomena* which he called *The Mirror*. One benefit to be derived from an exact mirror-image relationship of the earth and the sky was the possibility of plotting terrestrial seasonal changes with precision, of making, in short, a better calendar, a project of supreme importance in the waning archaic age. He travelled extensively; there are definite hints to this effect in Ptolemy and Strabo, and we hear of his presence in the Halicarnassus of Mausolus and his successors. In one way or another he collected the materials for his *Tour of the World* in seven books, the liveliness of which made it comparable with the *Histories* of Herodotus. He contributed more than any other single person, so far as the records show, to the organization of the *Elements* of geometry. He is thought to have resorted on occasion to writing in verse.

Scattered references to his opinions and theories evoke the image of him leading the inquiries of students of all kinds in Cnidus—mathematicians, physicists, astronomers, geographers—all participating no doubt in the liberal curriculum of the medical school. In his lectures he is said to have discussed "the gods, the world, and the phenomena of the heavens."

III

The emergency which prompted Eudoxus's return to Cnidus was, according to Lasserre's reconstruction of events, the crisis which followed a popular revolt against a too exclusive and much divided oligarchy, while the city itself was in the throes of facing up to an enormous building project. The Cnidians, needing leadership in rewriting their constitution and enacting new legislation, called on Eudoxus. He responded positively, with promptitude.

So far as they go, these propositions are perfectly convincing. Eudoxus's general success is attested in bronze, but in bronze generalities. No one, to my knowledge, has attempted to describe his performance in anything like plausible detail. To try to do that, we must begin by considering Cnidus in terms of its similarity with, and its ties to, the other cities in the long coastal and island chain of Greek centers.

Thales of Miletus, a century and a half earlier, had proposed forming a defensive league of Ionian cities in order to withstand Persian aggressions. Bias, another of the Seven Sages, countered with a proposal to move all of the cities, pots and wheels, goats and freight bottoms, to Sardinia, and to set up new cities there: a flamboyant but not impossible idea. But neither idea prevailed. Thales' easier one fell apart because of jealousy in regard to naming a center for the league.

But now in the lifetime of Eudoxus an eastern Greek federation had come into power. It was founded on a broader basis than the one proposed earlier. It was directed, however, not against Persia but in the opposite direction. And in spite of human nature and civic rivalries, it had prospered. Its victory over Athens in 355 B.C., in the Social War, proved how well it has prospered.

At first glance the picture of an alliance against Athens, against the motherland in general, shocks the imagination. But Pericles' destruction of Samos and the continuing policy of planting *cleruchies,* of evicting Greeks from their homes abroad in order to give outland property to the poor of Attica, had aroused primitive terrors among the inhabitants of the Aegean area. Then, after the Peloponnesian War, Sparta's turn at overseas rapine had been no less appalling. And so with a half-blind but sound instinct for the future in about 394 B.C., following the Battle of Cnidus, the eastern cities formed a society, a *Synmachikon* (SYN), which aligned itself with Thebes. Members of the federation issued local coinages with their own symbol on one side and the Theban blazon, the infant Heracles strangling serpents, on the obverse. Cnidus matched its head of Aphrodite with the pro-Theban Heracles sign; Rhodes, its rose; Iasus, its Apollo's head; Samos, its lion's mask; Ephesus, its honeybee; Byzantium, its bull; Cyzicus, its tunny fish.

Although these cities can be named as members of the maritime pro-Theban and pro-Persian society on the basis of their coinage, the revolt of Chios and Cos along with Rhodes, against Athens in 357 to touch off the Social War, must mean that they were also SYN places, for whom no coins have been found. Outside the eastern Aegean coastlands, coins of the infant-Heracles type issued by Croton and Zacynthus reveal how widespread was the discontent with imperialism—Athenian, Spartan, and Syracusan—in the affairs of Croton.

The SYN pieces are of Rhodian weight, according to J. P. Barron; others describe them as of Chian weight. Except for the fact that Rhodes gave leadership to the SYN society, the distinction is unimportant. The practical fact is that coins of this weight made them easily interchangeable with Persian money: two Persian shekels were equivalent to a tridrachm. The reason for the standard is clear: members of the society directed their commerce toward one another and toward the satraps and the Great King himself. To Athenians this arrangement was repugnant; it signified a loss of independence, a forfeiture of democracy. But in cold fact, although neighbors like Samos and Cnidus doubtless paid a tribute to Mausolus, and Mausolus paid a tribute to the king, still the tribute payers enjoyed more independence than was normally allowed rich but vulnerable settlements. The right to coin money was in itself a proof of effectual independence. In fact Barron,

The Infant Heracles Strangling Serpents: *the Theban blazon on the coinage of the Maritime League. The League was aligned at first with Thebes against Sparta; then after the upsurge of the fortunes and the renewed aggressions of the Athenian Empire, against Athens. The east Greeks used a double-siglos of the Persian standard for the type. The coin illustrated here is a silver stater from Croton in Magna Graecia.*

in *The Silver Coins of Samos,* entitles his chapter on the era of the rise of Mausolus "Fourth-century Independence." In referring specifically to Samos, Barron of course is describing the general situation in all of the eastern states.

Unfortunately we have to add that for Samos this pleasant independence ceased when Timotheus son of Conon conquered the island, dispossessed its citizens, and made an Athenian cleruchy of it in 365 B.C. It has been said, and by no less admirable a personage than Demosthenes, that Timotheus "delivered Samos from the garrisons of the Persians." Thus always the ignorance (when some rare Eudoxus does not happen along) and the distortions of politics! As a matter of fact, one should wonder what proportion of the oarsmen and marines in the Chian and Coan ships which destroyed the Athenian navy eight years later were exiled Samians.

A feature of the coinage of the early fourth century in the SYN area is the regular appearance of a local magistrate's name on each of certain important annual issues. A sequence of local names on the coins of Cnidus, as of Samos (before all coinage ceased with the arrival of Timotheus), is best explained by the thesis that the mint master was elected annually, and that his office in all logic would be only one of a number of elective offices. Strabo gives a general account of traditional practices in Cyzicus and Rhodes, which may have led to parallels sooner or later in Cnidus. Boeotia underwent definite constitutional changes shortly before Eudoxus was called to Cnidus. In view of the SYN connections with Thebes and Eudoxus's connections with Cyzicus, the direction of his reforms can be visualized with a good deal of clarity.

With the growth of the power of Thebes, there had come a swing away from the crumbling oligarchies toward new, more democratic organizations among the member states of the Boeotian League. In order to regularize these changes, a convention of about 375 B.C. established a broader base for the political franchise in the league, limiting it not to the top ranks of the landed gentry but extending it to embrace, as a probable example, everyone whose wealth allowed him to exist at least in the ranks of the hoplites; and then, as if to compensate for so much expansion with all of its inherent clumsiness, the league reduced the number of Boeotarchs from eleven to seven and the number of cantons similarly. The Boeotarchs constituted a council of generals. They, along with all other officials, including whoever was named master of the mint, were responsible to the General Assembly. These changes brought about a tightening of the inner organization but a broadening of its foundation. It was a good federal system, which was not neglectful of democratic processes.

The names of Epaminondas and other Boeotarchs entrusted with the mint which appear on the silver coins of Thebes in this period suggest how similar the constitutional procedures of Cnidus and of Thebes were to one another. In these circumstances it follows that Eudoxus, benefiting by the example of Cyzicus and the recent Boeotian reforms, instituted in Cnidus a balance of a greater popular franchise, which Aristotle implies was long overdue (*Pol.* 1305B; 1321A), with very definite consolidations in the central government.

These consolidations, as it turned out, were so drastic as to include a complete overhaul of the physical structure of the capital city.

At some point Cnidus decided to regroup its several centers in one big city. No one knows whether the decision had been made before Eudoxus's arrival or not. What is known is that in the decades preceding his return, first Rhodes in 408 B.C., and then Cos in 366—to mention the two closest neighbors of Cnidus—consolidated their chief settlements in new locations: sea-looking, easily fortified promontories at the tops of the islands, beside natural, or nearly natural harbors; and simultaneously Mausolus was intensely at work relocating Carian settlements in grand style on the Halicarnassus harbor.

The option that offered itself to the Cnidians was whether or not to build on the slopes above a shallow strait or low neck of land, hardly more than a causeway, that connected the mainland with the small island farthest out on the long Cnidian peninsula. The defensive and maritime advantages of the place were plain to see; so too were the hardships which would be occasioned in realizing these advantages. Eventually, in spite of the refractory terrain, this was the site adopted. Archaeologists C. E. Bean and J. M. Cook believe that the builders had to start building from scratch; American archaeologists, in a project sponsored by Long Island University, report that they are finding evidence of an earlier Greek city on the site. Though in all logic the problems of sailing a coast such as this demand early establishments in these coves, nevertheless building a city great enough to house the main elements of the Cnidian population was still a Gargantuan undertaking.

Why should there have had to be a new Cnidus at all? What ultimately was the concept that lay behind it? Frankly I can't quite believe that defensibility or maritime commerce could have provoked so revolutionary a move. The chances of war, the changes in commerce, were not suddenly so different from what they had always been. And on top of everything else the new location had the glaring disadvantage of putting the orchards and fields and famous vineyards some two hours' walk from the city gates; the sources of fresh spring water were nearly as far away. Wide paved roads and the remains of lofty stone culverts tell the story of the multitude of feet that had to tramp back and forth, morning and evening, from the houses in the city to the patches of land and the fountains out in the country.

Possibly there had to be a new Cnidus because there was a new Rhodes and a new Cos; because of the mysterious dictates of fashion. But there had been a new Cyzicus too, some centuries earlier, set up in an identical situation on the Propontus, which had proved to be a remarkably wholesome city. The duplication of the plan of Cyzicus at Cnidus seems to be more than a coincidence. If Eudoxus was in a position to impose the decision on the Cnidians to expend the multiple fortunes that it took to occupy the new location, he would have done so, I am sure. It would have been, however, as a physician and a man of varied worldly experience that he would have urged the enterprise forward.

No one knows when conscious knowledge becomes conscious enough to beget an intelligible form of expression. Malaria, of course, was the scourge on these seaboards, as it has been nearly everywhere in the world until quite recently, and it still hangs in balance in certain areas, like Ceylon, pending the outcome of the hysteria about chemicals. The Cnidians were as vulnerable as anyone else to the disease, and Eudoxus knew what the disease was. He also knew what caused it, I believe, and though his description of the specifics might not satisfy the contemporary ear, it could have been persuasive to the Cnidians, and very rightly persuasive.

The effects of what we call environment were apparently recognized from the beginnings of Ionian empirical observation and the forming of theory. Alcmaeon of Croton, whose connections were in one way or another directly with Pythagoras, said that when a body becomes diseased it is "sometimes affected by external causes, such as certain waters or a particular site or fatigue or constraint or similar reasons." At a slightly later date Empedocles, discovering that "the people of Selinus suffered from pestilence owing to the noisome smells from the river hard by, so that the citizens themselves perished and their women died in childbirth," diverted two other rivers in order to sweeten the waters of the first.

The point of view of Alcmaeon and Empedocles was typically Presocratic. It was also persistent. A century later the Hippocratic *Airs Waters Places* posts in its very title a quarantine notice. Its description of the water on a certain kind of site leads to a classic description of malaria: "Such as are marshy, standing and stagnant must in summer be hot, thick and stinking, because there is no outflow. . . . Those that drink it have always large, stiff spleens, and hard, thin, hot stomachs, while their shoulders, collarbones and faces are emaciated; the fact is that their flesh dissolves to feed the spleen, so that they are lean. . . . This malady is endemic both in summer and in winter" (Hp. Loeb I. 85).

Let us take the plight of the people of Caunus, on the coast some sixty miles east of Cnidus just north of Rhodes, as a concrete example of the general effects of malaria:

Although the country is fertile, the city is agreed by all to have foul air in summer, as also in autumn, because of the heat and the abundance of fruits. And indeed little tales of the following kind are repeated over and over, that

Straticonicus the citharist, seeing that the Caunians were palish green, said that this was the thought of the poet in the verse, "Even as the generation of leaves, such is also that of men"; and when the people complained that he was jeering at the city as though it were sickly, he replied, "Would I be so bold as to call this city sickly, when even the corpses walk about?" (Strabo 14. 2. 3)

The fine quality of the figs of Caunas was so famous that *"Cauneas!"* was the street cry of fruit-hawkers in Rome. With great agricultural profits at stake, the Caunians may not have thought they felt quite so sick as they looked.

Aristotle with his usual deliberate formation of his opinions, says, in a page which may have been the outcome of discussion with Eudoxus, that the rules for selecting a situation for a city are these: "It should be fortunate in four things. The first, health—this is a necessity." Next is convenience for political administration and for war, and finally the availability of good drinking water (*Pol.* 1330A–B). Cnidus could claim these advantages, if cisterns, which are moderately acceptable to Aristotle, and a lot of leg work could make up for the absence of natural springs on the new site, which few Greek cities had to any extent anyhow.

In any event reason enough for transplanting landlocked Cnidian towns to the city with the double sea front was, in one word, malaria. The ominous way of malaria was this, that if it did not sooner or later become a fatal disease in itself, it made its victim the easy prey of any other disease that might attack him. Of these, chest troubles were the most common. But malnutrition, complete exhaustion, wounds and demoralization—the everyday lot of smiths and soldiers and pirates and common people alike—wreaked an unnatural toll on the sufferers from the basic ailment.

There were no direct remedies; quinine came nearly two thousand years later with tobacco from America. Treatment was well-conceived: rest, warmth, and simple nourishment; and scientific inquiry was unflagging. The Cnidian school was accused of overrefining its distinctions between types of malaria or malaria-complicated diseases. If the charge is justified it would seem to indicate a Cnidian mathematical interest, in the different periodicities of fevers for instance, while the Coans were interested in the practical prognosis: the one was perhaps a little too detached, the other a little too close to the bedside manner.

The best defense against malaria was clearly recognized, if not consciously formulated. It was not just, "Stay away from swamps"; it was more subtle, and much more practical. When at the close of the past century the chain of the transmission of malarial parasites through mosquitoes from bird to bird and man to man was fully explained, then brilliant classicists like W.H.S. Jones, the editor of the Hippocratic writings in the Loeb Classical Library, were in a position to reinterpret some scandalous passages in ancient literature. The luxury-loving Sybarites, for instance, adopted the motto, "Let neither the morning nor the evening sun look upon your head," not simply because, as had been thought, the Sybarites liked to start drinking early and lie abed late, but because they were instinctively aware of the prophylactic benefits of avoiding the out-of-doors when mosquitoes were most active. T. J. Dunbabin in commenting on Jones's addendum to Sybarite history, notes that "this simple rule of health" was readopted in the last century in the malarial parts of Italy, the worst of which was still the plain of Sybaris.

With so much empirical experience behind him, Eudoxus could reasonably insist that the two hours' walk each morning and evening through the dry hills between the new city of Cnidus and its well-watered crop lands was not a hardship; to the contrary it was a health-giving regimen. Other cities—Cyzicus, for instance—had thrived best when they had submitted to like conditions. Or if a city had no place to move to, the marshes might be drained, as at Selinus, and in the fifth century at Camarina.

These measures were all expensive, probably in excess proportionately to sums we are prepared to spend for similar purposes. The decisiveness with which places like Cnidus acted contrasts with the reluctance of people during the centuries immediately past to do more than crawl like Sybarites under a mosquito net and take quinine: a defense which of course was not available to inland natives and the multitudinous poor.

Eudoxus's medical science probably did not go beyond naming certain marsh animals (*bestiae*) as the cause of illness: beasts so small that their presence could best be detected by a bad-water smell. The mosquito, I think, was not indicated. Nor need it have been, since it was innocent until it gathered microorganisms from carriers of infection. And the final irony is that the subtle *bestiae* of early medicine are sci-

entifically more descriptive of the villainous parasites, actually protozoa or unicellular animals native to the swamps, than the pharmakos
mosquito.

Though no detail of Eudoxus's medical science, except for a haunting notation on the value of both physical and mental exercise, has
come down in the records, we have to suppose that it reflected the geometric disposition of his work in general. And as it happens, there is in
the Hippocratic corpus one short work with a curiously geometrical
sheen which is hardly to be explained, as it usually is, as a display of
Heraclitean mannerisms. *Nutriment* is concerned with the intake, partial absorption, and outflow of that which nourishes—food, water, air
—in ways which are continually fluctuating. Health similarly is a state
of being which fluctuates along a lifeline that extends from conception
to a timely and normal death. These, as it were, are the coordinates of
existence. "Nature," the little treatise observes, "is sufficient in all for
all." Nature determines the imaginary lines from which it is disastrous
really to depart, though living consists in nothing other than following
the zigzags of small, compensating deviations. The manner is distinctly Eudoxan in that it aims to pair axiomatic nature with the irregularities of the actual. And this, I hold, is what Eudoxan philosophy is.

There is a tragic footnote to be added. In spite of the bravery of
ancient medicine, many sufferers failing to find direct relief, grew
impatient with the physicians and resorted to the priests of Asclepius.
George Sarton, in describing the imposing temple of Asclepius on the
island of Cos and the lateness of its date, spells out the unhappy turn
of later events in which the genuine doctors, refusing to be corrupted
by the demand for magic rites, departed from Cos and left the priests
of Asclepius to capitalize on the fame of Hippocrates. "The spirit of
Hippocratic medicine," Albin Lesky remarks, "shows the greatest
contrast imaginable with the practices of the priests as we know them
from Epidaurus." It seems to be a law of human nature, too often overlooked, that austere objectivity, such as that of Ionian science, de-
clines readily into pretentious sentimentality. For every Pythagoras,
there will eventually turn up an army of miracle-mongers, with a rare
Eudoxus standing here and there in between.

IV

If Eudoxus had been a pre-Socratic, which he is in every respect except the chronological, Aristotle would have said that his *arche* was geometry, just as for Thales it was water, for Anaximander the *apeiron,* for Heraclitus fire, for Pythagoras number. And Aristotle would have been right, or as right as he is in applying the overly simplified labels to the others. What we would have to specify for Eudoxus is that geometry constitutes the schematics, not the elemental constituent, by which the cosmos may best be described. For Pythagoras the schematics, not the elemental constituent, had been number: "In number all things find their fitting place"; but the possibility of a final quantitative description of the universe had eluded Pythagoras in the empyrean of irrational numbers. Eudoxus avoided the problem of trying to count where counting is impossible by manipulating figurative magnitudes rather than numerical entities: into his mouth we might put the words, "In determinate magnitudes all things find fitting place."

Before venturing into the pure geometry of Eudoxus, we would be better advised to characterize the geometrical Hippodamean grid plan for the new city of Cnidus, and with it some general geographical disciplines, as being practical examples of the geometer's art. The city plan of Cnidus, which Eudoxus sponsored or at least collaborated in, was a checkerboard of city blocks "oriented on true N," each just under 200 feet square, with main thoroughfares some 20 feet wide interspersed among secondary streets. The thoroughfares were completely paved, with sewers under the pavement. The terrain, lying as we said at both ends of a causeway, sloped upwards toward the ridge on the peninsula and the low peak on the little island. In conforming to the premise of the rectilinear grid plan, the streets resolutely climbed and descended the rises, with one of the main streets making its way on ramps and stairs from the theater on the commercial harbor sea front, passing above a Doric portico and the arcades of other merchants, to the Corinthian temple. Module after module of architectural units and open spaces with sea outlooks among them comprised the new city of Cnidus, and the long straight avenues tied the whole together.

The grid plan of course was not Eudoxus's invention but rather a

significant item in his heritage. The plan is said to have been the innovation of Hippodamus of Miletas, a gentleman of the preceding century who wore brilliant costumes and had elegant geometric theories
about the political advantages of dividing a city in equal thirds among
the soldiers, artisans, and husbandmen. Although his political system
was mistrusted, his vigorous ideas on city planning, which were probably derived from observing Asiatic and perhaps Italiote practices, led
to his being called to supervise the reconstruction of the Piraeus in
Attica; and soon afterwards he was enlisted as city designer for the new
foundation at Thurii in Italy, in which Herodotus and Protagoras and
other notables were also engaged. Strabo says that he drew up the
plans for Rhodes before its move in 408; but if so, it would have been,
like Isocrates' *Panathenaicus,* a work of extreme old age.

Applied to Cnidus the grid plan was especially radical because of
the amount of physical labor required to shape the broad terraces,
which are still evident today, and because of the vexing problem of
assigning property rights. The streets of Athens, despite their ultimate
focus on the top-heavy marble Acropolis, wound round at the pleasure
of interested landowners. The streets of Cnidus did not; and like the
streets, the houses: those of Cnidus are said to have been comfortable
but very modest, suggestive of a cohesive, moderately prosperous society. Civic monuments were well distributed. In the days when the
few gardens were nursed from cisterns, every vista must have been one
of graceful architectural profiles, with viney green plots here and there
and many bright marine interstices.

Of the monuments, one, the temple of the Aphrodite of Praxiteles,
was dug out of its ruins just a summer or two ago by the American
archaeological team. It was a round, open, marble pavilion on a high
terrace above the city and the encircling sea. The golden goddess of
sailors and of the planet stood with her smiling, meditative gaze and
her unabashed confidence in herself as the naked image of her sex on a
podium in the center of the temple, around which no doubt were the
beds of antique flowering shrubs that the pseudo-Lucian says were
planted there to greet the pilgrim, which still persist today as a patch of
wild thyme. The other monument, Eudoxus's observatory, has not
been found and probably never will be, because through the centuries
when it was pointed out to visitors it was described only as "a house
not much higher than the other houses." Yet for practical purposes

it must have occupied a site like that of the temple, perhaps on the hill-crest close beside it. For both the goddess and the astronomer looked far outwards upon the same phenomena.

V

Although the Hippodamean grid plan seems to have emerged spontaneously from the rigors of setting up a newly migrated colony or the need to put fallen oriental cities quickly together again, it became in the mind of Eudoxus a diagram to be applied not simply to the obdurate headlands under a maritime city, but to the whole world. No one before him had dealt consciously, so far as the records show, with geography in terms of a grid of latitudes and longitudes. Homer and Thales and Pythagoras may never have forgotten about the zones that range across the face of the earth, defining the bounds between habitable lands and the areas of intolerable heat and cold; and Hesiod's perceptions certainly included the precise turning points of the sun at the "tropics"; but Eudoxus was able to articulate still more evasive facts about geography in his *Tour of the World* because, according to Strabo, he was "a mathematician and an expert *both in geometrical figures and in 'climata'*" (9. 1. 2). That is to say, he imposed linear boundaries on the zones of the climates and intersected them with meridians. Dicaearchus, the other oldest geographer to propose something of the sort, was a follower of Aristotle and therefore later than Eudoxus and probably in debt to him. By the time of Eratosthenes, Hipparchus, and other predecessors of Strabo, the Eudoxan method had come into general use.

In the ancient system the base lines, equivalent to the equator and the zero meridian at Greenwich, traversed "the greatest length and breadth of the inhabited world" (Strabo 2. 5. 16). Since the first scientists were projecting their personal point of view onto the location of these axes, they naturally assumed that the axes intersected one another in the center of their world, and just as naturally that they followed the E–W, N–S alignments of the most famous landmarks lying within their purview. Specifically, the E–W axis, or geometrical *element* as Strabo calls it, ran westward under the Taurus mountain chain from the Eastern Ocean through the Gulf of Issus, passing over Cnidus and the capes of the Peloponnesus, through the Strait of Sicily, across Sardinia, and out between the Pillars of Heracles; the N–S line dropped from the mouth of the Borysthenes (Dnieper), southward through Byzantium and Cyzicus, touching the Cnidian peninsula and Rhodes, then Alexandria and Syene in Egypt, and finally Meroë in Ethiopia.

When the known world is thought to be quartered thus, with Cnidus at, or near the central point, then a Eudoxan fragment describing one of the most richly historic coasts in Greece becomes much more significant than it appears to be at first glance. The fragment is taken from Strabo (9. I. I): "Eudoxus says that if one should imagine a straight line drawn in an easterly direction from the Ceraunian Mountains to Sunium, the promontory of Attica, it would leave on the right, towards the south, the whole of the Peloponnesus, and on the left, towards the north, the continuous coast-line from the Ceraunian Mountains to the Crisaean Gulf and Megaris, and the coast-line of all Attica."

To the eye falling on an ordinary map, this "straight line" of Eudoxus's is astoundingly crooked. It provoked an excellent historian, E. H. Bunbury, to cry out against Eudoxus for seeming to lack that for which he had always been honored, geometrical good sense: "That such a man," Bunbury wrote, "should have arrived at conclusions so wide of the truth in regard to countries so well known, is indeed a striking proof of how little geography could yet be regarded as based on any sound and satisfactory foundation."

But a map such as Eudoxus must have visualized would have resembled the one accredited by Strabo to Eratosthenes, and depicted in a number of modern reconstructions. It shows a natural elongation of the oval containing the known parts of the world, with a systematic foreshortening of the extremities, particularly in the circle from the west to the northeast, where lay the most familiar parts of distant lands. Spain is shrunken; Britain lies in close under the Alps; Italy is relatively large, stubby and flat. The effect is that of a moderately spherical projection viewed from the point of intersection of the main axes of the world; on it Eudoxus's straight line looks like the conformation which strikes the eye of the air traveller coming down from the north: the coast of Italy falling behind as the coast of Albania comes up, which merges soon into the upper shore of the Gulf of Corinth, with Delphi at the top of its own gulf, and then the shore of Attica with Sunium at its tip. The choice of this great-circle route for a Cnidian on his way home from Italy to Cnidus would have been, in regard to distance alone, a matter of simple expediency proven by many voyages. "Corinth," writes Strabo in a context with a reference to Eudoxus, "is the master of two harbors, one of which leads straight to Asia, and the other to Italy." The sphericity of the earth was accepted as a fact by Eudoxus's Pythagorean predecessors; but the navigational phenomena that issued from it were probably understood only by geometers.

Eudoxus appears in the passage cited, however, to have been chiefly concerned with something more than cartography. His purpose in identifying the straight line of the waterway from Albania to the tip of Attica is to exhibit the rigorous geometry underlying the lax meanders of the actual coastline. His argument is that departures from the perceptible great circle compensate for one another. Rhium draws Antirhium out of line, and its unnatural protuberance is balanced by the hollow of the gulf below Delphi. The west coast of Attica would not be so concave if it were not for the concavity of the coast of Argolis opposite it. And so his argument goes, emphasizing the fundamental patterns in the coasts of the world.

Such simplifications are matters of common sense. The small, card-sized map of the Underground in London would disintegrate as an intelligible plan if it tried to show in scale every twist and turn of every route. The helmsman steers by the farthest appropriate landmark, not the closest: his "straight line," like the lifeline of health, is subject to repeated small adjustments. And so, on the grand scale, the structures which can be composed mentally must be applied to the looser structures which are evident to the senses. Eventually this victorious invasion of the mind into the realm of the senses results, for one pertinent example, in Eudoxus's principle of exhaustion.

The *Tour of the World* in other words is a study of the premise that all things, including the features of the earth, find fitting place in figurative magnitudes. The comparison between Eudoxus and Dichaearchus is revealing. Dichaearchus, as an early post-Aristotelean, is already a specialist. Surviving information characterizes him as a geographer whose individual contribution to the science was the calculation of the height of mountain peaks: remarkably inaccurate calculations, they appear to have been, which were applied to a random choice of eminences.

Eudoxus leaves literal geography the farthest behind, however, when he undertakes to recount, in archaic style, the legendary history and ancient mythology, the natural marvels and odd customs, which are attached to the places being considered. Thus the treatise recounted which heroes founded which cities; where adultery and incest were honored, where banned; who liked what foods: Heracles quail, Plato figs.

Although the notes on miscellaneous curiosities have disappeared for the most part along with the rest of the book, they seem to reflect the tendency in proto-classical times to turn the puzzling aspects of life into little illuminations. A geographer was like Zeus. When he lifted his eyes from his immediate concerns, he found himself contemplating the lands of the Thracian horsemen, and of the Hippemolgi that drink the milk of mares, and of the Abii, the most righteous of men. Strange places, strange people. And beyond them, the sphere of the whole earth and the heavens, needing some sort of rationale to explain it.

At this point the geometer of the Eudoxan sort and the astronomer became one and the same.

VI

The sphericity of the earth's surface was known as a sensory fact long before the fact surfaced in the mind persistently enough to demand intellectual attention. Homer, for instance, has Odysseus, who has been watching the Pleiades, Boötes and the Bear from his raft, discover shadowy mountains in the misty deep; and later, after swimming from the wreckage of the raft, Odysseus is said to catch sight of land close by when he is lifted up on a great wave: until then Phaeacia has been beneath the curve of his horizon, though he does not bother to think about it that way. Similarly, seafarers on innumerable transports, looking ahead toward their destination, could see the battlement walls and upper suburbs while the awaited city was still out of sight, and at night, the bivouac fires on the hillside while the glow of the camp arose from the nowhere that lay ahead. The elemental perspective seems always to come up out of the sea, or else, as with Thales, to be directed out over it. Either way, the image of the strange roundness of the world lingered in the nerve centers of Greek eyes.

The need to explain experience of this sort prompted the creation of a wonderfully appropriate mythology. In Hesiod, Earth herself brought forth the round sky "to cover her all over" with its reciprocal shape, and

> to be an unshakable standing-place
> for the blessed immortals.
>   (trans. Lattimore)

In a fragment of Euripides, sky and earth are pictured as being of one form, which by separating apart brought forth "trees, birds, beasts and those creatures whom the briny sea doth nourish, and the breed of mortals." This variation of the Aristophanes myth in the *Symposium* makes the important point: earth and sky are complementary one to the other.

The conception that the sky mirrors the earth, as Eudoxus implies by his second title for the *Phaenomena,* is no less scientific for becoming involved with mythologic imagery. In the terms of science, there are the corresponding polar circles, corresponding tropics, corresponding equators located both on the surface of the earth and in the celestial sphere; and the ecliptic is a geometrical tether that connects them. But it also follows that if the earth is the scene of an enduring mythology, so must the heavens be.

For us, there are naturally many difficulties in the way of reconciling Eudoxan science and mythology. In view, though, of the probable content of the *Tour of the World* and the explicit content of the *Phaenomena* as recorded by Aratus and witnessed by Hipparchus, it seems obvious that we can't ignore the fabulous, as I feel Lasserre has tended to do, nor to let it get out of hand, as Hertha von Dechend and Giorgio de Santillana seem almost to wish to do in dealing brilliantly with similar materials in *Hamlet's Mill.* Jung and Kerenyi and Walter Otto and others have demonstrated the immeasurable impact of constellation imagery on the psychic structure of the race: at least that much is clear, even though details remain obscure.

The myths which Eudoxus draws on ought to be studied for their range as well as their individuality, but strictures of space force me to consider only two episodes in which I imagine the author of the *Phaenomena* may have taken a personal interest. Both would tie in with the observations of a young astronomer in Egypt. The first is his treatment of the *Argo,* the ship remembered in the tragic legends of Cyzicus and

Medea Escorted toward Boarding the Argo. *This caption is one of my guesses as to the meaning of this fragmentary black-figure scene. Another is that it represents a bit of the choreography in a dance at Naxos in honor of Ariadne; in this case it would become a celebration associated with the constellation Corona. Or it may be presenting steps from the famous Crane Dance, first performed, on a happier occasion, at Delos: "which the Delians keep to this day, in which there are many turns and returns, much after the turnings of the Labyrinth" (Plutarch: Amyot-North translation). In any event whatever we choose to see here, it seems to give a glimpse of how the people of the myths looked in the eyes and the imaginations of sky gazers in early Greek times, and as a painting it adds a dimension, a human dimension, to what we have been trying to establish as a strictly* metrical *graphic art. The visualization of choral motion, as of animal motion, is a motivating force in an iconography such as this.*

represented in the constellation lying above the Tropic of Capricorn in the far south. In it the bright star Canopus, the "Egyptian star," associated as it was with the history of his observatory in Cnidus, stands like a seal on the brief page of his biography:

Beside the tail of the Great Dog the ship Argo is hauled stern-foremost. For not hers is the proper course of a ship in motion, but she is borne backwards, reversed even as real ships, when already the sailors turn the stern to the land as they enter the haven, and every one backpaddles the ship, but she rushing sternward lays hold of the shore. For so is the Argo of Jason borne along stern foremost. Partly in mist is she borne along, and starless from her prow even to her mast, but the hull is wholly wreathed in light [i.e. the light of Canopus].

(Loeb translation)

The device of using sky imagery reflecting the counterpart of a terrestrial scene for the purpose of describing a constellation, along with the intent to animate heroic memories, of Jason in this case, explains the sense in which a poem like the *Phaenomena* is said to be didactic. The author of *Titanomachia,* of an uncertain earlier date, is convinced that Cheiron initiated the education of the human race by bringing men to the knowledge of "oaths, sacrifices, and the schematics of Olympos," which is to say, to a degree of consciousness of broad moral obligations and intellctual familiarity with the star patterns covering Olympus. Something of the sort seems to be the intention of Eudoxus. But simply in practical terms, if the Argo can be seen in its resemblance to a ship, with its parts singled out by individual stars, then the constellation becomes as unforgettable as a design painted in a cup, and the old bugbear of communication is disposed of: one has only to name a feature in order to specify a star. There were advantages in visualizing a star as a detail in a mythological picture; the preference for coding the heavens with Greek-letter stars is indicative of the dominance of the needs of a specialized astronomy in modern times. But by some irradicable habit the names of the constellations themselves have hung on, even though the ability to see a Lion, a Bull, or a Bear, not to mention a Virgin, in the sky has become a withered area in the modern sensibility.

My second example of mythology in the *Phaenomena* works out in miniature the task which Eudoxus assigned himself for the whole book, a poem running to 1154 lines in the epic version composed by

Aratus. In describing the starry sphere in punctilious detail, Eudoxus correlates the risings and settings of the constellations with weather watching and calendar making and some stock taking of the general cosmological environment. In the collection of the *Fragments* there is evidence that from the days in Egypt and Cyzicus Eudoxus, following the example of Democritus (who was in many ways the most important of his masters), kept records of astronomical patterns in connection with meterological events. These preoccupations are apparent in the passage below (Aratus, ll. 402–430). I confess to transcribing the passage somewhat freely, in the interests, not of translation, but of total effect:

> While Arcturus wheels in his high arc, far beneath him,
> In the lower sky, under the fiery sting of Scorpion,
> The Altar loops in a path toward the Western Sea.
> It spins from the waves, because Night, our ancient nurse,
> Aghast at the ills of sailors, set it as potent warning
> Of storms to come. Ships wallowing helpless hurt her heart.
> She set this sign therefore, kindling it with beacon lights.
> Now when the Altar, low on the sea, by clouds encircled,
> Gleams forth in brilliant stars, great darkness above,
> Great darkness below, Night, sending South Winds,
> Delays the storm, unveils the Altar, gives cheer to crewmen.
> If quickly they lighten ship, fasten bulkhead and rigging,
> Look! Look! their peril is eased! though not passed by.
> For if by chance a black gust drop from heaven upon the sail
> In loud turmoil, they yet may steer downward under the wave.
> But if Zeus hear them, and a wind pass over with lightning,
> They then again may see each other toiling on the deck!
> Fearful also are the South Winds, till North Winds pass over
> With lightning.

The activities on shipboard when the Altar burns brightly in the stormy darkness are visualized with painful exactitude and imagination. But also impressive is the filiation of the mythology in this episode from the creation myth par excellence. Night it was who, as the offspring of Chaos, gave birth, after her union with her brother Erebus, to Aether and to Day, the purest elements in which, along with her own element, the mortal race subsists; but neither did Night fail to bring forth some subtler elixirs: Doom and Fate and Death, and Sleep

Aratus: Dread are the Stars that are Wheeled along without a Name. *The handsome monster in the foreground I presume to be a chimera. Since archaic animals were best known from their pictures in works of art, even the familiar ones are likely to reflect a communal consciousness rather than individual observation. Lions, though they were to be seen fleetingly in real life, come into view ordinarily looking like improvised variations on the dominant images that had been passed down through the civilizations of Asia Minor. The household dog, however, and the barnyard goat remain reasonably faithful to everyday recognitions. Chimeras naturally posed a special difficulty in that there were none of them anywhere about to be seen. The exceptions are the very few that appear in early vase paintings and the few on coins. In literature when they are mentioned at all they are monstrously unlike one another. Hesiod, whom the chimera painter followed, gives the chimera three distinct, fearsome heads. Here our painter follows Homer (Il. 6. 179–82): a lion-jawed, goat-bodied, dragon-tailed fire breather. The evasive outlines of the constellational figures, like the loquacity of Aesop's animals, seem to stem from a sudden decisiveness in the work of the human imagination. The vivacity of mind which discovers a visible chimera in a myth, or a centaur in the heavens, or for that matter an angle for the ecliptic on the terrestrial globe, emerges as a rude intrusion upon the conserved awarenesses which constitute the ordinary makeup of a human being.*

and Dreams. The Altar, we might say, is celebrated in tones of a tragic humanism, whereas the names of most of the other constellations invoke recollections of old colossal violences. The mythological groundwork of the *Phaenomena* cannot be attributed, in view of Hipparchus's evidence, to anyone except Eudoxus, although some scholars think that a so-called Stoic emphasis on Zeus may be the contribution of Aratus. While a quality of this kind could have been brought into an archaizing poem in which the gods are a part of the aesthetic tradition, the greater truth, it seems to me, is stated splendidly by Callimachus: "Though the style is Hesiod's, the vigil that wrought the poem was Aratus's." And the creation of the plot, of course, was Eudoxus's.

VII

In spite of the foliation of the Cnidian's geometry in extensive and important parts of Euclid's *Elements*, I gather that with close scrutiny the original style of Eudoxus will appear to be something quite apart from Euclid, something that sprouted from Democritus and bore its best fruit in Archimedes. The difference between the two styles is as simple as this: Democritus and Archimedes knew that their leading ideas referred back to mechanical models; while, needless to say, Euclid in his frugal Platonic coherence avoided concrete models as far as possible.

"Some things first became clear to me by mechanics," Archimedes wrote in a letter to Eratosthenes, "though they had later to be proved geometrically, . . . but of course it is easier to provide the proof when some knowledge of the things sought has been acquired by this method *rather than to seek it with no prior knowledge*" (my italics). This, in effect, is a denial of the *priority* of definitions, postulates, and common notions as the fountain source of geometric knowledge, and an affirmation of the power of the mind to transform verified observations into structures which demand recognition as axiomatic facts, which for convenience may be called axioms. "Eudoxus," Archimedes also said, "was the first to enunciate a proof of Democritus's discovery that the cone is a third-part of a cylinder, and the pyramid of the prism, having the same base and equal height." After Eudoxus had formulated his irrefragable proofs, the proportions of one to three for the solids in question could henceforth exist as axioms.

How Democritus of Abdera arrived at the initial proposition is not known, but his famous observation concerning the paradoxical "step-like indentations" created by cross-sections parallel with the base of the figures suggests that he could and probably did visualize the pyramid as a stack of laminations rising from a base of definite area to a peak of zero area at the top. It follows that his thinking must have ranged from ponderous architectural monuments, stepped pyramids in particular, to the figures of geometry, and that therefore the cube, rather than the cylinder and the prism, was the first of the models to force itself on his attention. If so, the most casual of investigations would have shown him that a cube, when cross-sectioned at its mid-point, reveals quite visibly to the observer the one-third proportion of the pyramid to the cube encasing it.

And then, considering the stepped pyramid as a purely geometrical problem, Eudoxus could have said something of this sort: "The line along the outer edges of the steps must be x distance away from the line along their inner limits. Now, while compressing the indentations in the figure and reducing it to more and more manageable areas, we discover that x can be forced to become smaller and smaller, while the laminations become thinner and thinner, until at some point the outside and inside lines come so close together that further reduction becomes incomprehensible." *But not impossible.* The mind must simply sit outside and wait while the process of exhaustion goes on to complete itself. To say that the lines finally coincide or become one line is meaningless. At this limit definitions of a line do not apply, and the question remains whether or not in the womb of things the embryonic steps do not continue forever to exist.

The enduring standing place, which Eudoxus discovered and from which he surveyed heaven and earth, can be described in words as simple as these: "If from the bulk of anything you take away a half or more, and from the remainder a half, and from it a half, and from that half a half, and so on, there will always remain some small bulk left over, which will be less than the least you set out or can set out but under the laws of exhaustion can never be obliterated." Nevertheless, the true, not fully materializable shapes toward which division and subdivision have been leading, as for example in the application of multitudinous tangents and chords to a circle—the best circle that can be drawn by the human hand—eventually a circle of unworldly exactitude is in fact evoked as an emergent reality in the inner consciousness. At this moment the curve of the circle and the straightness of the straight line are interchangeable. Eudoxus proves the propositions of the ratios of circles to one another, and spheres to one another, in the terms of squares and cubes, in a directly lineal, not curvilineal comparison. His inspired management of refractory finite particulars became an apparatus for dealing with what in one way or another he was always aiming at, and that was, of course, the conquest of the mystery of the physical makeup of the world and the conduct of the heavenly spheres.

VIII

Thus, since according to the theory of exhaustion, after innumerable particles of the outside world are brought into alignment, something clicks into a clear but evasive shape in the inner world of consciousness, I should like to consider for a moment that that something may be a poem.

To adhere as closely as possible to philosophical tradition, which in its need for coherence never ventures far from mathematics, I cite first of all the counsels of John Crowe Ransom to his readers, and of course to those who were once fortunate enough to be his students as well as his associates in letters. The shape that a poem assumes when it rises from the poet's consciousness may be studied best, he says, as an example of the Concrete Universal. As for the concrete: "The sensuous detail puts the poem in action." But the concrete is purposive in its action; it remains unfulfilled until it gathers about it a universal which is beautiful and moral and meaningful. Then it is finished. It becomes something more than and different from the sum of the palpable concretes and abstract universal. Ransom has followed Kant in recalling the beauty of a garden when its best season comes upon it. The gardener's hand was guided by a "geometrical Universal" while planting the plot, but in his mind was the "profuse detail and spontaneous-looking" foliage and blossoms which were to come; and when they do come, a principle in nature of active reciprocity makes the disparate coordinates of the planting and the profusion of the growth no longer disparate. "It is as if the plants obeyed the law of their placement only to exhibit their own freedom beneath it more luxuriantly."

Among the last citations in Mr. Ransom's "Observations on the Understanding of Poetry" to which I am referring, is the passage from Yeats's "1919" in which the impact of the image of a swan is accepted as a Universal with symbolic overtones; but the generalized image is admitted only as an occasion for converting it, as it turns out, into a definite, brilliant and mobile and transitory creature, an energetic lily-like bloom on the pond, by redefining it in a patchwork of astonishingly clearcut images. Only then, when this is done, does the original universal disclose its truly axiomatic character. I find it saddening to think that, in contrast with this, another potentially comparable poem, Bryant's "To a Waterfowl," should drift far away from any sense of reality into a mirror room of universal poetic phraseology, with only a slender introductory image to redeem it—that of the bird in its lonely, untranslatable flight in the evening sky.

T. S. Eliot's Objective Correlative, as must be self-evident, is a particularized Concrete Universal. An interesting difference is that Eliot, at this time at least (he was writing about *Hamlet*), was searching for a key by which to lock shut the empty passageway between a concrete narrative apparatus and the integrity of a unique emotion. Words are dangerous tools in this sort of discussion; neither moral nor emotional rightness suggests what I think we really want to say: therefore the value, in my opinion, of going behind all such terms to the fundamentals of discrimination, which would certainly seem in the light of a long history of thought to be centered somehow in the sense that there must be a boundless area of intuitive coincidences which is all inclusive and yet less than the least we can consciously lay out. In any event, the objective correlative, I believe, was suggested to Eliot by something that Paul Valéry had written, and Valéry's discriminations seem to have found their principles of order in his study of architecture, an art in which a substantial curtain and a deftly imaginative design vibrate harmoniously together.

Allen Tate, as most students of his work are aware, went through a period when he wondered whether, after having finished a poem, he would ever be able to write another. Which ought to be, but seldom is, a fear that should frighten every poet. Of course Allen Tate did always write another and a better and better poem. In any event I suspect that his perturbation was the outcome of a perfect sensitivity vis-à-vis the sensuous concrete and his unyielding conscientiousness about the integrity of the universal in which the poem must end, and also begin. As Radcliffe Squires has suggested in his study of the poems in question, the poet freed himself from his impasse, it seems, by allowing the universals to take the necessary way that the concretenesses had forced upon them. If as in ''The Eagle,'' the correlatives of the world's rot and God's hideous face occur in conjunct lines, that and only that is the necessary way of that particular poem. Only by that hard road can the grace of a good poem, or a good anything, be found, and there is inevitably a certain explosiveness when genuine thought and sense, those double worlds in our frail universe, come together.

Jacques Maritain, preoccupied with these matters, helps his reader, after confessing to his fondness for diagrams, by drawing what looks to me like three Chinese umbrellas raised one above and inside the other, so that, according to his notations, downwards from the soul which is at the peak of the outer umbrella there is shed a run-off of concepts and ideas, which have washed down through the intellect, the imagination and external senses. Within this umbrella there is a second which collects the organized images of the imagination. Meanwhile a third supports the two above it with the tendrils and reeds of sensation which find their way from the ground clear back up into the soul.

In this figure, which I trust I do not misinterpret, Maritain speaks, as is appropriate for him, of the soul, where the others spoke of the universal, the moral, the beautiful, or the emotional; and I, of the axiomatic. Construe these formulations as you may, the reciprocal exchanges between the inner life and outer experience are impressively alike in the several accounts.

Now, if I may be permitted to lead Eudoxus of Cnidus down across a vast expanse of ages, all of which have been more or less dark, along the royal roads of countless fallen empires, over many ancient seas and hitherto unknown oceans, I should like also to begin with a drawing, because even a poor drawing can sometimes catch the gleam of that first Promethean intellectual fire which would be all but washed out by even a moderate flow of words from this, one of the world's remotest provinces.

The drawings I have in mind will begin with a cube, a regular hexagon, somewhat larger and more perfectly shaped than a knucklebone, about the size of a boy's top, made up of strands of metal, open to the inside, so that its internal diagonal is in view: *OB* in the figures. This cube, if we visualize it as a two-dimensional object standing on an apex, displaying both of the extremes of its profile positions, would resemble figure 2, drawn as in Euclid 13. 15. If it is spun on its apex while in this position, the cube produces a series of elusive outlines. The six lateral vertices pass by, brushing the shell of an invisible sphere. They emerge and recede like wingtips at points opposite the one-third divisions of the internal diagonal, and they drag behind them a veil of intermediate positions which cannot be visualized with pre-

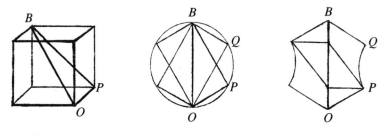

Figure 1.
Three-dimensional
cube, internal diagonal
OB

Figure 2.
Cube in two positions,
projected onto a
plane surface

Figure 3.
The shapes of a cube
in rotation

cision. The figure is hard to draw. Its every feature is transitory. It lies in an area like that in which the process of exhaustion takes place. In this case exhaustion clicks into a vision of duplicate cubes with edges *OP* and *BQ* entwined one within the other. The mobile combination moreover seems to yield up the formula for Eudoxus's lost solution, or an approximation of a solution, for the Delos problem. The radius at *Q* in figure 3 is the radial dimension for a sphere and consequently for an inscribed cube which doubles the volume of the first cube and sphere with radius *P*. Thus it seems that by working from the longest length in a "Platonic" solid—in a cube, its internal diagonal —Eudoxus coupled solids with spheres, and in so doing, he anticipated Johannes Kepler's *Mysterium Cosmographicum* (1596).

IX

In the study of the five regular solids inscribed in a sphere, Eudoxus (and perhaps other early contributors to Euclid's *Elements,* Book 13) undoubtedly had in mind the possibility of geometrizing the universe. That the sphere of the farthest heavens enfolded in its transparency a dodecahedron was a conviction with old Pythagorean associations; Socrates visualizes it as a boy's leather ball made up of pentagons sewn edge to edge, with the earth poised in the center, mirroring the distant celestial geometry. The fact, however, that in Book 13 all of the regular solids are inscribed without preference in the sphere, argues for the projection of all five of them into the celestial enclosure, with the cube, for premental reasons, perhaps being pivotal. Thus sphaeric is an appropriate mathematical geometry which offsets the ragged, loosely geometrical constellations and the paths of the wandering planets, just as the meridians and parallels of the earth offset the rough meanders of its coasts.

"Phenomena are glimpses of the unseen" is a proverb attributed to Anaxagoras, approved of by Democritus, and practiced rigorously by the first known master of Eudoxus, Philistion, the physician of Locri. For Philistion the unseen mechanics of the circulatory system, for instance, seem to have been rendered visible by experiments which followed the phenomenon of the pulse back to clear glimpses of the workings of the heart. It is manifest that in a similar way Eudoxus, for the first time in the history of empirical astronomy, regarded the aspects of the stars as phenomena which would lead him back to the invisible mathematical secrets of their organization: not, it should be emphasized, to ontological or teleological explanations of them, but simply to descriptions of their hidden articulations.

In tracing the flaming pinpoints to the mobile aetherial outlines of the magnitudes of the regular solids, Eudoxus of course could not make his flashes of unseen geometry fully visible; at best his inferences had to hang back in the tentative and theoretic—where they indeed may properly belong—in a science in which, for us as for the ancients, so much must remain inscrutable anyhow. That, in any case, was the irrevocable way of Eudoxan geometry: for just as the theory of exhaustion implied areas where the senses cannot follow the detail of convergence, so the superimposing of the sphericity of the universe on the apexes of solid figures occurs somewhere out of the reach of the human vocabulary. In fact, in this Eudoxan, non-Euclidean geometry, a sphere (or a circle for that matter) cannot be regarded as the complete Platonic form which it is under the rules of Euclid. Archytas, despite his emphasis on the circle, really reduces it to the track of a whirling object—a whistling toy on the end of a string, for instance, having the numerical values of the pitch of the sounds it emits. This was an insight which, since the laws of musical pitch had already been formulated, puts the emphasis on the pulsations which generate a circle, as well as an Einsteinean limit to the rapidity with which the pulsations may occur.

And after Archytas Eudoxus, as we know, could pursue the pyramid no farther than into a ladder of embryonic lines, or in the case of a circle into the vestigial imprints left by radii terminating at a place equidistant from their point of origin. The practicalities of the mind working with geometrical entities required a non-Ideal procedure; Diocles is happy to construct a ''curve'' by applying a straight edge to connect a series of points, a practice which has justly been said to prove that the Greeks acted as if they possessed a theory of infinitesimals, with no spurious logic attached to it. This puts them in one respect at least on an equal footing with modern mathematicians. And so the sphere, the great sphere of the universe, we must conceive as a mobile scaffolding of regular solids etching lacy designs upon it, while it itself consists in an even lacier system of infinitesimal platelets.

In the figurative Eudoxan way, we stand at the center of the universe watching the rotation of spheres which are rendered visible by the assembly of luminous bodies. Their courses are various, and though orderly they stand in a fluid relation to one another. The apexes of the solids within the spheres seem, figuratively, to etch out the plan of the heavens, the celestial equator and the ecliptic, the zodiacs and the polar circles. The main axis of the universe pivots on polar stars; Eudoxus mentions a northern polar star as if it were visible, though of course nothing of the sort was to be seen in the fourth century B.C. While the cube within the sphere of the fixed stars may be supposed to have supplied the principal axis as it revolved on its internal diagonal, some of Eudoxus's polyhedra must be imagined as revolving on axes of their own, with poles embedded, not in the north-south extremities of the universe, but in the particular mobile sphere which encased them. Thus, I believe, originated the theoretic side of the Eudoxan system of homocentric spheres, with its ability almost to account mathematically for the fluid motion of the planets in an abstract way.

"Now then," if we may borrow the idiom of Proclus, "what better way of explaining the fascination of the Delos problem for the ancients than its relation to astronomy?" If the cube is the cornerstone of the cosmos, and if it is rotating (as indeed it must be), and if in rotating it is seen to assume the shapes of duplication, then what are we to believe except that Eudoxus in his epoch-making *Phaenomena* named the awesome southern constellation the *Altar* because of its associations in his mind with the mythical Delian block of stone? The Altar, to be sure, is supposed, on no stronger grounds, so far as I know, than the words of a scholiast to the *Catasterismi,* to represent the object on which the gods swore when leaguing against Cronus. But the names of all constellations tended to gravitate toward the best-known myth which suggested a genealogy for them: the Kneeler, for instance, became Heracles; the Bird, the seducer of Leda. Though the fantastic idea of a bifold altar failed to survive in the legends of folklore, one philological detail implies that the Altar was visualized at first as a rotating object. In line 440 of Aratus's poem the Altar is referred to in these words: *antia dinotoio Thuteriou;* which seems to say that if it was not a turning Altar, it had been turned as on a lathe, and was only thereby suggestive of a rounded thing. Now a whirling movement in itself was a primary *arche* among the ancients—the *dinos*—and is alluded to quite clearly in Aristophanes. Moreover the archaic Ionic *dinotoio* is the genitive of the word which Parmenides applies to the spinning wheels of the chariot which bore him, with its remarkable swiftness, up into heaven.

At this point emerges the great contrast between a man like Parmenides and a man like Eudoxus. The goddess of Parmenides lavished her blissful favors upon him, with his right hand held lovingly in hers. But for Eudoxus there was no heaven except ultimately the heaven of this prayer: "that he might stand nere ùnto the sunne, for to learne the forme, the magnitude and beauty of that planet, upon condition to be burnt presently, as Phaëton was, with the beames thereof" (Plutarch, *Mor.* 1094B: Holland trans.).

X

The point of view which effectively rearranges the Eudoxan fragments on the ceiling beams of a Renaissance tower is the notion that experience is peculiarly coherent. For a polymath of the old school, life of course could hardly be otherwise than coherent; but as it happened Eudoxus was able to see a fairly complete overlapping of principles in his mechanical models—geometrical, medical, social, geographical, astronomical—which seemed to resolve nearly everything into interrelated axiomatic structures. In crude phenomena vistas opened up briefly which showed that things, for all intelligible intents and purposes, were as was to be inferred from their pertinent characteristics; an uncanny fact was this, that axioms of the same sort applied to phenomena of many sorts. These might be called the highly refined axioms of empiricism: the earth mirrored the skies, the skies the earth. "Nature," perhaps truly is, "sufficient in all for all."

In his every procedure Eudoxus seems to be determined to demonstrate the constant interplay between the sensible and the mental; or, in the vocabulary of Nicolas Bourbaki, between the constituents of "the double universe formed by the external world and the world of thought."

A truism holds that men of the same culture and of the same time will recapitulate, each in his own art, the qualities of the arts practiced by his fellows. Societies at any given time are what Leonardo da Vinci was in his own right and what Eudoxus most likely was in his.

I am thinking of Eudoxus and Praxiteles, and am imagining that they shared a fairly definable common ground in visual and tactile sensitivities, and may have been, speaking figuratively, what we may call collaborators.

We can place both men in Halicarnassus, and (though this kind of thing can never be proved) both at the same time: while the city was being remodeled and great men, sculptors and artists and poets and historians, were congregating there from all over the Hellenic world. As for Eudoxus, the habits of the day, the shortness of distances between places above and below the Straits of Samos, the unrecorded but inevitable intercourse among parties interested in the SYN Society—all this would have exerted a powerful magnetism on the projects of a man who was endlessly curious about the world. And Praxiteles, Strabo says, was in Ephesus soon after 356 B.C. working on an altar for the temple of Artemis, and then, according to Vitruvius, he came down to Halicarnassus some two or three years later to join the sculptors who were decorating the grandiose tomb which Queen Artemisia was building for the deceased Carian ruler.

Not long afterwards Cnidus, the city of Eudoxus on the next promontory south of Halicarnassus, acquired the Aphrodite of Praxiteles, which was beyond all doubt the most celebrated statue in the ancient world.

Why should we postulate this strange conjunction between the Aphrodite of Praxiteles and the Mathematician of Cnidus? Because of, in a word, the Eastern influences which converged here at exactly this time. An orientalizing disposition in all things is a pervasive mark of the proto-classical style which hung on along the Asiatic seaboard well after the naturalistic, self-assertive and emotional monuments of the Periclean age had made their appearance in central Greece. The impersonal geometry of the pyramid and sundial, the antique mythology of the constellations, the universal awareness of the mirror writing reflected between the heavens and the earth, the anachronistic Mausoleum itself, the nude, sex-motivated figure of Aphrodite herself, along with the low-keyed votive statuettes and the great Demeter, as well as the placidly seated old mother goddess; the aggressively organized medical studies, the coinage, the commercial accommodations . . . ; there is no end to the orientalizing traits that could be reckoned up. The concrete, the physical, the voluptuous, played on the minds of Cnidians in ways in which it did not play on the minds of Athenians. Or, to resist this crudely categorical contrast, let us say that the new art of Praxiteles with its exotic impact could not have been either fully appreciated nor seriously deprecated by the average homeland Greek. Compare Beazley and Ashmole, *Greek Sculpture:* "The life of many Athenians was an intelligent life, quiet-tempered, fond of pleasure and tasteful in its pleasures, taking things lightly, or as lightly as one can. There are only glimpses of this frame of mind in Plato, for he was too passionate, and too full of hatred; but there is something like it in the poets, comic and other, of the fourth century, as we know them from the pages of Athenaeus."

Modesty, it is said, forbad the people of Cos to purchase the nude

Praxiteles' Aphrodite of Cnidus: *the statue as recorded on a much-corroded bronze coin. This is a photograph of Percy Gardner's copy of Mionnet's cast: see bibliog. item 107, pl. 15, nos. 20 and 21.*

goddess. Whether Pliny is factual in recording this ludicrous episode seems quite doubtful. Aphrodite, as the deity of their city, properly belonged to the Cnidians. She was purchased by them, and she became their most cherished and valuable possession. Her suppliants came from far away; an oriental monarch offered a fortune for her. And yet, at best, we only have a very strong but rough idea of what she looked like.

It is only just, I am afraid, that in a study of the much fragmented work of a mathematician, the best representation of the goddess of his personal world should turn up on a battered ancient coin. But the Cnidian coin does show this: that the full profile of the naked goddess is turned pleasantly, following the hand which drops her chiton on a water jar, the other hand following the first, covering her sudden nakedness for the moment, while she herself is leaning in a contrary direction, starting to step down into her bath. I need not insist on the inadequacies of the extant marble copies or imitations of Praxiteles' statue. They are marred by the absence of the full-sized head with the well-ordered hair and the long neckline, by the unconvincing contours, and worst of all, by awkward, self-conscious, even coy gestures toying with the fact of her having taken off her clothes.

Although the sculptor of the Aphrodite was known in the scant records as "Praxiteles the Athenian," the birthplace of Praxiteles could hardly have immunized him from the seductions of the deities of Asia Minor, particularly since one of his first chronicled assignments was decorating the altar of Many-breasted Artemis in Ephesus; or if you choose to call the breasts eggs as many scholars do, the procreative fantasy is not less direct.

Where the Cnidian Aphrodite was created is not known, but as she was conceived in the Cnidian East, so was she probably translated into marble there. "Sculptors of olden times," says Apollonius of Tyana, "did not go around the cities selling their gods. All they did was export their own hands and their tools for working stone and ivory; and they provided the raw materials and plied their handicraft in the temples themselves."

The first nude female statue, a nude Aphrodite at that, after so many artfully and sensuously draped korai, was a challenge which Praxiteles met by avoiding the obvious, by carving the figure along geometric lines and not letting it swell out in voluptuous curves. Or such at least is the effect of the coin and of the tenor of ancient commentary. And at least one modern authority, Sheila Adam, describes how the Praxitelean artifice put "dents on the surface to enliven the appearance of the material," how it preferred "the linear to the plastic," how it was devoted to a "zigzag motive for giving a sharp definition to an edge," and above all how it refrained from giving "too high a polish to the flesh." These precepts ran contrary to the ambitions of imitators and copyists and the generations of lesser sculptors as a whole. The glyptic surfaces bespeak the mentality and sensitivity of a man not unlike Eudoxus. And of course they did not distract from the famous shimmer of the flesh nor the self-contained delicacy and repose of the goddess. Rather, they could have given her her unrivaled persuasive charm.

The Aphrodite was slightly over lifesize. She was placed so that she was standing on a podium in the center of a large, open, circular temple, in a position from which she could be viewed from all sides, with the sea and the sky glittering between the columns surrounding her. The temple was Eudoxan in its circularity. The stylobate blocks which formed the perimeter of the temple, the archaeologists say, were cut so that a circular edge was countered by an opposing straight edge: "a rather curious feature of the building,'' according to the archaeologists. Curious, yes, but precisely the combination of shapes which Eudoxus used in his examination of the properties of the circular.

Although any similarity of this sort is probably no more than a coincidence, still I see no way honestly to modify the premise that the mentality, the sensitivities, and the performance of the several arts and sciences harkened back to obscure shades where the hand and the eye come together with the mind, invisibly, but always, no matter which the route taken, always in the same way. Let that vibrantly winged image of Eudoxus's whirling cube, and all that it suggested to him, be compared with a poem. I think that the indwelling likeness in the motion of the cube of Eudoxus and the swan of William Butler Yeats cannot be denied, even though it is not easy to affirm exactly what it is.

> Some moralist or mythological poet
> Compares the solitary soul to a swan;
> I am satisfied with that,
> Satisfied if a troubled mirror show it,
> Before that brief gleam of its life be gone,
> An image of its state;
> The wings half spread for flight,
> The breast thrust out in pride
> Whether to play, or to ride
> Those winds that clamour of approaching night.

XI

Eudoxus had three daughters, Actis, Philitis, and Delphis, and a son apparently, to prolong the calling of the family in medicine. Nothing would be pleasanter than to have some knowledge of Eudoxus as a person, something beyond the fact of his astonishing and bewildering passion for learning and his easy acceptance of a clamorous world. I wonder whether these apparently contradictory traits were really twin aspects of the prestigious interplay of the physical and mental which colors all of his work.

One touchingly personal, completely unique, reference to him can now, in view of the new chronology, be identified with confidence. It is a remark which Demosthenes introduces in the late letter known as *Sons of Lycurgus,* and is of double interest because it rounds out, it

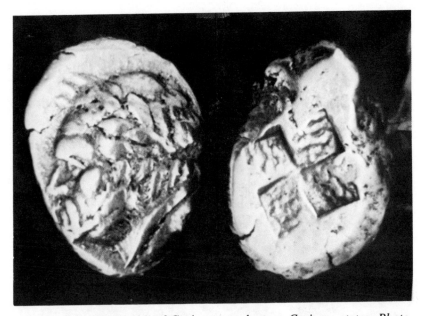

A Standard for the Wealth of Cyzicus: *an electrum Cyzicene stater. Photograph of a coin in the Norman Davis Collection, the Seattle Art Museum, courtesy of the museum. Xenophon reports that Greek mercenaries were induced to enlist in the army of Cyrus by the promise of a Cyzicene a month in wages: see Norman Davis,* Coins and Cities *(bibliog. item 110). Mr. Davis notes further that the electrum stater was used, in the case of the example before us, to commemorate an elderly man who had died recently, some citizen of Cyzicus, or other man who had honored the city, with a worthy memorial in the form of a portrait. The distinction of the man represented here is evident; the fact that he had died not long before is indicated by the laurel wreath he is wearing. The coin is dated 350–330 B.C. We have every reason to suspect that the man may have been Eudoxus.*

seems to me, the life stories of both men, at least from the time of Demosthenes' first oration, *On the Symmories,* to the era of the dominance of Macedonia. When finally that dominance was complete, reprisals fell on Demosthenes and his friends, including the innocent sons of Lycurgus (Lycurgus himself having escaped his enemies by dying in 324 B.C.). Demosthenes, though on that belated voyage which could end nowhere except in his suicide, chides the Athenians for their habitual mistreatment of their benefactors. He mentions how few the

number of good leaders had become, death having carried them off, wantonly in the turmoils of the times, or by natural causes. He names some of the men who had been lost to the Greeks more or less recently. Among them, surprisingly at first glance, he names Eudoxus. But then we notice that beside Eudoxus's name he puts the names of Euthydicus and Ephialtes, both of whom belonged to Demosthenes' anti-Macedonian party; Ephialtes, in fact, died in 334 B.C. while leading detachments of Persians who were helping in the futile efforts to defend Halicarnassus against the siege which Alexander had mounted against it. In that one phrase, which singles out a man who had lived, after those early days in Athens, in distant Cnidus, as a famous man who had served his country well, Demosthenes' estimate of the character and prominence of Eudoxus is reflected vividly.

Three Portraits Waiting for Positive Identification: *the lower half of pl. 7 in* G. F. Hill's *Select Greek Coins, 1927 (repr. 1976). The coin on the lower right is like our Cyzicene in the preceding photograph, possibly from the same die. Another, the upper one, has been generally accepted as a portrait of the Persian satrap Tissaphernes, in the regal headdress worn by dynasts under the Great King. The one on the lower left portrays the same face as its companion to the right. It too is an electrum stater of the same period, and the head on it too is distinguished by the symbolic laurel wreath. The Phrygian peaked cap is its feature of greatest interest. A fourth portrait coin, which I do not illustrate, is a Lampsacus gold stater (Jenkins, fig. 292) which appears to be identical with the foregoing as a picture of an elderly man in a Phrygian cap; he too is wearing a wreath, which may be an olive wreath: Lampsacus—to make connections clearer—was itself a member of the* SYN *Maritime League, a partner in the League's affairs. The semi-Hellenized Tissaphernes was obviously a leader in the practice of adopting vivid portraiture on coins. We can reasonably suppose our bearded man led a public life not unlike that of a satrap. From the point of view of Cyzicus and Cnidus and points between, Eudoxus would have been such a man. The Phrygian cap, I believe, is an attribute given him to identify the cultural band across Asia Minor, from Byzantium and Cyzicus to Cyprus and Rhodes and Cnidus, which Eudoxus represented, and represented well. He just about has to be the man on the coins.*

Another tradition made Eudoxus famous as a hedonist, and yet, and in spite of it, in Aristotle's judgment, a man of admirable character. The epithet of Hedonist of course may imply no more than Aristotle's uneasiness in face of the fact that Eudoxus seems to have espoused no metaphysical doctrine.

Eudoxus did espouse a late-flowering civilization. On those outer shores of the Aegean Sea there might have arisen, as Bury imagined, a renovation of the architecture of human life. Instead, as time went on, a dead hand fell on each of the disciplines to which Eudoxus had brought an astonishing vitality. In medicine, there eventually arrived Galen and the stagnant doctrine of the humors; in mathematics, Hero of Alexandria, whose mechanical models were more often than not merely frivolous toys; in astronomy, Ptolemy, the most uselessly ingenious and rigid of men. Aristarchus of Samos and Archimedes stand alone, far off the beaten track.

Alexander the Great had overturned the normal gaming tables of history. He had slashed his way through all the Gordian knots that were foreign to him. In this connection, an uncommon sort of documentation suggests with appropriate concreteness and symbolism the extent of the rupture of the new age from the old. "The period B.C. 371–335," wrote Percy Gardiner, referring incidentally but exactly to Eudoxus's years of maturity, "is particularly interesting for Asiatic coins. Many Persian Satraps were allowed to issue money. . . . And several cities, Cyzicus and Lampsacus especially, struck an abundance of coin. And this coin is the more valuable because it represents the highest limits attained by Graeco-Asiatic art. In the next age the art of Asia is flooded and destroyed by that of Athens and Sicyon, so as almost to lose its individual character, except when it returns in copies of the semi-barbarous statues of oriental antiquity."

To the coins of the friendly cities of Cyzicus and Lampsacus there might well be added the beautiful silver tridrachms of Cnidus with the serpents struggling with the infant Heracles on one side and the serene head of Aphrodite on the other.

True, Alexander the Great did found the immortal city of Alexandria, where a wealth of documents was preserved. They were preponderantly Attic and upper Aegean documents however: the education of the young conqueror had been notoriously conservative, and only a few records of the scientific discoveries of such men as Eudoxus ever found their way, and then seemingly by chance, like flotsam and jetsam, to the placid reservoirs of the Librarians of Egypt.

EPILOGUE

Scene: Hades. ALEXANDER THE GREAT *and* PHRYNE.

PHRYNE.   You could learn it from all the Thebans who lived in my time. They will tell you that I offered to restore the walls of Thebes which you had ruined, provided they inscribe them as follows: Alexander the Great had cast down these walls, the courtesan Phryne rebuilt them.

ALEX.   Were you afraid that future ages would forget what profession you followed?

PHRYNE.   I excelled in it, and all extraordinary people, of whatever profession, have been mad about monuments and inscriptions.

ALEX. It is true that Rhodope preceded you. The usufruct of her beauty enabled her to build a famous pyramid still standing in Egypt, and I remember that when she was speaking of it the other day to the shades of certain French women who supposed themselves well worth loving, they began to weep, saying that in the country and ages wherein they had so recently lived, pretty women could not earn enough to build pyramids.

PHRYNE. Yet I had the advantage over Rhodope, for by restoring the Theban walls I brought myself into comparison with you who had been the greatest conqueror in the world; I made it apparent that my beauty was enough to repair the ravages caused by your valor.

ALEX. A new comparison. You were then so proud of your gallantries?

PHRYNE. And you? Were you so well content with having laid waste a good half of the universe? Had there been but a Phryne in each of the ruined cities, there would remain no trace of your ravages!

—Fontenelle (trans. Ezra Pound)

Opposite—Colossal Kouros Head from Samos:
Archaeological Museum, Istanbul.

7

SAMOS: SOME SEQUELS

Scene: Hades. SOCRATES *and* PHAEDRUS.

SOC.   If ever I run into this Eupalinus, I still have something I want to ask him.

PHDR.   Maybe of all of the blessed shades he is the most unfortunate. . . . What would you ask him?

SOC.   To explain himself a little more clearly about buildings which can cause him to say, "They sing."

PHDR.   That word haunts you, doesn't it?

SOC.   It is one of those words which fly to the spirit like workers to the hive.

—Paul Valéry

IN 1964 SAMOS was a pastoral island in which the richness of its history in early times was so evident, it seemed to me, that nothing could blur the images one took home with him. There could not be anything at all doubtful either about the glory of its leaders in the first forward motions of our wobbly civilization. The wreaths of the rivals of the Samians —even Thales and the great Milesians, the witty Bias of Priene, that rebellious intellectual, Heraclitus of Ephesus—the wreaths of even them, though handsome, were thinner and a little drier than those worn so nonchalantly by Eupalinus, Anacreon, Aesop and Pythagoras, Theodorus, Democedes. The world knew these men for what they did, as well as for the poor echoes of what they may have thought.

But in the nine years following 1964, while the sun had been sinking in its familiar appointed slots in the folds of Mount Ampelus, the island had grown a little older and not so remote as it had been. It was not less beautiful; poorer, alas, or at least more dependent on travelers' checks, but in general as beautiful as ever it had been. Nevertheless something of the fragile edge of its character seemed to be wearing away. Perhaps the imperious demands of the *Now,* the *Now* of cruise ships and touring buses, was marring the sculpture of its landscapes. Perhaps the sinister, world-encircling cloud of political affairs was hanging a little more darkly over its foam-girded, green fastnesses. Or perhaps what I was uncomfortable about was unreasonable—quirky and self-indulgent. In any event one thing is certain. By the edict of nature, the "I" of 1964 was not the "I" of 1973, nor the earlier "we" the "we" of the present.

No doubt the only way to renew an old passion is simply to move back, to settle in and take her as she is without bothering about detailed inquiry. But since 1964 some questions about Samos have been buzzing in my head which, I am afraid, would make me not the most gracious of returning lovers. On the surface the problem which has been troubling me is remote and inconsequential. It is this, only this: what happened between the fall of Polycrates and the beginning of the Hellenistic Age? What was the fruit, in Samos, of those two centuries that came and went a long time ago? The answer seems to be this: nothing . . . nothing of compelling interest, I mean. After the early flowering, the tree turned sterile.

And yet, all that which had begun in Samos in archaic times, and had been beautiful, had continued to grow and to ripen in a normal fashion in certain neighboring places, places not far off, but, then as now, on the wrong side, the Asiatic side, of the Straits of Mycale. For the example that lies nearest at hand we must consider Eudoxus of Cnidus, as we have said, the last immediate descendant of Pythagoras of Samos.

There is tragedy in what I am saying. The summer of 1973 was the fiftieth anniversary of a disaster which took place at Smyrna, now Izmir, and ended in the Treaty of Lausanne, July 24, 1923. During the preceding year the remnants of the Greek population in Turkey had stood on the quais of Smyrna and wailed at midnight, hoping to be evacuated from their fallen city. They wailed and kept on wailing, Ernest Hemingway says, until they were stupefied by the blinding searchlights on the idiotic warships of the Great Powers. The grinding harvest of corpses, for which neither the Greeks nor the Turks were really responsible in the first place, runs parallel with the inane blood-letting on these same coasts centuries ago when the great Hellenic powers tried time and again to get a stranglehold on Asia Minor and the wealth of its dynasts.

And again in this year of grim anniversary, the searchlights were playing, not on the quais of Smyrna but on Samos, and they were Greek searchlights. Patrols clacked heels on the pavements. Every Samian was named and numbered and required to attend lectures. Loudspeaker announcements came as if from the lion's mouth in the central square; military music cascaded down the narrow streets. The Colonels were putting on an election. If you asked in the polling place for a blue and white ballot on election day, you were voting for the Colonels and their version of democracy and Greek ethnology. If you were to ask for a black ballot, you were voting against them. You had to vote.

Naturally, in our conversations with old friends, none of these sore dilemmas were delved deeply into. We heard countless variations on William Faulkner's speech at Stockholm. The Greeks will endure, as they had endured through the past. Until the last ding-dong of history clangs, they will be found prevailing, still prevailing over adversity, in their own way. But nobody, it was obvious, was eager to translate the announcements which issued from the loudspeakers. Nobody speculated in our presence on the drama which would inevitably occur when every person between twenty-one and seventy years of age would be seen marching across the neighborhood polling place with either a ballot dressed out in the blue and white national colors in his hand or else with a defiant, unconcealable ballot in black and gray. Nobody referred to this detail in the election procedure: we had to read about it in the *Herald Tribune*.

On the other hand, nobody pronounced the name *Watergate* with that small twist of a smile which we could have expected from any national connected however remotely with NATO; nor did anyone ask us in a genuinely troubled voice about the USN *Independence*, which was anchored in the very center of the naval political show in the old Athenian roadstead, the Phaleron harbor. Nobody mentioned the CIA.

It is true that some other charming Samians were impelled to deride us gently for what they took to be our American national policy. This became a particularly tricky obstacle when we paused to talk to the gregarious winos who inhabited the local quarters of the co-op winery's retail store. The only plea that I could honestly resort to was a plea of ignorance about international affairs, and a keen appreciation of their Samos Sec. It was not hard to settle differences, imagined or otherwise, over a bottle of Sec or rather, in this case, Samos Doux.

And yet, in spite of the furor over ethnology—furor! fraudulence: I saw a governmental employee blackmailed into buying an expensive, garish set of books on *The Ethnology of the Greek Democratic People!* But happily I had also noticed that the speedy, trim caiques were making their usual ferry runs back and forth from Greece to Turkey, from Samos to Kusadasi, from Bodrum to Cos. This seemed to be as good a season as any to start a backtrack in time: to visit what was left of the city of Bias and of the twin cities of Eudoxus, to traverse the luxurious area which Heraclitus had abandoned, to try to reconstruct the outlines of the grid of the Miletus of Hippodamus and from the present Bodrum the Halicarnassus of Mausolus and his masterly architects, the birthplace as well of the historian Herodotus; and to see more or less incidentally some other sites which had once figured spectacularly (like Didyma) or more modestly (like Iasus) in glories and humiliations.

Fortuna Holding the Archaic Hera in her Hand:
Imperial bronze coin from Samos.

II

Bias of Priene and Thales of Miletus, Hippodamus of Miletus and
Herodotus of Halicarnassus and Samos and Thurii, Eudoxus of Cnidus
and Cyzicus: the early, the middle, and the late generation of geniuses
among the grand innovators in the affairs of the Asiatic seaboard. Why
should it have been that in contrast with men such as these the Samians
should have dwindled into obscurity? Where originated their want of
motives or their lack of resources?

To make just the least bit of sense out of this crooked page of history
I feel obliged to refer briefly to Samian troubles during the late sixth,
the fifth, and fourth centuries B.C.

Herodotus himself, having spent the earlier, decisive years of his life on the island, makes an extraordinary remark to the effect that the Samians, at a period of about two or three generations before his own time, began to act as if they had ceased to value freedom, as if they were indifferent to independence and consequently were dull in their regard for worthy accomplishment. An additional oddity in his account is that, despite his intimate knowledge of the island, the Heraion and its fittings, he gives us not the slightest sense of the contemporary scene, not even hinting at the incomplete state of the great temple on which he expends copious praise. His first excitements stem from clear-cut scenes of early achievements and violences; his final emphasis is on the island as a backdrop for the defeat of the Persians in the battle of Mycale.

What provoked Herodotus into his cynicism was the scramble for despotic power that followed the death of Polycrates. The greatest among Samian citizens plotted the destruction of a certain Maeandrius, who was legally deputy governor and inheritor of the tyranny, even though Maeandrius had announced himself, in all good faith apparently, as wanting no more than a priesthood and a caretaker's role while a constitution granting equal rights was being drawn up. There followed a mass of assassinations among his opponents and then the arrival of a Persian army which acted in support of Syloson, an exiled brother of Polycrates. The Persians enjoyed immediate success. But while their dignitaries were seated in their thrones under the citadel celebrating the treaty they had signed, a mentally unreliable brother of Maeandrius turned the garrison men loose, and the principal Persians died in their own blood in their thrones. At this, Maeandrius devised a way to make his own escape; most of his countrymen were by no means so fortunate.

This story in itself represents the massif of the *Histories* in a miniature way. In the ethos of Herodotus there recurs at all crucial moments a man of oriental grandeurs seated in high place while he observes a triumphant pageant and exults in his might; or contrarily he is seated aloft to witness the evidence for great dejection. The man may be Croesus or Darius or Xerxes, or many another, including the unnamed invaders of Samos.

Retribution always follows swift upon the moment of glamorous vision. The Persians were slain. Then it was Samos's turn to be well on

the road toward complete depopulation before their destroyers relented
and the netting of the island came to a halt. Nevertheless its inhabitants had been thinned out so thoroughly that a proverb came into being: "King over a realm without subjects," referring to Syloson,
brother of Polycrates.

The island was populated again in due course. Before long we hear
of an event which may come as a surprise. The engineer who contrived
the bridge on which Darius, the Great King, crossed the Bosphorus
was Mandrocles, a Samian—a term which of course may refer to his
place of origin or of his residence. However it was, Mandrocles still
thought enough of Hera and her Samian temple to erect a noble dedication from the rewards which had been bestowed upon him. Within the
massive walls he placed a tablet which read:

> Upon the fishy Bosphorus, such bridge
> Mandrocles put afloat that gained a crown
> Of honor for him and for the Samian Hera,
> And pleasure for the heart of the Great King.

Above this plaque was a picture. Darius was depicted as sitting high on
a throne, looking down on his enormous, many-colored army crossing
on the gigantic, ominous footpath that led from Asia into Europe.
Herodotus was much impressed with the picture, and he probably
recognized the ancient Ionian suavity and genius which were latent in
the whole thing, just as we do. He probably felt too something similar
to the wonder we feel in looking at the new suspension bridge which
exploits a geographical quirk that is as impressive today as it must have
been in the days of Mandrocles.

Of course no one would have known better than Herodotus that
Ionian suavity and genius may work at various levels of moral recti-
tude. The Samian sailors did not make a good showing in the battle of
Lade, the loss of which led to the destruction of Miletus at the hands of
the Persians and the long, crippling onslaughts of Darius and Xerxes
against all Greek lands. The sailors from Samos had provocations.
Some of their allies were mutinous. And they themselves could not
have been certain whether they preferred to support their former tyrant,
a son of Syloson, or to help the tyrant of Miletus who had imposed his
dominance over their people in Samos. Beside all that, these men were
sea-roaming traders by nature, and they had found the seaports which

the Persians controlled rich and hospitable. A large part of the Samian fleet, confused in its purposes, fled from the battle.

The choices had been bitter, and the outcome forbidding. Many Samians who possessed the means to do so migrated to Magna Graecia: a course of action like the one which had earlier been proposed by Bias of Priene and which the Phocaeans had resorted to wholesale. For Samos the emigration meant dissensions and losses.

Then there followed the Persian wars and the Aegean Treaty Organization, with its own dramatically confused wars culminating in a costly defeat in Egypt. Quickly on the heels of this disaster, in which Samos must have been the greatest loser, the ATO treasury was moved from Delos to Athens. That the transfer of the enormous wealth of a league of allies should have been authorized by a Samian motion is particularly ironic, since the next major political action which Pericles and the Athenians undertook was the destruction of Samos itself, economically, and as an autonomous political and military power.

During the Peloponnesian War Samos was a pawn, but a pawn which became powerful and was played for high stakes when finally it was the last, lonely Athenian naval base overseas.

Clearly the fifth century B.C. was not a good century for Samos or anything Samian. But in order to give perspective to the events of the following century let us reconsider Pericles and his part in the Samian War. At issue originally were the merits of hostilities between Samos and Miletus which were being waged over certain territories that may also have been claimed by Priene. Often in earlier times the two larger powers had embroiled themselves in contentions over croplands in the Maeander valley close by the city of Priene. Samos had been accustomed to dispatch farmers into its Asiatic *peraia;* the antiquity of this practice seems to be attested by an ancient electrum Samian coin discovered in an area in which the Prienians may also have raised their crops. In exactly the same way Miletus reached inland for farmlands bordering on the holdings of Myus, until finally, because of malarial conditions, the Myusians moved into Miletus and shared their country homesteads with the Milesians.

When actions which disregarded the necessarily vague boundaries erupted into violence, serious warfare sometimes followed. Plutarch in his *Greek Questions* tells us that once upon a time the Prienians, after fighting sporadically against the Samians, threw themselves into a real battle and slew a thousand of the islanders; but six years later when the Prienians engaged the Milesians in the legendary Battle of the Oak, they lost "practically all of the best and foremost of their citizens." On this occasion the sage Bias, like Aesop, found himself unexpectedly acting the part of an ambassador. He was dispatched from Priene to Samos, where he is said to have won considerable benefactions for his people.

And so now in 441 B.C. in just such another collision, the Milesians, finding themselves badly worsted by the Samians, appealed to the Athenians, who had assumed certain privileges as a sort of caretaker of independent Miletus, at the moment when Pericles sought power. Athens arbitrarily ordered Samos to yield control over the Maeander valley to Miletus. Samos refused. Under the basic ATO treaty Samos, as an autonomous ally of Athens, could reject the intervention of Athens or any other power. Pericles and the Athenians did not stop to seek out some method of achieving impartial arbitration; they made war. They made war against Samos with a suddenness and fury which revealed their real intentions, which were to crush their one rival in the new world of Athenian imperialism. And they succeeded, though at no small cost. The walls of Samos were leveled, the fleet surrendered, hostages taken. The islanders were compelled to pay instalments on a fine amounting to the impossible sum of 1,276 talents. Those people captured, the Athenians branded like cattle.

And Miletus really gained nothing in its own right from the Samian War. It fell successively to the Spartans, the Persians, and finally to Mausolus.

With the Spartan victory over the Athenians in the Peloponnesian War, Samian coinage (but rather strangely no other monuments that I know of) reveals the effectual return of independence and prosperity, which lasted, as we said in an earlier chapter, until the invasion of the Athenians once again, in the person of Timotheus and the colony which claimed squatter's rights as a cleruchy from Attica in the households of the exiled Samians.

In the power politics of ATO there was always in the posture of Athens something that was pretentiously noble and at the same time transparently predatory, whether the stance was vis-à-vis Sparta or vis-à-vis its Aegean partners. Toward Thasos, Lemnos and Imbros,

Melos, Mytilene and Samos, and Chios, one would assume that there would be at least a reasonable amount of fair play and friendship. In most instances there was nothing of the sort. I think that what we notice instead is the crude licentiousness of its disproportionate popularity in its form of government. In this particular form of democracy, bigotry and shortsightedness easily took over, as Aristophanes went to great pains to show.

The fate of Samos—and not Samos alone—eats at the conscience so insidiously that one is likely not to be sure of the extent to which his objectivity is failing him. Consequently, I am going to insert here a careful statement made by a most distinguished archaeologist and scholar, and an authority on Chios, John Boardman, which should cause not a few classicists and historians and philosophers to ponder some common assumptions a little more thoroughly. After remarking that a splendid earlier initiative in the arts of sculpture and architecture began to weaken noticeably on the island of Chios, Mr. Boardman explains the decline in these compact, intense terms:

The great achievements of archaic Ionian art are of the period of Lydian and Persian interference, trade rivalry, and fitful assertions of independence. But the political misfortunes, massacres, and deportations left Ionia without the enlightened patronage for the arts which she had previously enjoyed. In the fifth century Ionian artists and artisans were still at work, but in what had become the provinces of the Athenian empire there was less scope for their skill than in the empire's metropolis, and in the east.

"And in the east!": the Asiatic borderlands along the straits, toward which in our purposes we were already bound.

What we were leaving behind was an unimaginative, inartistic present-day example of the dominance of the leading Greek metropolis. What we have been asserting is that nothing good can come out of a cleruchy, or of any enforced military dominance of one place over another. In a cleruchy, as in any police state, householders lie awake a good part of the night, listening. And yet, paradoxically, the unnerving, monstrous darkness of the cleruchy in Samos seems evidently to have educated one unique human being to a degree which allowed him to become comparable with the heroic Samians of the archaic age. Epicurus, growing up in the cleruchy and knowing only the opaque

doctrines of the Athenian philosophical schools, went as a young man
to the good Asiatic Ionian centers, Colophon and Teos, where he began the long studies in which he recast an honored physical theory,
the atomism of Democritus, into a guide for the dispirited.

True, it took innocence to do it: a faith in the inexplicable, fortuitous
swerve in nature and some little juggling with terms like *up* and *down*.
But inexplicable swerves or gaps in things are not to be denied at some
extremes of our experience, and while Epicureanism is worth long contemplation, it also has the dubious distinction of being the first example
of introversion and specialization in feelings as such, which comes
readily to mind. The spirit alone—the spirit of love, peace, content-
ment—is the target of the philosophy.

And yet, after all, in the ashes of a cleruchy the ancient glory of
Samos comes to a not inglorious end.

Remembering Epicurus, and not forgetting Lucretius, my wife and
I set off for Turkey, where, despite strange gods and strange prophets,
we knew we would find our fellowmen enjoying as we did the shower
of atoms which surrounds each of us alike. We would pick up the trail
of the past. We would consume the bread and, if not the ouzo, then
the raki of the present.

III

Jude of *Jude the Obscure,* needing someone to come to his aid, finds
himself compelled to say to himself: "But no one will come, because
no one ever does." I respect Thomas Hardy for attributing to Jude this
essentially Muslim sentiment. When caught in the currents of the great
whirlpool, the lonely swimmer reverts wholeheartedly to despairing
ultimate recognitions, be he Muslim, or a forgetful Greek, or a lapsed
Calvinist. But, given fair health, a modest travelling budget, and a
decently eager curiosity about certain villages and their remote past,
there is always, without fail, someone who comes to help. Often he
is a Turkish boy. He studies English for a few hours every week in
school.

Often his name is George. In the village of Bayrakli it was George
Kurtulus, age twelve, who appeared from nowhere and by simple
intuition saw that the strangers standing hot and doubtful at the closed
gate of his little farmyard were looking for the excavations of ancient

Smyrna, which the strangers seemed to know must lie somewhere out of sight up on a slope covered with the rich foliage of vineyards, blocked out here and there by the houses of the farmers. And so after George had cheerfully explained us to his family and the next-door neighbor, we looked down into a broad cavity at the rare geometry of ancient foundation stones. The significance of the various tiers of stonework was beyond our science; but the outline was easily imaginable of the well-ordered, the earliest perhaps of the orthogonal, deliberately designed cities in Aegean history: Ekrem Akurgal, J. M. Cook, and other diggers and historians have reconstructed the modular image of the ranging walls, the straight streets, the temple on a raised terrace balancing the fortified gateway to the docks, which in the imagination hovers now over the shimmering green on the inland hillside.

It was very hot. George's capering on the embankments of the excavation turned, when we were ready to go, to heroic efforts to help us find transportation from the stifling village back to Izmir.

This was the pattern of many of our days. But before long there came a day which was exceptional. A rose gardener, who as a sideline operated an excellent small hotel in the midst of his rose garden on the beach at Erdek, had intuitions which ran more strongly toward plants and people than the business of booking guests and rendering them their bills. As a result of our host's eccentricity, a young man came to us when we were sitting in the shade in the garden soon after our arrival and introduced himself. He was Ahmet Toygar of Ankara, but during college sessions he was a student in the United States, a youthful Turk, a Muslim, a lover of his heritage with all of its diversities and contradictions; and besides, he was a rebel, irreconcilable toward the practice of making women labor in the fields, impatient with the mechanical backwardness of his people and the emptiness of their debates on whatever subjects happened to spring from the coffee cups in the cafes.

These qualities led Ahmet into a dilemma, as we were soon to discover. Should he follow his first intention of entering the school of electrical engineering on graduation, or should he turn toward the social, probably the political sort of thing? He was quiet, compact, intent, modest. We could not tell ourselves, nor least of all him, that he was facing the problem that every young man faces: what should he become? He was caught between the claws of technical specialization pressing in on him from one side and some sort of missionary work pressing him from the opposite. In Turkey the context for original work in engineering would probably never exist: other nations had got too far ahead. A context for originality in politics was hardly in sight either, for the same reasons.

But this only dramatized the question for which we were seeking an answer: what would the world be like if there were not this slippery chasm between mechanical techniques and the controlled well-being of social units? If it were not for people like Thomas A. Edison and Guglielmo Marconi on the one hand and on the other hand such men as Walt Whitman and Frank Lloyd Wright? The Ionian sort of civilization bypassed, or never arrived at, specialization as we know it. To look at what was left that revealed the quality and some of the secrets of that distant, unmechanized world was the desire, the lust, that had brought us to Turkey, where the flesh of the past was not so completely veiled as elsewhere, or so, at least, we hoped.

Our little hotel in the rose garden on the beach lay in an area which once would have been a suburb of the metropolis Cyzicus, where Eudoxus had established one of the best-documented, many-faceted schools of ancient times, a singularly compact early form of the true university, where all studies are pursued. But of a city which had "a perimeter of about five hundred stadia" according to Strabo, few traces are to be found, and those not easily by passengers who came unarmed with a command of the Turkish language. Names like Eudoxus, or Cyzicus itself, are beyond the range of the usefulness of the ordinary phrase book. We had begun to feel helpless when Ahmet came to us in the rose garden.

For Ahmet the complete disappearance of an imposing place where generations had passed their lives was a fascinating phenomenon. I suppose that his tradition is more preoccupied with the whims of fortune—the here today gone tomorrow—than ours as yet has had reason to be. And besides, he had this sly, bemused question to tease us with: were such things written on the forehead? Whatever the answer, we set out with the Toygar family car, thanks to his parents, to explore the area of the phantom city as thoroughly as we could.

In the village of Erdek there is an outdoor museum, a fairy's circle of well-carved but mostly badly damaged marble pieces, with the blue Propontis, small boats and scattered shrubs in the background. The collection contained nothing of great interest: the choice finds had been transported to Istanbul where we had already seen them. But by tracking down the man who was in charge of the display, Ahmet gathered the information that was necessary for the reconstruction of something resembling the city plan of Cyzicus and for locating the few monuments which remain above ground.

Thus armed we were able to find the track which circles around upwards toward the heights of a metropolis which in the area of the Propontis was rivaled only by Byzantium. The ironies that turn up in the world of archaeology are endless. Modern Byzantium (i.e. Istanbul) is not the largest city in the world of course, but it could claim to be the noisiest and most bustling; Cyzicus—as it has persisted in the village called Artake—the quietest. In Istanbul contractors building a wing to the archaeological museum sift through every shovelful of dirt, hoping to collect artifacts before laying the footings. On the site of Cyzicus the four-inch spikes of a cultivator drawn along slowly behind a little horse turn up sherds in the olive orchards everywhere along the paths; but elsewhere the growth of the brush has become so dense that nothing more than the shape of a depression gives away the location of the theater. The small stones and the irregular chunks of marble which remain on the hilltop make one suspect that the theater, the paved arcades and larger buildings, were regarded as convenient quarries yielding ready-cut materials for the construction of Istanbul. It is said that stone merchants operated in this way in places as distant as Cnidus on the lower corner of Asia Minor.

Though there were a few ruined monuments—the pair of towers, for instance, called castles by the natives but really piers at the ends of a huge arch in the Roman aqueduct—the beauty of Cyzicus was at present a rolling overlay of olive groves. Never have I seen prettier. The best of my own trees at home have looked no more splendid, and alas I never find painted sherds on the ground beneath them. Indian pestles once in a while but never a marble kouros.

There is as a matter of plain fact a marble kouros, the torso, somewhat battered and completely deprived of the extremities, but still revealing the fully rounded yet robust belly and shoulders, hips and thighs, of the eastern Archaic style, which has made its way onto the schoolground on the edge of the village that had once been Cyzicus. It lies on its back in a fringe of weeds among other impressive fragments that reflect in their dull white gleams the pride of old Ionia and the strict floral preoccupations of the Hellenes in general.

But hopscotch played here in the confines of a space fenced off loosely by some awesome stone work is probably not different from hopscotch played anywhere. To the little children we were what seemed to impress them as awesome, or, to a pair of bigger boys, comical because of the fuss we were making. While the boys snickered, an old man shuffled off at high speed to his house to find some coins he had hoped to sell us. But somebody else showed up with an enormous loaf of bread and a chunk of delicious cheese, which was shared among us all. We took turns at admiring a perirrhanterion inside the glass-paned front door, and then we went on our way.

These were a great, hospitable people, these olive growers. When a large piece of marble kept snagging the teeth of their cultivators, they dug it out, got help, and dragged it to the schoolhouse, where people who were interested could come to see it.

When on another day we went to see how the world looked out in

Where Once the Long-walled City of Cyzicus Stood:
the main street in the Turkish village Asağiyarici.

An Archaic Dedication
which Preserves an Eastern
Composure. *Despite the
battering of centuries, the
torso in the schoolyard still
has the power to evoke an
image of a full-bodied
eastern beauty translated
into marble.*

the area of the much-envied Satrapy called Daskylion, another boy
named George seemed to be waiting there to help us. Our interest in
Daskylion was twofold. It seems probably to have been the site of the
first Greek habitations in the region of Cyzicus, the place where the
strangers venturing up from Miletus at about the end of the eighth century decided to settle down. The first bands of those who were to become colonists seemed to have pushed inland. The natives and their
women lived inland, and where there are other men, and women, the
daring, lonely strangers are bound to show up. Besides, if we take
Troy as an example, we must think of horse breeders and metal workers; first, the pastoral life and small industries behind defensive walls:
then, with the accumulation of resources, could come the thought of
building ships and trading in other places, and the urge to move from
Daskylion to a place like Cyzicus. At the same time the place left
behind, judging by the wars fought among the Persians for possession
of it, we knew must have had a likeness to a royal pasture and hunting

park, with nothing at all which resembled the agoras and sea moles and chained harbors beloved of the Greeks.

The difficulty for us was not in finding Ergili, the village somewhere on the green horizons of which once stood the half-Hellenized housing complexes of the Satrapy, the difficulty was in finding the site itself. When we passed a garden patch where some women were working on the edge of the village, we noticed the boy. He was standing up among the bending women, his eyes were following us as we passed slowly by, and while we were still backing up, he was starting slowly across the field to meet us. His very style of approach told us what we wanted to know: within a radius of five miles nothing much would have escaped his attention, certainly nothing so out of the ordinary as a lot of digging on a hill among the farms.

He got into the car. Some minutes later he led us along a boundary line between two plantings of chickpeas toward a slight rise of land which was nothing like the impressive mound that one would expect

Architectural Fragment beside the Torso of a Marble Kouros: *a part of the schoolyard collection at Asağiyarici of some recently unearthed debris from Cyzicus.*

great Daskylion to be built on. But the landscape was deceiving. Suddenly, from the embankment along the archaeological pit, the view was a view of miles and miles of the heartland of Turkey, the royal plantation and game preserve—with fewer trees now, less cover for game, but obviously the domain which the satraps called Daskylion, and fought for their dynastic rights to it.

To the north in the distance was Manyas Lake, Bird Lake, and a densely populated bird refuge; to the left just below us was the ochre-colored river carrying the outflow from the lake, wandering through shored up dikes and directed through sluices under a modern bridge. In these directions and even more distinctly in the other two, were the green and gold geometries of croplands, jeweled now and again with round shade trees.

It was like Cézanne, it was like Brueghel. One field was being harvested. Men were following the swing of their scythes, women were following behind, tying the wheat into sheaths. Minuscule motions and rhythms in miles and miles of an oil painting floating in the soft air.

There was a question nevertheless: the color of the river, the evidence of the effort to keep it securely between firm banks. The skeletons of human beings, as analyzed by the Smithsonian Institution, show that malaria was active in the Near East as early as the Early Bronze Age. If people suffered from malaria at the inland site in the colonizing period, the Greek settlers, abandoning any claim to Daskylion, may have made their move to the Cyzicene peninsula quite abruptly, where the benefits of familiar coastal winds would have been self-evident; and some centuries later Eudoxus of Cnidus would never have failed to notice the advantages of the geography at Cyzicus and its likeness to the geography at new Cnidus.

So far as I know malaria no longer troubles the people of Turkey. But apparently the habit of living in elevated, wind-swept villages still persists. The workers, women in multilayered, loose clothing, ride to the fields in a four-wheeled trailer drawn by a tractor. The women are graceful and inclined to be vivacious; the man at the wheel of the Massey-Ferguson is always gravely aware of his responsibility and importance. Through a long, long noon hour, the women gather, hands busy, heads together, in little groups in the shade of a tree. Brueghel.

IV

After Cyzicus came Cnidus by the rule of the logic of the inquiries set down in these chapters. But to go to Cnidus required going first to Bodrum (ancient Halicarnassus) which in itself was a most attractive prospect, though one which presented difficulties. The chief problem was this: how to find transportation across the twenty-five miles of the Aegean that lie between Bodrum and Cnidus? The archaeologists from Long Island University had not arrived as yet; and we understood that there was practically no sea traffic to the almost deserted site. The only solution in all likelihood would be to hire a caique to carry us across. We had rented a car, and having departed long since from our young friend Ahmet, foresaw the awkwardness of knowing no Turkish in a city where few other languages are spoken. The boy who seemed always to show up in a crisis could hardly be expected to come along and help us through this one.

Nevertheless it was the ubiquitous young boy who came to our aid when we found ourselves coming out of a tangle of streets onto the waterfront of the harbor at Bodrum. We knew where we wanted to stay: at the hotel named in commemoration of Herodotus; where else could it be on this trip? Stopping at the curb to puzzle over the Turkish *Hachette,* I noticed the boy. He was standing in that familiar position, his head bent a little to one side, regarding us curiously. Through the open window I extended a hand, palm up as if reaching for something, and said, "Otel Herodote?" He smiled, glanced over his right shoulder toward the inner side of the harbor, shook his head, and said something while he was coming to the door to get into the car with us. Following his gestures, we followed the ins-and-outs of an esplanade and pulled up in front of a tall, rather plain white building carrying across its front in clear lettering the name *Otel Herodote.* The boy had disappeared by the time we recognized where we were.

The proprietor of the Herodote spoke serviceable English. He showed us the docks on the opposite side of the harbor where a passage on a boat might be obtained: there they were, the line of caiques and ferries and yachts of all sorts. But to get to that part of Bodrum proved to be almost impossible in a car, even a little Turkish Fiat. The streets, directionless, bazaarlike, were charming but not negotiable.

The Two Faces of Cyzicus: *Cyzicene silver tetradrachm, c. 350 B.C. Veiled head of Persephone; lion's head with signature of the city KY and tunny fish; obverse and reverse (photograph courtesy of Numismatic Fine Arts, Inc.). The two sides of this coin represent the fantasies and realities which are central to our story. The lion is in his fiercest pose; he has been the heraldic antagonist of man and beast throughout the centuries, and as such he is shown tearing a bull apart on the earliest coinage of Sardis. A drama like this is a possible reality. But repeated encounters with images of such fierceness set up a compensatory reaction; just such a head as this is metamorphosed into gentle fountain spouts at Samos. His claws become the feet of furniture. In Aesop he becomes ponderous and slow-witted, and among the stars only a glittering arched phantom. On the obverse Persephone, Kore, the lovely girl, may leave a cold touch on our hearts as the good seasons pass away; yet the ancient effort was directed always toward presenting her as the most beautiful of women, as she is here, with her necklace and droplet earrings and crown of barley heads escaping from her scarf. All this adds up to about as true a representation of the human lot as any which we are likely to be able to think of.*

We arrived at our destination on foot. It proved to be a small waterfront plaza. Travellers evidently arrive in Bodrum by boat and leave by boat; or else, ever since motor traffic replaced saddle animals and caravans, they have used their feet and handcarts to come into the center of the city.

Facing on the Plaza was the office of a forceful travel agent who spoke some French. Through him we found our captain. We looked at his sturdy caique with its Italian diesel engine and the usual stabilizing

Marble Plundered from the Mausoleum at Halicarnassus. *The grandiose tomb of Mausolus was an enormous Doric columned pyramidal structure, from which, after an earthquake, or following deliberate destruction, marble column drums found their way into the walls of the Castle of the Knights of Rhodes at the mouth of the harbor at present day Bodrum. Barbaric though the Castle may look from the outside, it has sunny terraces and flowering gardens inside and, as of recent times, galleries decorated with fragments of the friezes which, at the behest of Queen Artemisia, sculptors came from all over the Greek world to execute.*

sail, and made our trade: 7:00 A.M. to 7:00 P.M. the third day later; from the Herodote pier to Cnidus and back; six hundred Turkish lira: forty-two dollars.

Meantime, we had the leisure that one owes to so modest, and yet so rich in provincial restaurants and small shops, and so leisurely a place, as Bodrum. We found we were relaxing enough not to continue to be horrified by the dominating Castle of the Knights of Rhodes nor to be distressed by recognizing the stones which it had cannibalized from nobler buildings, the Mausoleum in particular. We just have to get

The Wine-dark Sea at Sunrise off the Cnidian Cape. *This composite of utterly barren shadows on the Triopian headlands with so many lively palpitations on the surface of the sea, sped many a traveler landward, toward the metropolis and medical school and observatory of Eudoxus, or toward the games at the festival of the southern Dorians, or toward one or another of the centers of the worship of Persephone. Though the nature of the goals of ancient visitors have mostly faded into deep obscurity, the sea day after day is as alluring as ever. On the surging horizon the little knob at the end of the peninsula is the island district of the old city of the Cnidians.*

used to things like the wailing on the quais of Smyrna, or on the walls of Troy. In all truth the castle is a beautiful museum, once you are inside, with flowering gardens in its courts. And Izmir is a gracious, volatile yet peaceful city, despite the unforgettable wailing.

In this interim we saw our captain at the cafe where the captains of the odd-looking little fleet congregate. Real conversation was impossible, but the warm gestures of communication were not; particularly since a young boy was sitting with our captain, his son. The boy smiled slyly at us. We were his old friends, the people he had guided to the Otel Herodote. We could tell that he was telling his father about it. Later we found out that his name was George.

Approaching Cnidus from Bodrum in the early morning, you see the peninsula rising in featureless grayish lavender, shadowed as it is, from the flowing bright faience of a sea which is studded with golden wavelets. Then, as you come closer to the tip of the claw, details begin to come into view. In the notch which separates the elongated land of the Cnidians from the little island at its extremity, the contours of narrow parallel terraces on both sides of the inlet mark starkly the depressions that two thousand years ago were the busy avenues of a city which has utterly disappeared, building by building, visible stone by visible stone, through the succeeding centuries. The compact naval harbor forms a shallow recession at the base of the notch. The modern white lighthouse makes its small exclamation point on the upper end of the island.

The caique rounds the rocky point, because the docking place is on the far side of the notch. Now the sun begins pouring onto the ragged breakwater and above it into the aligned terraces, each with a marvelous variety of steepnesses and white dapplings here and there, where stand the trophies which the archaeologists have brought up from below ground. And the sun glows in the hollow concave of the theater. Here is where the crowds seated themselves, exhilarated, noisy, to watch performances which took place in front of an illusionary painted background, surrounded at a little distance by the realities of the freight-bottoms in the commercial harbor. Out among the ships with variegated fittings, and up over them, were the two blue dyes that may be obscured from time to time but never fade.

We were shown the utmost courtesy by the Turkish archaeological officer in charge of the site, by the local gendarme, and by everyone, which is to say, the restaurant man, and the lighthouse keeper, who attends not only to his flare but a flock of a large species of ducks, perhaps because they are reminiscent in a feeble modern way of the geese of Aphrodite.

In one respect my earlier conjectures—or perhaps wishful thoughts—proved to be wrong. The "island" rises too high for Eudoxus to have set up an observatory anywhere near the temple of Aphrodite. His concentration on the southern constellations, which was inspired no doubt by his early studies in Egypt, predicates a choice of a location on the southern ridge of the city, on a height opposite the sanctuary of

The Terrace of the Rotunda of the Aphrodite of Cnidus. *The compact ancient naval harbor is in the foreground; the island of Hypocrates, Cos, is on the left horizon.*

the golden goddess. If so, we may imagine that the steady light of Canopus, the Egyptian Star, complements the wandering blaze of the White Planet.

We took home with us a handful of the wild thyme that grows beside the base of the circular temple of the Aphrodite of Praxiteles. Our herbs have an unmatched freshness, as indeed they should have, being descendants, as they must be, of the shrubs which Lucian praised as being symbolic of the goddess's direct, ever renewing beauty. Also, I would add, of distinctiveness and vital simplicity, an intimacy which balances against the imponderable sea views, the two harbors, the open waters and the stars, toward which the goddess addressed herself.

Going home, with our captain bent catlike over his tiller, it was Cos this time that rose lavender and dull out of a gold glinting sea. Then he turned us northwards, threading the surging winds, toward Bodrum.

Head of Aphrodite in the Style of Praxiteles. *Izmir Museum. This marble head of Aphrodite is reported to have come from a statue that stood originally in "Cyme-Nemrud." Cyme, a famous Aeolic city not far north of Smyrna (Izmir), raises no problems. It was the birthplace of Hesiod. Having acquired a reputation for being the home of a slow-witted people, it became the butt of jokes: its fault apparently was only this, that it made no effort to levy taxes, in the high-handed way of Polycrates, on shipping passing through its waters. Eventually it became malarial and had to be abandoned. The building materials that would have been lost were given over to the construction of other settlements, among them Aegae, now the village of Nemrud, or Nemrud Kalesi. In 1924, at the site of Cyme, French archaeologists found evidence of an Ionic temple of Aphrodite. I have no doubt that the marble head in Izmir was once a part of the cult statue that stood in this temple and that it was moved with the moving of the city to Nemrud, where it suffered its part in later destruction. Remembering the transactions in sculpture on this stretch of coast, one must guess that it was related to the Aphrodite of Praxiteles; perhaps a copy, perhaps a work of Praxiteles' own hand. The shadowed eyes and cloudy setting for the strong mouth are unlike anything to be seen among the faces of the poor existing Roman copies of the Cnidian original. The expression of infinite compassion is a well-attested attribute of the Aphrodite Euploia of Cnidus.*

V

Towering Didyma! though splintered, towering, and smothering to death in the sun like the giant Talus on the axis of a busy village.

Great Miletus! How fallen, how sunken, how buried! I quote from Virginia's journal:

We set off in our orange buggy, first to Didyma, which had splendid huge columns and walls that enclosed an area that appeared to be about an acre or more. . . . Then on to Miletus in the heat of the day—an enormous area on the Maeander-silted delta, where there had once been a seaport. Only in the early 1900's were the archaeologists able to dig here. The ground is still spongy underfoot, probably much is still buried. In Miletus we were accosted by a small girl and a boy, offering us small sweet pears, which we accepted, then producing two illegible copper coins. H. bought one. The boy about twelve years old, was angry because H. wouldn't buy the second. He came back a bit later with a perfectly beautiful large baby bird with feathers the color of the Aegean; according to the Peterson book probably a rock thrush. He showed us how he was going to wring its neck. We couldn't decide whether he was trying to force us to buy his coin or to pay him for not killing the bird. We threw the bird into a tangle of brush and chased the children away. No friendly young George, this one!

Then Priene, the gem of the Maeander!

Off we went, directed by our beer host, across the bottom of the still marshy delta to Priene. Oh Priene!—built on a promontory backed by high straight cliffs and higher mountains, and overlooking the great wide valley. I was entranced with it. A long, long approach avenue—hard going, going up steeply on slippery stones, on worn marble, to the temple of Athena at the top, where Ionic columns still stood. . . . This city, moved several times, was built on a grid plan, orthogonally. An almost intact council chamber; closer to the rim of the city, a temple to Zeus. In every area, stone flooring, steps and walls outlining the basic plan. Wind-swept and high. The most impressive we have seen, this gloriously Greek city.

Priene from an architectural point of view is probably the most prestigious single city left over from ancient times; adored by visitors like ourselves, feared by students taking Architecture I; a unique phenomenon, it raises questions like, what really is it? how did it come about? I start with two premises which are not always accepted, and since they are by no means self-evident, may continue to be subject to debate. One, Priene is not Hellenistic. Two, Priene is not strictly speaking a Greek city but rather a late Ionian city.

The fact about Priene, the one fact worth bothering about, is that it is a *planned* city, totally planned and built according to plan, from the articulation of its surface masses down to the finest detail in its decorative moldings. The city was moved. It was moved from an unwholesome location in the boglands to the elevated bluff. This circumstance made coherent planning a reasonable act. Though a reasonable act of so great a magnitude is unusual in the history of the world, this one had its parallels on these coasts at this time, witness Cnidus. Elsewhere one possible parallel may have been the settlement Thurii in Italy; if so, the names of the architects of that exploit refer directly back to the Ionian context: Hippodamus of Miletus, Herodotus, Protagoras.

In thinking of Priene as a planned city we have to postulate time-consuming preliminaries. First would come the selection and survey of the site, the drafting of plans, the tremendous labor of creating at least the earliest of the six main terraces running east and west, with tons of earth to be gouged out of the slope and settled behind retaining walls, and ample passageways established to connect one level with another. And the first thing not to be overlooked would be the formidable task of prospecting for marble, mining it, and collecting it in an enormous stockpile.

Priene is said to have been founded in about 350 B.C. Its origins at that date or even a few years before would be none too early for dating the crowning architectural work of the city, the temple of Athena Polias, as the master archaeologists Theodor Wiegand and Hans Schrader have done, at 344 B.C. Of course a date for a temple does not mean the temple is completed: that is always a state of affairs which is to come about later, if ever. At any rate Alexander the Great's dedication of the structure in 334 B.C. is interesting as an example of his presumption in inscribing in hallowed, archaic Greek form the announcement that he, the half-civilized Thracian conqueror, "*King* Alexander dedicated this temple to Athena Polias," which is to say to the Athena of that peculiarly civilized urban expression, such as it became at its best at a relatively late date in Ionia. The famous dedication makes only one truth clear: Priene, new Priene, had become a considerable place in pre-Hellenistic times.

It was a considerable place as a culmination of the greatness achieved by eastern Greeks living in harmony with their eastern neighbors. Today the most conspicuous feature of the small metropolis is the visible richness of the employment of the Hippodamean grid design in laying the place out. But since the worth of the orthogonal plan for a city has often been challenged, mostly in recent times on the romantic grounds that it is indifferent to nature, to the beauties of natural contours, and is inflexible to the demands of the environment, a quick comment becomes necessary at this point. The problem is philosophical. Le Corbusier believes that man must assert himself against nature, find ways to exist in his cultural, de-natured being. The distinction is the same as that which Claude Lévi-Strauss makes in defining elemental civilization: it is the cooked rather than the raw, table manners rather than snarling contention over food. Opposed to this point of view is the instinct of a Frank Lloyd Wright, of a *Sunset Magazine,* of a Californian, to bring the outdoors indoors, to let the habitation and its contents seep away into the landscape. The latter view appears, historically speaking, to be immature; I am wondering whether our rootless young people, who roam like the Sea Peoples of old, have not been confused by the loss of a distinction between indoors and outdoors, cooked and raw, in architecture, as in most of the other arts.

Another objection to the grid is that it is too stiff to suit the spirit of the Greeks, the Ionians, or any other vigorous people. On this question I quote Ferdinando Castagnoli:

From the viewpoint of urban aesthetics such a rigid geometric plan may seem surprising. . . . Yet the Greek creation (not Hellenistic since it appears as early as the fifth century) is not really alien to the Greek spirit, which sought through mathematics the precision of temple architecture and in some cases of sculpture as well. The rigor of geometric subdivision was maintained even in difficult geographic situations, on steep slopes, as for example in Rhodes and Olynthus first, then in Soluntum and Priene, among others. Interesting scenic effects were often obtained this way.

The grid has superior beauties when it occurs on rough land. In Priene from the center of the agora one looks up at the upper structures of the delicate yet soaring temple of Athena Polias, and up into the theater, and all around at a lacework of other structures, with out beyond them the green and gold fields of the well-watered valley.

A city on flat land, so far as I have been able to notice, has nothing to gain by any fundamental rejection of avenues and cross-streets running at right angles, and a lot to lose. Even a curved avenue in a subdivision fails to enhance the appearance of the house across the street or the one next door.

We know a lot about how Priene came into being and by inference a startling amount about the history of the period. Pytheos is the architect of Priene. He designed the temple of Athena, and becoming so absorbed in analyzing the properties of the Ionic order, he wrote a treatise on the temple. His concern was with symmetry in particular, which meant agreement among parts of the work, and agreement of the parts and the work with a general scheme. This we know from Vitruvius. It follows from the tenor of Vitruvius's account and from the manifest evidence presented by the ruins of the city that Pytheos, working from the temple as a focal center, imposed a symmetrical plan, an "agreement," on the array of public constructions and private dwellings. A planned city needs a planner, an architect, who will not accept potluck contributions to his art.

We have introduced the name of Pytheos without preliminaries. As every reader of Vitruvius knows, Pytheos and Satyrus were the architects who designed the Mausoleum in Halicarnassus. While that structure was moving toward its physical and artistic completion, Pytheos undertook his assignment at Priene; it can't very well be otherwise since his work at this time, in these places, is a matter of well-documented history. In accordance with this pattern, it is a likelihood—but only a likelihood—that Satyrus performed a similar service in the building of Cnidus. Priene could be called a foundation of Mausolus's; it has been called that, whatever the exact meaning of the term. Cnidus and Miletus were unquestionably close attachments to the dominion of the Carian dynast and his successors.

Pytheos made two noble contributions to the concept of what inevitably must be involved in the art of architecture. Vitruvius expands his interpretation of the master's principle of symmetry into the familiar realization that the proportions of the human body can be regarded as a standard for relative dimensions which will give satisfaction to the human being in his sense of physical things. The principle can hardly be denied; it has been important, as important in the mind of Leonardo

A Five-part Hymn to Pytheos, Architect of Priene: *the extant fragment of the colonnade of the temple of Athena Polias. Contrary to Ionian custom, this temple was built on a height, so that although it was not large it dominated its city, which itself was planned with the clarity and simplicity that these columns suggest. Once again deep-seated Greek traditions had been able quickly to reform themselves; here a height was chosen for the temple because of the need to move the city, in its whole Ionic complexity, up out of the encroaching marshes. Thereupon the aesthetic form of Priene underwent drastic adjustments to take advantage now, not of the shelter of well-watered flatlands, but of the openness of craggy heights.*

as in the mind of Le Corbusier, and yet it is no self-propelling, self-revealing solution to the problems of architecture.

A tighter, stronger, somewhat similar principle, which is more challenging to the present discussion, has come out in the course of measuring up the proportions which Pytheos actually built into the Ionic temple of Athena Polias. Briefly stated the dominating dimensions are 1:2 and 2:3 and 3:4. The temple supported its entablature on six columns on each end and eleven on each side. If those figures look unsymmetrical, they are not: the temple measures from the centers of the corner columns exactly 60 by 120 feet. Counting from center points again, the columns are 12 feet apart; each rests on a plinth 6 feet square and 6 feet apart. This series of ratios is precisely 1:2. In the entablature the handsome water spouts, lions' heads in their shape, go by threes, with one over the eye in each volute in the Ionic capitals and one at the midpoint of the space between volutes; these features consequently, at 4 feet apart, are as 4:6, or 2:3. The architrave itself is laid out in threes, with the plain fasciae beneath and the decorated members above. In comparison with these sets of twos and threes, the visible column diameters are as fours in proportion to the 6- and 12-foot units: the eyes of the volute, at 4-foot spacings, matching the basic diameter of the columns. In height the columns are more than 9 times, and less than 10 times their diameter: they are fluid, floating multiples which, unlike other dimensions, soar freely into an upwards perspective.

The governing proportions repeat one of the first shimmering discoveries that came floating up into the conscious mind, Pythagoras's mind according to earliest history. In musical tones there can be recognized an underlying design composed of octaves, fifths, and fourths. Vitruvius said: "The concords, termed in Greek, *symphoniai,* of which the human voice will naturally form modulations, are six in number: the fourth, the fifth, the octave, the octave and fourth, the octave and fifth, and the double octave. . . . Their names are therefore *due to numerical value.*" And considering the slender columns, we might add that on these staunch proportions many intricate harmonics may be imposed.

If any temple that I know of can be imagined really to sing, it must have been Pytheos's at Priene, and in the flower bed of fallen marble, it is still Pytheos's at Priene.

In his lost treatise Pytheos made such extraordinary claims for his art as an architect that only the shade of Eupalinus could be expected immediately to agree with him. His claims in any case were too radical for a man of great learning and good Roman commonsense such as Vitruvius to submit to. "An architect," Pytheos asserted, "ought to be able to accomplish more in all the arts and sciences than the men who, by their own particular kinds of work and the practice of it, have brought each single subject to highest perfection."

To this Vitruvius is compelled in his blunt honesty to say, "No; Aristarchus, Aristoxenus, Apelles, Myron and Polyclitus—men such as they, philologists, musicians, painters, sculptors—will always surpass the architect, be he ever so well informed, in their own specialities."

But will they? Will they always? At this point the encyclopedic banality which Vitruvius had a certain taste for has taken him over. Only the hollow pronouncements of academicians of the most unregenerate sort will insist thus on the rule and ignore the fertile exception. After all it was an architect, Michael Ventris, who broke the Linear B case, and established his findings "in spite of the opposition of established archaeological authority" (*Ency. Brit.*). It was an architect, one like many another who was more often than not at leisure, Leonardo da Vinci, who outstripped every specialist at his speciality. The first-rate astronomer of his times and leading authority on public works in England, and mathematician, was an architect, Sir Christopher Wren. It was an architect, a late comer—perhaps significantly a late comer to the profession—Nikolas Lobatchewsky, who overturned traditional geometry with sound non-Euclidean theory; who checked a plague by following Hippocratic practices based on Hippocratic intuitions; and built a great university.

My purpose is not to praise exceptional men; there are far too many who come to mind, and doubtless thousands who do not; my purpose now, as it has been earlier, is to explore the state of mind, the physical feelings, the nature of an education, the fabric of a society, which will be able to utilize the many-faceted powers that dwell within us. Since these powers dwelt conspicuously in many less materially fortunate individuals than we are, some simple uneasiness ought to make us stop and ask: couldn't we somehow manage to expand our own horizons?

I am not entertaining hopes for anything arbitrary such as the familiar "breadth requirements" as antidotes to specialized training, nor for anything so formless as the undirected, merely tutorial concept of higher education, but for a return (if possible) to the implications vested in the very term *university,* where in theory, in learning to play the lyre, we learn to play on all seven strings in even the most elementary lessons. I mean that every student should be trained, mentally and physically, as if, on first surmise, he might intend to become an architect, with the whole world his laboratory, with his hand and eye and intelligence all engaged as equal spies grappling with the future. The earliest record of a specific collection of books which a Greek thought worth bringing together is classified under the following headings: Medicine, Architecture, Geometry, Astronomy, and *Rhapsodia,* which is to say, recitable poetry. I can hardly imagine a better survival kit for civilization. One might add Music; but where would music be without the others? At all events the broad, acutely pointed discipline that Pytheos envisioned has seemed only recently to have sunk down out of reach beneath the overgrowth of detailed knowledge.

The rewards of contemplating Priene and the art of Pytheos, like the gold of Croesus, are more than any greedy mortal can carry away.

What we can carry away is, ironically enough, largely available only as the result of ancient misfortunes. Priene arose out of the swamps, and because of the swamps life eventually died out within it. But the swamps protected the marble as the centuries passed by. Even when Theodor Wiegand arrived in 1895 as a young archaeologist he found everyone suffering to a greater or less degree from the fever of marshes, and his chief, Karl Humann, mortally ill. A short time later he died.

Wiegand and the surviving scientists at last were prepared to ship crates containing a portion of the architrave, with capital and plinth, back to their sponsoring museum in Berlin. At this point they were very nearly defeated. Wiegand reports in a letter that the road to Söke was very bad, with numerous swampy stretches breaking across it, so that despite the strength of twelve oxen their forward progress ceased again and again. "Several of the fine Turkish draft-animals just lay down and died." In all they spent fourteen days traversing the nine miles to Söke, the point where adequate facilities for transshipment began.

One of the greatest marvels in the history of Ionia is the magnitude

In a Planned City Plans Call for Accommodations for Continued Planning: *a commodious, geometrically balanced auditorium which presumably housed the assemblies of citizens to whom special councils made their regular reports. It faced southward, out over the Maeander valley, and was roofed over in order to provide protection as much from the heat of the sun as from bad weather. On its flank there was an open theater of impressive proportions for so small a city. Athena Polias, Athena of the City, seems to have presided over a great deal of peaceable discourse.*

of the adversities which had constantly to be overcome, and were overcome.

VI

The return to Samos from the ancient Samian *peraia* was a return from the land of eloquent phantoms to the hospitable *kali meras* of the present. The elections over, the old peacefulness exuded around the ridiculously enthroned lion in the central square. There was the leisure now really to look at things, and to do some wondering; to admire and to entertain fewer doubts.

Take Pythagorion for example. The quai at Pythagorion bristled with the mostly useless masts of a fleet of highly varnished private yachts. But the people who had tied up in the home port of Polycrates' boar-snouted navy were not themselves discordant with the scene: no amplified sound-boxes blared from their trim vessels, as had happened even in Bodrum. I gather that a modern yacht is like an automobile; when you buy one you buy what the manufacturer produces; and certainly boats like the honest native caiques are too slow to bring you to Samos from afar.

In contrast with this shining flotilla there was only the poorest remnant of the local small-boat fleet at the foot of Polycrates' deep-sea mole, and no caiques were being built. The sea had become sterile, we were told. When there were no fish, it was useless to build fishing boats.

Nevertheless my old friend with the restaurant at the corner of Main and the Embarcadero had lamb, and fish sometimes, and octopus always. And cucumbers and tomatoes and salad greens and bread and ouzo. And so life was not so bad, neither for us nor the people who came ashore from the yachts.

The tunnel of Eupalinus, Costas Ptinis had told us with untranslatable excitement, was being reexcavated, opened through the mountain again by a team of Italians! And so it was. We descended into it and found it looking like a basement corridor in a warehouse, stretching forth dingily under a string of electric light bulbs. One by one laborers came by us, each carrying a basketful of earth on his shoulder. We stood aside to let them pass at the points where the aqueduct was bridged over. With all this activity going on the magic of the tunnel had fled like the ghosts of the crusaders from the castle at Bodrum. But a new magic, a magic of newly processed iron water mains, lay in a ditch which was cleft along the line of the ancient conduit: the bountiful springs of Agiades, it appeared, would once again refresh the old metropolis and prepare it, not for a siege of Spartan or of Athenian soldiery, but for the invasion of the dazed hoards that would come on speedy air-conditioned tour buses.

Samos we noticed was already under a mild siege of the contemporary Sea People, the idle, long-haired, blue-eyed, befringed and bejeweled compatriots of ours. Once in Pythagorion one of them, probably overhearing something that Virginia was saying about an object in a clutter of junk in a shop window, asked us about a coin he was wearing on a string of beads. I'd noticed this man some moments earlier; and more particularly, much more particularly, the two bizarrely draped, handsome young women he had with him; more particularly because, at some time or other, on some such an occasion, one of the young women may turn out to be my daughter; but not this time, not on this occasion. The coin was no puzzle. It was a large bronze Artemis of Ephesus, a delta Neokor, a good coin, a very good coin, I could assure him. I asked to see the other side. Though the Emperor's portrait was unmarred, I couldn't read his name.

"What about the beads?" the owner of the coin asked. "I think they're just rosary beads. What do you think?"

"I don't know much about beads," I said.

On another day, having rented a car, a blue Fiat this time, on our way to or on out beyond Koutsi, in the deeply shaded, un-Greek freshness of the mountains near the inn, I saw on the roadside a small pile of heavy, crooked timbers like those which had astonished me nine years before. They had been freshly squared off with an adz. Obviously they were lying there waiting for a truck to come and pick them up and carry them to a shipyard. So somewhere the old Homeric boat carpentry was still going forward. I thought of several places, Ormos Koumeika, for instance; but it proved to be nothing so remote. The exotic shipyard was at Kokkarion, a sequestered town on the north coast, just around the bay from Vathi. We had failed earlier, it seemed, to drop down to a certain section of the seafront.

The main road passes through an open, upper section of the small city, which is elegantly weighted with white red-roofed houses, each set in its tiny park above a larger park that was eucalyptus bordered.

The Timbers for a Ship
Hewn by the Woodsman's
Axe *"lie in rows until
picked up to be built into the
well-wrought ship"*
(*Apollonius Rhodius,*
Argonautica). *A roadside
in Samos, 1973.*

Virginia, enthralled as usual with natural wonders, asked a native of
Kokkarion about eucalyptus trees on the island—eucalyptus trees on
Samos! He was delighted to tell us in the picturesque Italian he had
picked up while living as a camp boy with the Italian soldiers, that
his father, as it happened, had been in Australia and when he returned
after the war, he brought the trees with him and planted them there,
where they had become the wonder of everyone and that moreover if
we were serious about wanting to see the shipyard, all we had to do
was to walk down the hill from the eucalyptus grove through the village to the waterfront.

   Walk down the hill, he said; but the next day from the road beside
the grove, seeing the lay of the land quite clearly, I advised Virginia
to drive on for a short distance and then to swing back along what must
be a quai that skirted the cove at Kokkarion.

   We did, and moments later, there they were, a pair of unfinished
caiques. Gracefully ribbed, skeletal, painted a bright orange, they
soared like transparent flying carp on their stays, glittering in the light
of the late afternoon, and foreshortened a little by the boat builder's
house. A string of laundry—many-colored children's things—looked
like the pennants of a man-of-war stretching between the prow and the

white house. On the tips of both prows were large crosses. They were simple wooden crosses, also painted orange, but the horizontal member was underslung in the Byzantine style. We turned off the ignition and walked toward them from the car.

Nothing in the fashioning of Homer's broad-beamed, ox-horned freight ships had changed, not since 1964, nor since the archaic age, nor since those dim times of Homer himself, unless it were the use of standard five-eighths inch bolts rather than pegs in the mortised joints where the ribs start their sweep upwards toward the topmost wale of the sheeting. But then, metallic pins have forever been a common means of locking abutting surfaces together, whether they were monumental marble or fine cloth or anything in between; and since several of these craft were bigger than those which village shipwrights ordinarily built, they were being prepared no doubt for the strains set up by the new heavy-duty diesel engines. Otherwise the builders conceded nothing, nothing in the way of craftsmanship and design, to the practices of the modern world. And why should they? in the small self-sufficient enterprises of the island communities, why should they? And yet, how precarious the balance, how unlikely, the survival of these scattered, rich, insular centers of life!

We edged on down to the brim of sea, viewing the vessels from the stern, and then along with them several more which we had not seen at first. The clothes on the line flapped in the breeze, a man on a ladder was stroking the side of the nearest caique with a stubby plane. Someone shouted across to him from the next hull. The planer left off his planing and joined the two others. Then the three of them began fitting a mortised rib into a notch in the kelson. It took many moments to shave the butt of the rib to exact dimensions, trying it and cutting it down little by little until finally it could be pressed into place. The men straightened up with their hands still on the timber, studying its harmonious alignment in the string of other ribs with an air of quiet triumph. Such a triumph need not be a great triumph, but no matter how frequently it occurs it makes a workman smile momentarily in his heart.

The approach along the waterfront having been rough, we drove on, at my suggestion, to the next corner and turned uphill toward the main road. The little street that we entered curved round in a moment and narrowed into a steep strip of paving with pleasant small houses

The Work of the Shipwrights of Samos: *Kokkarion, 1973*.

crowded in on both sides and people in the middle of the foreground, seated or standing, enjoying their evening relaxation. Farther along, a vine with purple blooms stretched across from house to house so that nothing was visible beyond it. My heart fell. I got out, peered ahead, looked back, and did the only thing I felt I could do. I appealed to the two or three people nearest me, not too vocally, but making manifest my embarrassment at their discovery of a dusty blue Fiat trying to thread a way between their thresholds. They were taken aback, I could see, not angry, just cold, until they too looked down the street and up the street and began to appreciate the difficulty I was in. They were the ones who decided against the hazards of the reverse gear. So with a convoy of aids we moved up the street, getting chairs and stools and children and such miscellaneous debris out of the way, lifting and skidding the gaseous little Fiat around the sharpest corner, wriggling through another block or two of the passage upwards, until I could see open daylight ahead.

There the resident Kokkarions left us, wishing us well while I was trying to express our eternal gratitude. Trudging forward with the Fiat under my left hand, like a farmer leading the family cow to his neighbor's bull, I emerged into the glare of the crowded small central square of Kokkarion.

Our entrance there caused a bluster of response from the cafe tables, curbs and benches, where the young Sea People had been reposing. I might have anticipated something of the sort, having seen them with their packs and fringes moving out through Samos to descend with migrational instinct on tranquil Kokkarion for the duration of the summer. Of course the last thing they expected to see was a man leading a rented Fiat through the golden light of their secluded encampment. The walls of their isolation had been breached ruthlessly.

For once I had a slight inkling of what might be contained in two particular packs which Prometheus, according to Aesop, had hung on a creature such as me. The one which he had put in front, in which I could plainly see the faults of others, seemed sometimes to contain, as I had noticed more than once, a profusion of soiled sandals of many sorts; the pack in back with my faults in it, though it was ordinarily hard to see into, seemed to swing around just a little at this moment, giving me a glimpse of a pair of L. L. Bean's Skeet Shooter's shoes, prime leather in quality but somewhat inflexible in leaping dikes of weeds and marble in the Heraion. Where I had seen only empty blue eyes in empty steel spectacle frames, by twisting a little I could see the arbitrary precision of a massive-lensed Japanese camera. In the front pack there were the herbs of Morpheus; in the back, a book containing indecipherably intricate time charts. The present rose like a child's balloon from the front; from the back, some part of the dead curriculum of the past wanted to pull every adventure down.

The next day we returned the Fiat to the garage owner, and a few days later were on board a flight for Paris, following the great circle of Eudoxus of Cnidus, inscribing a line from Athens to Delphi to Corfu to Brindisi to Switzerland, with the snow-studded Alps lying as within a small saucer. Then Paris and Cornwall and Ireland; then an enduring, timeless shelf of clouds, until suddenly Greenland arose in a great rift, exposing—wonder of wonders—more white, enormous icebergs than there are ships on the sea, or skyscrapers in all the cities of the world. Finally, as the light of the day ebbed, came the unbudging contours of the mountainous desert and then another green fringe edging another ocean, with implanted in it at some secret places a mud-brick complex where the citrus and the palm are restored, and the olive; and plataea architecture thrusts forth an Islamic window.

Full circle. Such was the full circle of 1973.

CONCLUSION

Scene: Hades. CLOTHO *and* MEGAPENTHES.

CLOTHO.   Come along with me, Megapenthes.

MEGA.   No, no, if you please, Clotho. Let me return for a little while, and I'll come to you of my own accord, without troubling you in the least.

CLOTHO.   What do you want to go back for?

MEGA.   I beg you to give me a special permit to finish my palace. The way it stands now it's hardly more than half-finished.

CLOTHO.   Half-finished! What isn't? Come along.

MEGA.   May I speak privately to you, Madam? I could offer you . . . certain unique inducements.

CLOTHO.   Still confident in the powers of inducements! Charon, use force on him if you must. I don't think he will embark of his own accord.

MEGA. (*shouting to the Shades*).   I want you all to bear witness to this! this violation of what is right! The walls of my city are almost complete! So are the docks! I ask for no more than a small extension of my time. . . . A matter of a few days only!

CLOTHO.   Don't worry, Megapenthes. Somebody will take over where you left off. And he'll probably never be able to finish everything either.

—Lucian

WITH SO MUCH that in its own way is perfectly clear, it is tempting to try to conclude a discussion of this kind by asserting: "Thus, as we have seen, the Greeks thought and built and worshipped, and fashioned many beautiful things."—and then to give those topics predication by summing up the ancient accomplishment in a few suitable paragraphs, alluding at least to familiar topics such as the Polis, Paideia, Democracy, the Mysteries, and so on. But for me anything of the sort would be totally out of reach. What we have been attempting to do is at most to assemble some clippings of written fragments and some fragments of modern photographs and, after arranging them in a harmonious structure, to tape them together, hoping that from this sketchy model of a notable experience some interesting suggestions as to the shape of our own experience might be forthcoming. Our model has had a certain wholeness, but also a vibrancy and flexibility which defy formulation and negate the possibility of saying, for example, what the role of religion in it actually was. Final pronouncements became a smothering tissue of terminologies and biases. But nevertheless from the whole model a certain amount of meaning may burst forth here and there.

We can remark that the greatest oddity of the experience was no doubt its avoidance of dogmatism. Of the other faiths and philosophies and disciplines which have touched the modern world most directly, it appears that each has presumed to build on a rock: on a theos, a prophet, a trinity, or following Aristotle on an intellectual *arche*, which in his brilliantly individual case was God as the source of the goodly working of the cosmos. The objective of each system was to establish structural finality, to create a coherence which would be wanting in no respect and to which there could be no exceptions. The Ionians betrayed no such compulsions. Even in speculative inquiry, they were casual about finalities.

For example:

Aristotle said about Herodotus that his archaic (and Ionic) way of writing his prose in the *Histories* was out of date (*Rhet.* 1409A). The historian's style, he said, was loose and free-running, the goal of the narrative was never kept in sight; the stopping point came only when he ran out of subject matter: Aristotle found the whole thing extremely unsatisfactory. What Aristotle required was a proper beginning and a proper ending, with the period in the middle held to a direction which is foreseeable at a glance. The difference between the two methods, or the two styles, he adds, is the difference between the indefinite and the definite. Or between, as we would say, archaic openness on the one hand and classical finality on the other.

But in certain situations the definite is not possible nor desirable; the indefinite is necessary and deeply to be preferred. The work of Herodotus, from my point of view, is actually a perfect case in point, but it is by no means the only one: I think of Ludwig Wittgenstein's preface to his *Philosophical Investigations,* in which he says, "I have written down all these thoughts as *remarks,* short paragraphs, of which there is sometimes a fairly long chain about the same subject, while I sometimes make a sudden change, jumping from one topic to another. It was my intention at first to bring all this together in a book whose form I pictured differently at different times. After several unsuccessful attempts to weld my results together into such a whole, I realized that I should never succeed. The best that I could write would never be more than philosophical remarks; my thoughts were soon crippled if I tried to force them on in a single direction against their natural inclination. And this was, of course, connected with the very nature of the investigation." And Wittgenstein's investigations, needless to say, were directly concerned with the very processes of mind which enable us to put words together and perhaps to make sentences out of them and possibly even books.

Wittgenstein's patient acceptance of the fragmentariness of the ways of consciousness has, like a rare and beautiful coin, an obverse in the worried resistance with which Albert Einstein met the implications of fragmentariness in atomic science. The staring vacancies, the irrational congestions and decongestions in the structure of matter, which could only be accounted for along nondeterministic lines by quantum theory, led him to put his perplexities in these words: "Some physicists, among them myself, can not believe that we must abandon, actually and forever, the idea of direct representation of physical reality in space and time; or that we must accept the view that events in nature are analogous to a game of chance."

We can hope that Einstein's faith will be rewarded and that Wittgenstein's skepticism will not completely silence us, but only chasten us,
in our efforts to speak. At the same time we can suspect that at one
frontier after another difficulties will continue to haunt us, that the
patterns which things reveal under scrutiny will always have their
resemblances to a cast of the knucklebones or the inscrutable coun-
tenances of the gods.

A BIBLIOGRAPHICAL ESSAY

IF THE FOLLOWING DISCUSSION is to be of interest, I must restrict myself quite severely. No mention on my part of an estimable work may mean that, had I time and space for distinguishing shades of agreement and difference, I would have said something about it, or it may mean that I was ignorant of it, or too little acquainted with it to allow inclusion. H.D.F. Kitto's two works, *Greek Tragedy* and *Form and Meaning in Drama*, might have gone without the recognition they deserve because of the normal inclination to avoid difficult distinctions; the reader, however, who considers the complexity of Euripides' *Ion* will discover for himself why I prefer to put a slightly unconventional emphasis on this drama and several others much like it. On the other hand, Albin Lesky's *A History of Greek Literature* (trans. by J. Willis and C. de Heer, 1966) is so studious of detail and so uniformly capacious and well recognized, that it might have been taken for granted.

As a general rule I keep the texts of the Loeb Classical Library, published by Harvard University Press, before me, though on occasion I have turned to the texts published by the Association Guillaume Budé (Paris) and from time to time to both. Translations are usually identified; if not, I suppose I am largely responsible for them. In some instances one or another of the standard translations of an ancient text dominates all other alternatives as, for instance, the Oxford translations of Aristotle, edited by J. D. Ross.

Being formally untrained in Greek has had one great but not too welcome advantage: I have been forced to spend sizable parts of many working days digging into Liddell and Scott's *Greek-English Lexicon;* and that παράδισος has rewarded me with trophies with which otherwise I might not have come home.

Instead of footnotes it seems more convenient to gather general references together here with critical notations under general headings.

I HISTORY AND GEOGRAPHY OF THE GREEK SETTLEMENTS

ANCIENT SOURCES

1 Herodotus, *The Histories* (Loeb and Budé). There are also several standard texts in translation which serve ordinary purposes.

How and Wells, *A Commentary on Herodotus* (Oxford Univ. Press, 1928).

An Elizabethan translation of Books 1 and 2 of the *Histories* by B. R. (Barnabe Rich, 1584) is jaunty and archaic in its bearing, though falling short of the elusive seriousness of the original. But, as Andrew Lang, editor of a reprint of Book 2—the fabulous Egyptian book (1888)—said in his preface: "B. R. tells a story with a point, with breadth; above all, with enjoyment. Of what other translator of Herodotus can we say so much!" Would that we could say so much for most translators of the classics!

2 Thucydides, *History of the Peloponnesian War* (Loeb, Budé, and others).

A. W. Gomme and others, *A Historical Commentary on Thucydides* (Oxford Univ. Press, 1956 and later).

Thomas Hobbes's translation follows the Greek in a particularly appropriate and agreeable idiom. Unfortunately the modern edition, edited by D. Grene (Univ. of Michigan Press, 1959), which on the whole is first-rate, omits Hobbes's introduction, with its trenchant, highly individual political views and its studious but still shaky inquiries into ancient geography.

3 Diodorus Siculus, *The Library of History*.

4 Strabo, *The Geography*.

5 Pausanius, *Description of Greece*.

6 Athenaeus, *Deipnosophistae*.

7 Plutarch, *The Parallel Lives*.

8 Plutarch, *Moralia*.

Diodorus is a comprehensive chronicler; Strabo has the admirable ancient gift of combining history and geography and legend. Pausanius leans toward monuments and legends. History is incidental to legendary anecdotes in Athenaeus; it is ever present in the work of Plutarch. The lively concreteness of these books makes lapses into bad information not really bothersome. To the contrary, cultivated misinformation, as in chronology, can be a negative form of good information. Sequences such as Eusebius's list of the sea powers which preceded the rise of Samos as a thalassocracy form a substantial outline, however mistaken some of the details, for plotting the course of the archaic age.

MODERN HISTORIANS: GENERAL

For me the meticulously projected, patiently assembled pages of a much outdated work have been in their broad sweep quite to my purpose:

9 George Grote, *A History of Greece,* 12 vols. (1846–56; rpt. Everyman, 1907).

An only comparatively modern history, dating from the beginning of the century, initiated the use of archaeology and numismatics while retaining a sweeping objective outlook. Fortunately this work has been rendered thoroughly serviceable in its recently revised edition:

10 J. B. Bury, *A History of Greece to the Death of Alexander the Great* (1900; ed. and rev. by Russell Meiggs, Macmillan, 1955).

11 N.G.L. Hammond, *A History of Greece to 322 B.C.* (Oxford Univ. Press, 1959).

This history is the output of the newest, intensively specialized study of every shred of historical evidence. Though one has the sense of the author's being nailed to the scholarly journals with their Athenian point of view—see the handling of the actions of the S Y N League during the Social War—still, on the whole, the narrative avoids fragmentation and pursues its way with coherence and forcefulness.

MODERN HISTORIANS: THE EARLY SETTLEMENTS

12 A. J. Graham, "Patterns in Early Greek Colonization," *Journal of Hellenic Studies,* 91 (1971), 35–42.

13 John Boardman, *The Greeks Overseas* (Pelican, 1964).

14 A. R. Burn, *The Lyric Age of Greece* (E. Arnold, 1960).

In addition to these selected titles, contributions to the revised edition of *The Cambridge Ancient History* have been appearing in the form of fascicles, which are in themselves excellent, and to which are attached extremely useful bibliographies. For example:

15 John M. Cook, *Greek Settlement in the Eastern Aegean and Asia Minor* (Cambridge Univ. Press, 1961).

At the other end of the spectrum of useful, recently published hand-books are the *Hachette World Guides* (Paris), which could legitimately claim to be the most indispensable of tools.

MODERN HISTORIANS: EARLY LITERATURE

The selection of titles for this category would have to be massively inclusive or reduced to the very few which imposed themselves on the writing of certain passages in this book. I have chosen the latter course.

16 C. M. Bowra, *Greek Lyric Poetry from Alcman to Simonides* (Oxford Univ. Press, 1935; rev. ed. 1961).

17 G. L. Huxley, *Greek Epic Poetry from Eumelos to Panyassis* (Harvard Univ. Press, 1969).

18 J. A. Davison, *From Archilochus to Pindar* (Macmillan, 1968).

MODERN HISTORIANS: IONIA

19 G. L. Huxley, *The Early Ionians* (Faber and Faber, 1966).

20 J. M. Cook, *The Greeks in Ionia and the East* (Thames and Hudson, 1962).

21 T. J. Dunbabin, *The Greeks and Their Eastern Neighbours* (Society for the Promotion of Hellenic Studies [SPHS], 1957).

These three books vary in their emphasis from a resourceful but noticeably prosaic study of the ancient record in the first, to expositions illustrated with archaeological data and reproductions of works of art in the other two. Since both ways of presenting history are desirable, the works listed above complement one another.

MODERN HISTORIANS: MAGNA GRAECIA

22 T. J. Dunbabin, *The Western Greeks* (Oxford Univ. Press, 1948).

23 A. G. Woodhead, *The Greeks in the West* (Praeger, 1962).

The first above, a recognized model of excellence, concentrates on the early period; the second, a much-needed general account.

MODERN HISTORIANS: SPECIAL SUBJECTS

24 A. Andrewes, *The Greek Tyrants* (Harper Torchbook, 1956).

25 Russell Meiggs, *The Athenian Empire* (Oxford Univ. Press, 1973).

26 C. W. Fornara, *Herodotus: An Interpretative Essay* (Oxford Univ. Press, 1971).

27 Claude Mossé, *Athens In Decline* (Routledge and Kegan Paul, 1973).

28 W. W. Tarn, *Hellenistic Civilization* (Meridian, 1952).

Among the niggling questions left behind by Herodotus is the question of any intelligent Greek's true estimate of the Persian Empire—always bearing in mind as crucial evidence the careers of Themistocles and Xenophon. We can see a degree of "Medizing" as normal among the more mobile, free-spirited Greeks; and among the instinctive antagonists of the Athenians—the Thebans, for instance—it was a predominant trait. The premises on which the Athenian Empire rested, in other words, were not so universally accepted as orators liked to pretend. From its beginnings, from its aggressive rise to its sorry decline, the empire was always immoderately self-interested.

The Peloponnesian War is the turning point in a case history beginning with the fall of the tyrants, rising to a height with Mycale, and ending, but not quite, with Alexander the Great. Professor Meiggs's history thus has a pertinence which includes, or perhaps really centers on, early and late Ionia, and Magna Graecia as well. We are left in no doubt as to the scope and the character of the Athenian Empire.

We have a niggling question about the position of Herodotus himself, Herodotus vis-à-vis the warfare of his own times. The reader will know quite well, I am sure, that I regard Herodotus above all as an imaginative Ionian. This point of view resembles quite closely a thesis which I discover is developed conclusively in Charles Fornara's book *Herodotus.* Although Herodotus, apparently a sometime prominent resident of Athens and an enlisted colonist in Pericles' new foundation at Thurii, never lets current history obtrude in the *Histories,* still Professor Fornara convinces me that the historian is thinking of his own present, and Pericles' present, when he recounts the efforts of the

Athenians to persuade Gelon the Syracusan to join them in their mighty efforts to defend themselves and the Greek peoples in the time of the Persian wars. Gelon, in the dialogue as Herodotus reports it, begins with a favorable reply that has conditions tied to it; and then, becoming aware of the complete inflexibility of the Greek envoy's position, Gelon says: "Friend Athenian, it seems to me you will have rulers but no one to rule. Since you insist on having the whole without compromise, you must go back empty-handed. . . . But tell them that *they have taken the Spring out of the year*" (see pp. 82–83). The concluding phrase is Pericles' own phrase, one that he had used in a funeral oration. Herodotus, whose recitals of his work were of public interest, could not have been unaware of the impact that this passage would make on an Athenian in the midst of the suffering occasioned by the Peloponnesian War.

The background for the political embarrassments which have troubled many of the pages of *Persephone's Cave* could hardly be put in language more understandable to me than that used by Professor Mossé to conclude her *Athens in Decline:*

The concept of the *polis* was, originally, that of a community of free men, living in perfect autarchy under the protection of the gods and defending themselves against any attack from the outside. Needless to say this ideal concept was never realized at any moment in Greek history, for very soon, and at a very early stage, the need for supplies of grain and common metals imposed upon the Greeks a system of relations which implied division of labour, slavery and social inequality. The history of Athens is typical in this respect, since as early as the sixth century B.C. she found herself involved in a complex system of relations, which hastened her evolution towards democracy, a democracy that presupposed slavery and the exploitation of her Aegean allies. From that moment, the apogee of Athens contained within itself the elements of her decline. Deprived of her allies, Athens was condemned to provide for herself the resources which would enable democracy to survive and to protect itself; and to accomplish this she must give up the traditional ethic of the *polis,* that autarchy of which some theorists were still dreaming in the fourth century, and to seek an opening onto the outside world, to develop her industry by a large-scale recourse to slave-labour, to attract foreign traders and integrate them into the civic community. A few men, towards the middle of the fourth century, were intuitively aware of this new necessity. But there were too many obstacles to its fulfillment, some due to the very structure of the essentially rural civic society, others to the general conditions of the

Aegean world, to the threat from Macedon and, later, to the great upheavals caused by the conquests of Alexander, and others again to the political regime itself, to that democracy which had constituted the greatness of Athens and which now doomed her to die.

This analysis, as I say, is understandable. But its deterministic alignments are doubtful. One must have doubts about "the greatness of Athens" as an equivalent to its early democracy. One must reject the implication that slavery, in these centuries, was as destructive to Athens as her betrayals of her allies. And finally in trying to assess the failure of Athens, no one can ignore the success of some other leagues of the times—the Achaian, for instance (see Pausanias, Book 7) and those of the Achaian foundations in Italy; the s y n federation in the eastern Aegean; and the league that Thebes enjoyed, especially under the leadership of Epaminondas, and continued to enjoy until Macedon came into the picture.

We cannot ignore examples, not of imperialism, but of, elsewhere in the world, groupings which favored unselfish decisions and "a community of interest in upholding the federal principle and not the partisan spirit of democracy as opposed to oligarchy" (Hammond: 1959, p. 504). Nevertheless, on the whole unfortunately, it has been the Athenian who has ruled over history, not his gentler Ionian or Achaian cousins.

II MYTH

ANCIENT SOURCES

29 *Hesiod, Theogony;* and incidentally, *Works and Days,* astrological fragments, etc.

30 *Homeric Hymns.*

31 Pindar, *Odes.*

32 Callimachus, *Hymns.*

33 Apollonius Rhodius, *Argonautica.*

34 Apollodorus, *The Library.*

35 Ovid, especially the *Metamorphoses.*

36 Lucian.

Beginning with Hesiod, a large part of ancient literary work is dominated by myths. One can make a somewhat similar claim for Homer's epics, but they are not quite the same as those works which in the whole or in important parts revolve around a myth as such. The same rule holds for other fragmentary epic or choral work and for the drama. The ancient historians and geographers named in section I above often cloak some of their pages with a cloud of mythology. But the integrity of myth as myth is conspicuous in the works which I have enumerated. These, then, are primary sources for mythological information. They are, of course, very different one from another, ranging from the exalted genealogical roster of the gods and the roles they enact in Hesiod's epic pageant to Lucian's wily caricatures.

For the purposes of this book the Greek myths are evasive, ever-present illuminations that hover around the more substantial stuff that comes under scrutiny. Mythic allusions make their way into the contexts of the whole range of the written record, from geometry to astronomy, from living athletic champions to the populations of Hades. In looking at works of art, statues and coins, painted pottery and architectural friezes, we encounter myths presented in a graphic form, on the presumption that we as viewers will have the ability to recognize the myth depicted. Although this is a challenge in which complete success will often lie out of reach, we can hardly avoid trying to dig out the elementary grammar of the phenomenal ancient narratives. Sometimes on the vases the names of the protagonists in the scene are set down in archaic script. Whether the artist intended the names to be helpful or was indulging himself in the naive love of labels would be hard to say. In any event they are worth noting with care because they lead to the recognition of what became traditional scenes in which no names appear. See:

37 Jane Henle, *Greek Myths: A Vase Painter's Notebook* (Indiana Univ. Press, 1973).

Thus it is apparent that after the authors listed at the head of this note, art books appear to be of greatest usefulness. They enable the reader not only to identify but to check the visual impact of a mythological personage in a mythological situation, with presumably reliable commentary on the part of an editor to supply pertinent information. Not all books are equally capacious, or reliable. The fol-

lowing are compact, wide-ranging, informative volumes in modest
black and white:

38 John Boardman, *Athenian Black Figure Vases* (Thames and Hudson, 1974).

39 John Boardman, *Athenian Red Figure Vases: The Archaic Period* (Thames and Hudson, 1975).

Art books with luxurious color reproductions are more immediately
impressive, of course, than analytical handbooks. An account of a very
few volumes on Greek art in general which are notable for their illustrations is reserved for a later section in this brief inventory of materials.

MYTH: MODERN HANDBOOKS

This leaves us with the problem of the modern handbooks which set
out to expound the Greek myths. They are surprisingly few; and among
them the Bulfinches and the Gayleys on the bookstore shelves are
really useless. Among those left in the popular market is

40 Robert Graves, *The Greek Myths* (Penguin, 1955).

This work, in my opinion, is of unrivaled value as a brief index covering the chief events in a given myth and the chief ancient writings
which dealt with it; but as an assessment of what the story meant,
whence it was derived, how it figured in the everyday thoughts of the
Greeks, Graves's vivid compilation is one toward which a great deal of
skepticism should be directed. The author embraces the rampant phantoms of Sir James Frazer, Jane Harrison, and the Cambridge ritualists,
and adds to theirs a few ritualistic phantoms of his own.

41 Veronica Ions, *The World's Mythology in Colour* (Hamlyn, 1974).

This is an extravagant but effective picture book with the inevitable
impoverished text of a wide-ranging survey, to which Jacquetta
Hawkes contributes a thoughtful short introduction.

The standard reference works such as the *Oxford Companion to
Classical Literature* have their place, but have room for no more than
grotesquely attenuated outlines. The unhappily out-of-date dictionaries
of Sir William Smith, even a ragged copy of the voluminous, totally

antiquated *Classical Dictionary* by Charles Anthon, can be fascinating to anyone searching for an additional clue to a mystery or wondering about the contents of many now forgotten ancient books.

MYTH: SPECIAL STUDIES

Among the many notable studies of mythology the following, I believe, are as comprehensive as they are different from one another, both in regard to their premises and execution:

42 G. S. Kirk, "Greek Mythology: Some New Perspectives," *Journal of Hellenic Studies,* 92 (1972), 74–85.

This is a model of detached inquiry into the fundamental nature of the Greek myths as literate expressions.

43 J. G. Jung and C. Kerényi, *Essays on a Science of Mythology* (1949; Torchbook, 1963).

From the point of view of the newer psychological schools, the Jungian assumptions almost alone are finally persuasive.

44 Walter F. Otto, *Dionysus: Myth and Cult* (Indiana Univ. Press, 1965).

Very effective on the always extant, imponderable connections between myth and religion.

45 C. Lévi-Strauss, *The Raw and the Cooked: Introduction to a Science of Mythology* (Torchbook, 1969).

An anthropologist using the heavy-equipment of his profession makes a great deal of sense of the place of mythological patterns in the formation of society.

As a counterbalance to the above speculative studies, with their weighty abstractionism, I propose a brief return to the best evidence of all: an example of Greek mythology actively at work; because finally the most important question to be asked of the Greek myths is, How did they contribute to the arts of the Greeks and therefore to the arts of anyone of us? The following fictional work, technically a novel, puts on display, with all of the resources of a deeply imaginative state of mind, the legendary sufferings and intimations of divinity of Heracles:

46 Caroline Gordon, *The Glory of Hera* (Doubleday, 1972).

Of a character different from any other inquiry into the character of

Greek fantastic, mythological, and religious impulses, are the closely documented and brilliantly reasonable lectures delivered originally in Berkeley, California in 1949 and prepared for publication shortly thereafter:

47 E. R. Dodds, *The Greeks and the Irrational* (Berkeley: Univ. of California Press, 1951).

This book departs from the conventional specialist's work by admitting as one the evidences from archaeology, anthropology, psychology, and allied sciences. The result is a healthy iconoclasm toward Orphism, vegetation magic, annual king burials, and several other shibboleths which are proving to be not so revealing as once was thought.

And finally:

48 P. Freidländer and H. B. Hoffleit, *Epigrammata: Greek Inscriptions in Verse from the Beginnings to the Persian Wars* (Berkeley: Univ. of California Press, 1948).

As for the above, no commentary in words could possibly be more descriptive of archaic elegance, I think, than the verse inscriptions which have been found incised on some of the ancient marble works of art.

III   ART

GENERAL REFERENCES

A representative collection of some of the most interesting objects of early Greek art is presented, with the highly visible illustrations which the newest techniques have made possible, in a number of lavish folio volumes. Among them these two are especially valuable for the high quality of the texts as well as the pictures:

49 Pierre Demargne, *Aegean Art: The Origins of Greek Art* (Paris, 1964).

50 Jean Charbonneaux; R. Martin; and F. Villard, *Archaic Greek Art 620–480 B.C.* (Paris, 1968; and London: Thames and Hudson, 1971).

The distinctly original reports of the late curator of the Louvre, Jean Charbonneaux, have made a special impact on many interested observers, including myself. Therefore I add the titles of several less-imposing tomes than the volume from the French series, The Arts of Mankind, ed. André Malraux, which is indicated above.

51 J. Charbonneaux, *L'Art Egéen* (Paris, 1929).

52 ———, *La Sculpture Grecque Archaïque* (Paris, 1939).

53 ———, *Greek Bronzes* (Viking, 1962).

Penguin Books sponsors a fine series called "Style and Civilization," which includes:

54 J. Boardman, *Pre-Classical: From Crete to Archaic Greek* (Penguin, 1967).

Similar in style but of wider scope:

55 J. Boardman, *Greek Art* (1964; rev. ed. Praeger, 1973).

The following are comparable, uniquely impressive but inexpensive reference works:

56 E. Akurgal, *The Birth of Greek Art* (Methuen, 1966).

57 E. Homann-Wedeking, *The Art of Archaic Greece* (Methuen, 1966).

58 K. Schefold, *Myth and Legend in Early Greek Art* (Abrams, *ca.* 1966).

Of these titles, the last is remarkably graphic and informative in spite of the moderate size of the format.

Three highly relevant reference works, which are also highly technical, give great depth to certain matters which are touched on at crucial places in the general studies:

59 J. Boardman, *Island Gems: A Study of Greek Seals in the Geometric and Early Archaic Periods* (SPHS, 1963).

60 H. Frankfort, *The Art and Architecture of the Ancient Orient* (rev. ed. Pelican, 1970).

61 K. Branigan, *Aegean Metalwork of the Early and Middle Bronze Age* (Oxford Univ. Press, 1974).

PAINTERS AND PAINTING

62 Ernst Buschor, *Greek Vase-Painting* (Chatto and Windus, 1921; rpt. 1971).

63 E. Pfuhl, *Masterpieces of Greek Drawing and Painting,* trans.
    J. D. Beazley (Macmillan, 1955).

64 J. D. Beazley, *Attic Black-Figure Vase-Painters* (Oxford Univ.
    Press, 1956).

65 J. D. Beazley, *Attic Red-Figure Vase-Painters,* 3 vols. (Oxford
    Univ. Press, 1963).

66 Arthur Lane, *Greek Pottery* (Faber and Faber, 1948).

Arthur Lane's small book is companionable, though rich in the details
of an educated discipline. The others are technical in effect and perhaps
dated. A study which seems to be dated, however, may in the long run
turn out to be less dated than some of its immediate followers, which
may have had a modish success of their own for a brief period of time.

As for these introductions to vase-painting, the most cherished of the
arts that have survived the destructive centuries, the first was prefaced
by the numismatist Percy Gardner, who eloquently pleads the case for
the unsurpassed beauty and community of feelings which the Greeks
attained in this art and, I might add, in related arts in these exceptional
centuries, including the art of numismatics itself.

GREEK SCULPTORS AND SCULPTURES

In presenting free-standing figures and figures in deep relief, Greek
sculpture does not resolve itself into outlines as simple as those which
describe vase painting. Notable is the fact that after a sequence of
centuries archaic sculpture with its well-known features—the celebrated smile, the asymmetric foot position, and in reliefs the incongru-
ous torso and profile alignments—gave way in the classical period to
attempts at physical naturalism along with documentary details.
Among the results there arrived eventually the famous portrait statues,
the quality of which is revealed in the copies in the form of the busts of
the dramatists and philosophers that have survived. These are not
examples of great art. The helmeted Pericles, for example, is a dull
exploitation of the archaic Athena portrait on the coins. The full exploitation of this unhappy narrative portrait art was left mercifully for the
Romans to make the most of.

In the Asiatic area certain restraints held the storytelling classical
"ideal" in check, with the result that the colossal Mausolus of

Halicarnassus has dignity as a portrait of a human being and the Demeter of Cnidus as the figure of a goddess. Both are now in the British Museum, thanks to the resourcefulness of Sir Charles Newton. East Aegean portrait coins are equally self-contained, equally striking at the small end of a scale set by the colossal marbles.

67 G.M.A. Richter, *The Sculpture and Sculptors of the Greeks* (Yale Univ. Press, 1970).

For archaic standing figures see fig. 20ff., male kouroi, and fig. 144ff., female korai; archaic relief, fig. 519, grave stele of an athlete; Mausolus, fig. 330, and Demeter, fig. 331.

68 ————, *Kouroi* (Phaidon, 1960).

69 ————, *Korai* (Phaidon, 1968).

The urge toward storytelling took an irreversible hold on the imagination of the Hellenes, and the Laocoon was its unsavory fruit. With so many inconsistencies in the Greek tradition, books on sculpture have been obviously hard to write, and my list, I am afraid, must reflect this fact. The late Gisela M. A. Richter herself, in spite of her profound knowledge of sculpture, confesses to the unsettled state of affairs by trying painfully to balance the traditional praise of the Laocoon group against modern misgivings (see item 67 above). There is a somewhat similar conflict between the realistic anatomical emphasis which Miss Richter belabored in the interest of setting dates for the kouroi and the korai, and their triumphant stylized beauty as great archaic figures. Much more objective, in my opinion, and more richly informative is her study of archaic gravestones; and this besides, is one of the later works which are illustrated with the fine black-and-white photography of Alison Frantz:

70 G.M.A. Richter, *The Archaic Gravestones of Attica* (Phaidon, 1961).

71 Ernst Buschor, *Altsamische Standbilder,* vols. 1–5 (Berlin, 1934–61).

This five-part trophy erected by the leader in the archaeological conquest of Samos demonstrates for sculpture something that he and his colleagues had discovered was true for architecture. The Samians were the first, the greatest of innovators.

In 1965, in connection with the art of the Ionians, I had occasion to object to certain articles in the *McGraw-Hill Encyclopedia of World*

Art, including Professor R. M. Cook's "Greek Art, Eastern," (1963). I shall repeat the gist of my remarks here, mainly in the spirit of caveat emptor, but also in acknowledgment of a widely held aesthetic point of view which differs profoundly from my own. Professor R. M. Cook's concern is with the tall Ionian goddesses or their attendants whose figures have reminded some eager observers of "tree-trunks," of whom the Hera of Cheramyes in the Louvre is one example and, on the other hand, with the impressively clothed Asiatic dignitaries, of whom the Lydian gentleman in the Vathy museum is a fine example:

What troubles Professor Cook is the "neglect of the structure of the human body" and the preference for "the sleek undulations of fat and tricky folds of clothing" which he sees in the work of the Eastern sculptors, while in the same decades the mainland Greeks were concentrating, so much more sensitively, "on the anatomy of bone and muscle," which is to say, on naturalism. . . .

Sentiments of distaste like these seldom come out so strongly in the columns of an article in an imposing encyclopedia, nor, as I happen to think, with quite so much banality (*Sewanee Review,* 73 [1965], p. 510).

It is pertinent to add that the Samian Hera, in the opinion of the curator, the late Jean Charbonneaux, was "one of the most beautiful marbles in the Louvre," a museum which has always been well aware of its ownership of the Venus of Milo and the Victory of Samothrace.

72 Sheila Adam, *The Technique of Greek Sculpture in the Archaic and Classical Periods* (Thames and Hudson, 1966).

Often a precise study of the way a thing is done, such as the one listed above, tells more about the accomplishment than a lengthy discussion, with its inescapable subjectivity, of the thing itself. In item 72 we follow the marble from the quarry, step by step, to a finished statue, noting on route the variety of tools and techniques that have gone hand in hand with changes in emphasis and artistic taste. The result is an enlarged sense of appreciation of the Acropolis korai—Number 682 in particular (p. 73 in item 69 above)—at one end of the time span, and at the other end, the Mausolus of Halicarnassus, with, in the form of an appendix, a supremely interesting discussion of Praxiteles. To me it is a fact of some interest too that the sculptor of the early Athenian kore is as much engrossed in Professor Cook's "tricky folds" in the Ionic costume as was the creator of the much later Mausolus. Since

Sheila Adam wrote on the practices of the sculptors with the counsels of Professor Cook in mind, we may assume that verbal expressions on matters of taste are probably always much more complex than they may sound to the ear. With doubts as to its rhetoric, I suggest the value of a compact, learned, and wholly conventional work:

73 Robert M. Cook, *Greek Art: Its Development, Character, and Influence* (Weidenfeld and Nicolson, 1972).

SCULPTORS AND SCULPTURE: MAGNA GRAECIA

The Attica-oriented point of view has dominated the modern imagination so completely that Magna Graecia exists in a shadow nearly as thick as the one the Athenians sought to create in their desire to obliterate Thebes. The obscurity which presently covers the West exists in spite of Pindar and Aeschylus and Plato, in spite of the well-attested triumphs in philosophy and the more vaguely recorded triumphs in science, in spite of Heraclean archaeological monuments. There is a staggering need for rudimentary insight into the workings of the west Greek mind. Two treatises, mainly on sculpture and the related arts, present points of distinction which begin to bring vague impressions into a sharper focus. The first is a handsome, well-documented folio. The second concentrates closely on observable traits which differentiate the art of the rich outposts from that of the homeland, revealing in special the small massivenesses of the coroplast's expression. The fuller, more rounded shapes that seem to mold themselves decisively in terracotta carry over naturally into the local limestone, while marble, since it was not available from local sources, was not present in sufficient quantities to create intensely nervous images in the sculptor's mind, such as those which had excited the artist elsewhere. The decisiveness with which the Italiote sculptors utilized their resources carries over visibly into architecture, it seems to me, and would inevitably be conducive to the development of empirical sciences.

74 E. Langlotz, *The Art of Magna Graecia: Greek Art in Southern Italy and Sicily* (Thames and Hudson, 1965).

75 R. Ross Holloway, *Influences and Styles in the Late Archaic and Early Classical Greek Sculpture of Sicily and Magna*

Graecia (Institut Supérieur d'Archéologie et d'Histoire de l'Art, 1975).

Several curious features which mark the art of Magna Graecia include an extraordinarily bold use of stylization in the treatment of archaic subjects: both Europa and the bull assume an extremely archaic posture in the metope relief from Selinus (item 74, pl. 8; item 23, pl. 11) and in the pairs of running girls shown in relief on sandstone, from a treasury in the Heraion at Paestum (see chapter 5, fig. 11, p. 184. A lively Ionic charm is evident in these figures: the source of the style is made certain by the use of egg-and-dart decorative borders. On the other hand, the coins of the same area in the same period, while persisting in intensely archaic stylization, are unusual for their delicate workmanship and powerful presentations of mythical subject matter: on a stater from Croton, for example, a tall Apollo shoots a lofty, upreared python through the opening between the legs of an even loftier tripod (item 112, pl. 472).

Much is left along the ancient coasts of Magna Graecia for study in the future, and that which lies at the heart of it seems to be Ionian. Miletus went into public mourning when Sybaris fell in 510 B.C. to the men of Croton, says Herodotus, adding that within his knowledge no two cities were ever so close as Miletus and Sybaris: "The Sybarites did nothing after the Athenian manner" (item 1: 6. 21; also item 6: 519B, C).

IV ARCHAEOLOGY

Like mythology, archaeology does not lend itself to general books of great interest. An exception is probably the following, though I think it barely suggests the sense of fine discriminations that agitate the spirit of the person who is in the act of scanning an object from which the dust of several millennia has just been brushed away, or the overpowering lust of a Heinrich Schliemann in the act of cutting away a copper barrier with his own knife in order to get at the golden treasure of Priam in a tunnel under ancient Troy's crumbling fortifications; alone, down under the earth, before breakfast.

76 Paul MacKendrick, *The Greek Stones Speak* (Mentor, 1962).

The opposite extreme is the two volume collection of interesting short passages, following a hundred pages of admirable introductory discussion, taken from a wealth of fine archaeological field reports, which incidentally includes the passage from Schliemann's *Ilios* which I paraphrased above:

77 Jacquetta Hawkes, *The World of the Past,* 2 vols. (Knopf, 1963).

The publication of important individual achievements in the field is another matter, and the number of distinguished volumes is unlimited. Without pursuing a return to Schliemann, I shall mention only a few. The first by the excavator of Ephesus is remarkable for the courageous inferences that the scholarly scientist drew from the evidence which the digging had turned up:

78 D. G. Hogarth, *Ionia and the East* (Oxford Univ. Press, 1909).

The second, a publication by many hands, appeared between 1910 and 1926:

79 *Sardis* (American Society for the Excavation of Sardis, 1910–26).

A survey of recent work by Harvard archaeologists on the site at Sardis provides the stimulus for

80 J. G. Pedley, *Sardis in the Age of Croesus* (Univ. of Oklahoma Press, 1968).

This study has the merit of seeing history in all of its cultural forms, just as plainly as an architectural pattern, in a conglomerate collection of stones as the reward for archaeologists, though unfortunately the tone of this presentation of some extremely fine research into the arts of ancient Lydia is unremittingly academic and dull.

The older *Sardis* (item 79) belonged to the severe tradition of exhaustive archaeological reporting, to which has recently been added the monumental publication of a site which on the surface of things was not overly interesting:

81 Karl Lehmann and Associates, *Samothrace,* 8 vols. (Pantheon, 1958–69).

These studies present the archaeological discipline at its best. Regardless of the unimpressive character of Samothrace in comparison with Sardis or with Samos, the schooling which the personal devotion of the late Karl Lehmann, and that of his wife Phyllis Lehmann, made available to a young staff of assistants is proving to be of great immediate importance: the excavations at Cnidus are going forward under the direction of Iris Cornelia Love, who, with some of her fellows, learned the delicate art of extracting the frailest of objects, large and small, from tons of earth in the halls of the great gods of Samothrace.

For the future the findings at Samothrace may become a basis for a comprehensive review of one of the most powerful cults in all of Greece, the cult of Persephone, which appears to have carried its black chthonic luminosity from the Triopian headland outwards in all directions, including Magna Graecia (see item 31, Pin., *Nem.* 1. 13; item 22, Dunb., p. 64). At a fairly late date the cult, or something closely akin to it, began attracting spectacular multitudes of pilgrims to Samothrace: one wonders exactly what its magic was, whether it was the response to an imbedded irrational trait in all Greeks or whether it was a new craving for the decadent heroic festivities that seem to have been a part of Hellenistic imperialism (see item 28, Tarn, p. 316). Whatever the impetus, the chilling awesomeness of the Persephone-Hecate deity at Samothrace is counterbalanced by the warm sensuousness of the Persephone-Aphrodite goddess at Locri.

SPECIAL STUDIES BASED ON ARCHAEOLOGY

J. M. Cook: item 20 above.

82 J. M. Cook, "Greek Archaeology in Western Asia Minor," *Archaeological Reports for 1959–60* (SPHS, 1960).

83 J. M. Cook and D. J. Blackman, *Archaeology in Western Asia Minor 1970–71* (SPHS, 1971).

84 W. Leaf, *Strabo on the Troad* (Cambridge Univ. Press, 1923).

85 George E. Bean, *Turkey Beyond the Maeander: An Archaeological Guide* (Rowman and Littlefield, 1971).

The last of the titles above deals in acute detail and in splendid clarity with Iasus, Bodrum, and Cnidus, but because of the concentration on the early development of Caria, Miletus and Didyma and Priene unfortunately fall by the wayside.

For Asia Minor in general the annual reports of Machteld Mellink in the *American Journal of Archaeology* are especially to be noted.

The title of the following is ample to identify a first-rate brief survey:

86 Margaret Guido, *Sicily: An Archaeological Guide* (Faber, 1967).

87 ———, *Southern Italy: An Archaeological Guide* (Faber, 1972).

In contrast, an intensive, lavishly illustrated, completely expert guide:

88 S. Moscati and M. Napoli, *Civiltà sul Mediterraneo* (Instituto Geographico de Agostini, 1971).

Among many articles in archaeological journals, one recent comprehensive survey brings surprising information concerning the extent of activities now going on in Magna Graecia and the abundance of new discoveries of Greek-native interpenetrations, which demand a reassessment of common assumptions and at the same time suggest motives for explosive events such as the sudden disappearance of Siris:

89 A. D. Trendall, "Archaeology in South Italy and Sicily, 1970–72," *Archaeological Reports for 1972–73* (SPHS, 1973).

Especially remarkable in this account is the number of projects that the Italians themselves have undertaken. Men and women and institutions are not enervated by economic confusion and political uneasiness: they continue to press home their superior archaeological skills. In the midst of wars the French have become mathematicians once again; the Germans, when denied the field by hostilities, have stayed at home and made new translations of Euripides; when troubled, the Italians seem to scatter to the ancient fields and start digging. *Laborare est orare*.

The opulent city of Sybaris has been the subject of several recent archaeological detective stories in *Museum*, a publication of the Museum of the University of Pennsylvania. The most recent,

90 O. C. Colburn, "A Return to Sybaris," *Museum* (1976),

is particularly incisive in its approach to a dismally obscure page in the history of Magna Graecia. The story is no longer just a detective story: having found Sybaris, the author and his colleagues found some of the furniture of Sybaris, which enlarges the sketchy picture of a unique western Greek civilization.

V ARCHITECTURE

91 Vitruvius, *On Architecture*, 2 vols. (Loeb, 1962).

92 Vitruvius, *The Ten Books on Architecture*, trans. M. H. Morgan (Dover, 1960).

93 Vitruve, *De l'Architecture, Livre IX,* ed. Jean Soubiran (Budé, 1969).

94 H. Plommer, *Vitruvius and Later Roman Building Manuals* (Cambridge Univ. Press, 1973).

According to Vitruvius (7. Pref. 12) architecture appears to have been that art which called forth more treatises in early times than any other, including the Hippocratic arts of medicine. Books by architects started appearing, Vitruvius says, with Theodorus of Samos, and proliferated thereafter. This would substantiate the claim of Pytheos, builder of Priene and author of one of the many lost treatises: architecture is the sovereign art. Architecture produces that remarkable facility in which the statues, the painted vases, the votive objects in bronze, or ivory or gold, are cared for; the tabernacle of the image and the backdrop for the dance and the choric recitals, the home of the festivals. Architecture also sets forth the principles for laying out cities and setting up domestic and public establishments, so that they will be correctly positioned for protection against the day-to-day foibles of the weather and the enduring patterns of the seasons. The towns will be planned for healthfulness and convenience, having control over drinking water and sewers, the marketplace and croplands, pastures and fisheries, and the harbors for seagoing commerce. They will be strong if attacked. The assembling of these requisites requires the architect to deal pragmatically with the sum total of natural phenomena, say Vitruvius-Pytheos, and this requires him to be conversant with all knowledge, from the eternal laws of astronomy to the obscure biology of what we in our lingo call protozoa.

Though it is hard to imagine, in *The Ten Books* Vitruvius is in hot pursuit page by page of the fulfillment of this ideal. The learning of Vitruvius is enormous, partly second-hand though, as is to be expected. It is concrete, therefore it may be ready for practical application; it is speculative and well informed, therefore challenging in a Hellenic way to the imagination. The two final titles above (items 93 and 94) annotate these matters of learning for certain sections of the treatise. The second includes an effective introduction showing the Roman reliance on Vitruvius for, for example, the particulars of building aqueducts that would respect the hydraulic demands of the system and the health of those for whom it was designed. For conveying drinking water, lead pipes must be avoided: "Leadworkers even look unhealthy, plumbers are deformed." Hardest to imagine is a man with a genius resembling that of Archimedes remaining always so consistently pedestrian. Perhaps he is most perfectly a representative of his times and of the genius of the Roman Empire.

MODERN HISTORIES OF GREEK ARCHITECTURE

Ancient architecture worked with a wider and more exact range of empiric data than the other practical arts. This fact probably accounts for the large number of indisputably fine texts that are at hand:

95 William B. Dinsmoor, *The Architecture of Ancient Greece* (1950; rpt., Biblo and Tannen, 1973).

96 D. S. Robertson, *Greek and Roman Architecture* (Cambridge Univ. Press, 1969).

97 A. W. Lawrence, *Greek Architecture* (Penguin, 1962).

98 Helmut Berve; Gottfried Gruben; Max Hirmer, *Greek Temples, Theatres and Shrines* (H. N. Abrams, 1963).

After books of the high quality of the first three of these, it is unfair to pronounce the last, item 98, superb. But while the others are its equal in the development of detail, the last is closer to archaeology, to the work of the builders, to the landscape itself. To these tangibles the photography of Max Hirmer contributes a full share, as it has contributed to other books, including item 74 above.

ARCHITECTURE: SPECIAL APPLICATIONS

99 Birgitta Bergquist, *The Archaic Greek Temenos* (Gleerup, 1967). This text is written in a technical jargon which I find unreadable; enough data, however, is decipherable to make the drawings of the temple enclosures add up to an exciting display of a coherent architectural convention.

For brilliant and quite credible reconstructions of the arrangement of buildings on some famous sites, mainly those occupied by temples, see:

100 C. A. Doxiadis, *Architectural Space in Ancient Greece* (1937; MIT Press, 1972).

Of particular interest in the context of the present book are the studies of the Samian Heraion, Priene, and the great seaport city of Miletus.

The following extends some very thorough architectural investigations at Chios to many aspects of the history of the eastern Greeks:

101 J. Boardman, "Chian and Early Ionic Architecture," *Antiquaries' Journal*, 39 (1959), pp. 170–218 (with 35 plates).

Three modern books are expert examinations of the basics in a subject which, to our great misfortune, still remains largely in the Limbo of Ignorance and Perversity:

102 F. Castagnoli, *Orthogonal City Planning in Antiquity* (1956; MIT Press, 1971).

103 Paul Lampl, *Cities and Planning in the Ancient Near East* (Braziller, 1968).

104 J. B. Ward-Perkins, *Cities of Ancient Greece and Italy: Planning in Classical Antiquity* (Braziller, 1974).

And for the most instructive aspect of any art, techniques and materials have a priority all their own:

105 A. Orlandos, *Les Matériaux de Construction et la Technique Architecturale des Anciens Grecs*, 2 vols. (Paris, 1966, 1968).

VI NUMISMATICS

Since temples and coins are the great and the small among the visible survivals of material things from ancient Greece, it happened not unreasonably that early in the modern Renaissance, when Hellenism acquired its new vigor, the first striking production was, in fact, a book on temples and coins:

106 Thomas L. Donaldson, *Architectura Numismatica* (1859; reissued with supplementary materials under the title *Ancient Architecture on Greek and Roman Coins and Medals*, Argonaut, 1966).

Architectura Numismatica is the work of a man who had been a premier architect in London. As a traveling archaeological explorer, a forerunner of the great Sir Charles Newton (cf. item 67 above), he had stopped in his circuit of the Mediterranean to draw the first accurate groundplans of ancient structures at Olympia, Halicarnassus, Ephesus, and elsewhere. His observations led him to study ninety-two coins depicting temples and similar monuments. To his carefully engraved copies of the coins, he added vigorous commentary. His genius for combining the image on a coin with his sketches of actual ruins leads us straight to the sovereign injunction of archaeology: let the hand and the mind work together as if they were one.

From the year 1883:

107 Percy Gardner, *The Types of Greek Coins* (1883; reissued with title *Archaeology and the Types of Greek Coins,* Argonaut, 1965).

Margaret Thompson, in the introduction to the new issue, makes the point which is most pertinent to our own concerns: "The avowed purpose of Gardner's essay was to provide a kind of numismatic textbook. . . . He could not have foreseen that archaeology and numismatics were destined to establish their closest relationship not in the lecture hall but in the field." She adds this sagacious advice: "Gardner's chronology is not as outmoded as one might expect." Though refinements are being busily argued in and out of the time charts, no one has presumed really to redraw the basic calendar.

As for architecture, so for sculpture. Supporting documentation, sometimes unique documentation, for the exact appearance of a statue is often based on an image stamped on a coin:

108 F. W. Imhoof-Blumer and Percy Gardner, *Ancient Coins Illustrating Lost Masterpieces of Greek Art: A Numismatic Commentary on Pausanias* (*Journal of Hellenic Studies* 1885–86–87; enlarged and reprinted, ed. Al. N. Oikonomides, Argonaut, 1964).

For our purposes, we must begin with a coin from Miletus and a coin from Cnidus, both illustrated in item 107 above, to gather an impression of what the celebrated Apollo of Canachus at Didyma and the Aphrodite of Praxiteles looked like.

For a much later parallel with these pioneering books on numismatics, the reader should see a brilliant compact volume:

109 J. G. Milne, *Greek and Roman Coins and the Study of History* (1939; rpt. Greenwood Press, 1971).

A coin is a badge of a city. In one way or another each good coin tells as much as it can in symbolic fashion about the people and the place represented. Hence the stirring impression made by the several hundred superb photographs, supported by an array of grand enlargements and informative commentary in the following collection:

110 Norman Davis, *Greek Coins and Cities* (from the museum collection, Seattle Art Museum, 1967).

These are two of the most reliable and inclusive handbooks on Greek coins:

111 Charles Seltman, *Greek Coins: A History of Metallic Currency and Coinage down to the Fall of the Hellenistic Kingdoms* (London, 1933; 2nd. ed. Methuen, 1955).

112 G. Kenneth Jenkins, *Ancient Greek Coins* (Putnam, 1972).

The first of these standard works is a high-spirited, well-documented, modestly produced volume; the second is thoroughly academic and richly produced. The first is the work of an adventurous student of many aspects of ancient culture; the second is by the Keeper of the Department of Coins and Medals in the British Museum.

Of particular significance for several of the chapters which come together to form this book, two items are outstanding:

113 John P. Barron, *The Silver Coins of Samos* (Athlone, 1966).

114 G. L. Cawkwell, "A Note on the Heracles Coinage Alliance of 394 B.C.": *Numismatic Chronicle* 16 (1956), 69–75.

Both authors are extremely alert to the historical framework for the coinage. J. P. Barron is generously informative about a long, complex series of events in which Samos found itself centered during the era when it was free to operate its own mints.

VII SCIENCE: GENERAL

The standard gathering from ancient scientific writings,

115 M. R. Cohen and I. E. Drabkin, *A Source Book in Greek Science* (Harvard Univ. Press, 1958),

remains a convenient introductory survey of a great variety of subjects.

Fairly brief but quite adequate accounts, with the inevitable dubious passage cropping up here and there, are readily available:

116 Marshall Clagett, *Greek Science in Antiquity* (Abelard–Schuman, 1957).

117 Giorgio de Santillana, *The Origins of Scientific Thought* (Mentor, 1961).

118 B. Farrington, *Greek Science,* 2 vols. (Penguin, 1944–49).

The highly individual, detailed, and enormously inclusive learning of George Sarton enlivens each of some six hundred pages of unconscionably small print in a Norton paperback:

119 G. Sarton, *A History of Science: Ancient Science Through the Golden Age of Greece* (1952; rpt. Norton, 1970).

VIII   MATHEMATICS

120 *Greek Mathematics,* ed. I. Thomas, 2 vols. (Loeb, 1939–41).

These "selections illustrating the history of Greek Mathematics" are especially useful for the display of the Greek texts treating many of the ancient cruxes, the "Duplication of the Cube," for an obvious example, and for one less obvious, Hero of Alexandria's method of approximating the cube root of a number, which probably reflects an arithmetical study of the duplication problem. The editor has attached some unusually serviceable notes to this Loeb volume.

121 *Archimède,* ed. Charles Mugler, 4 vols. (Budé, 1970–72).

122 Archimedes, *Works,* with *The Method of Archimedes,* ed. Thomas Heath, with introductory chapters (1897, 1912; rpt. Dover).

Although ancient texts do not come readily to hand, the number of critical histories of mathematics is exceptionally large, and they are distinguished as a whole by their excellent quality.

123 Thomas Heath, *A History of Greek Mathematics,* 2 vols. (Oxford Univ. Press, 1921).

124 ———, *Greek Mathematics* (Dover, 1963).

Of these item 124 is a shortened version of the preceding classic, a classic, however, with a flaw: Sir Thomas avoided overburdening himself with problems of chronology and biography. The prominence of a text such as Euclid's *Elements* causes the great ship *Mathematica* to list dangerously, until an Apollonius of Perga comes aboard to make it list the other way. Meanwhile any individual mathematician, any

Eudoxus of Cnidus, appears and disappears as if he had nothing much to do with the whole thing.

125 D. E. Smith, *History of Mathematics,* 2 vols. (1923; Dover, 1958).

126 Ettore Carruccio, *Mathematics and Logic in History and in Contemporary Thought* (Aldine, 1965).

127 M. Kline, *Mathematical Thought from Ancient to Modern Times* (Oxford Univ. Press, 1972).

128 Nicolas Bourbaki, *Eléments d'Histoire des Mathématiques* (Paris, 1969).

Each of the four studies, in the order given above, covers the long history of Western mathematics, and each shows increasing concern with the philosophic burden that the mathematician finds he must submit to. Each comes to an end in its own sort of perplexity, and the better the book, it seems, the greater the perplexity.

The geometricians, though they seem to have tried instinctively to skirt philosophic dilemmas, encountered grave troubles from the beginning, which the labors of Euclid concealed but did not cure:

129 Euclid, *The Elements: The Thirteen Books of Euclid's Elements,* ed. T. Heath, translated from the text of Heiberg, with introduction and commentary, 3 vols. (Dover, 1956).

While I believe it is true that Eudoxus tamed the Irrationals so that Euclid could proceed comfortably in one field; nevertheless, anxieties about axioms and postulates, and finally about the nature of space itself, haunted the imaginations of all who became interested, and led eventually to the revolutionary reconsiderations with which we are gradually becoming fairly well acquainted.

The Heiberg text of Euclid with the commentaries which Heath assembled, is one of the superb acquisitions of modern times. The recent translation of Proclus enriches these documents still further:

130 Proclus, *A Commentary on the First Book of Euclid's Elements,* trans. with introd. by Glenn R. Morrow (Princeton Univ. Press, 1970).

Geometry, the only paramour among the sciences that Plato acknowledged in public, has received an impressive register of tributes from mathematicians of all ages, and most eloquently from those of

modern times, beginning perhaps, so far as articulate discussion becomes evident, with the arguments of such opposite numbers as René
Descartes and Thomas Hobbes, though Kepler's *Mysterium Cosmographicum* (1596) is not so much a treatise on the new Copernican
astronomy as on the astronomical precepts which still seemed to be
harvestable in the old field of Pythagorean geometry.

From our point of view, the need for a coherent account of the ancient interplay of geometry with mathematical and astronomical thinking is served especially well by two books:

131 Paul-Henri Michel, *De Pythagore à Euclide* (Paris, 1950).

132 François Lasserre, *The Birth of Mathematics in the Age of Plato*
     (American Research Council, 1964).

And in view of the steady advance of new forms of geometrical
conceptions in contemporary efforts to understand the ways of the
universe, the biographical chapters in the following collection are
fascinating:

133 E. T. Bell, *Men of Mathematics* (Simon and Schuster, 1937).

It is truly a fact that having some sense of a man named Lobatchevsky
or another man named Riemann helps to bring a subject matter which
is otherwise discouragingly abstruse to a threshold where the mind
does its first act of recognition. By the force of deep habit we say to
ourselves: ''All *that* he overwent; so also may I.''

For me mathematics is like an immortal family of related cogitations, which the mathematicians have begotten one by one, each cogi-
tation upon the body of another; so that the wonder is, that for this
immortal family, the begetters are all mortal. If from mortals come
immortal offspring, then something has happened which exceeds the
reasonable expectations of any human being. I hope this concept is not
treacherously mystical; not too close to Plato. That it is a Pythagorean
concept, I gladly acknowledge.

To the best of my knowledge mathematical intuitions are not a
function of the individual personality, not of the discrete being that
has his own infinite set of vital statistics, but of forces which he still
shares with his ancestors and has acquired through familarity with the
intuitions of others by a form of mental imitation. In any event a mood
which suggests something of this sort about the mathematical intellectual life seems to have pervaded the minds of a group of relatively

younger French mathematicians known as the "Bourbaki School." The central members of this large group have published a collection of essays which are highly varied in their content and yet are thematically, or philosophically, closely related: this fact in itself, I believe, is warrant enough of the unparalleled originality of the Bourbaki people:

134 *Great Currents of Mathematical Thought,* 2 vols., ed. F. Le Lionnais (1962; rpt. Dover, 1971).

The essay in this book which encouraged me to write about "the family of related cogitations" as a premise for mathematical thinking, and in fact for any coherent sense of mathematical history, was particularly chapter 5, "Intuitive Approaches toward Some Vital Organs of Mathematics," by Georges Bouligand. But of equal interest running toward other objectives are many chapters, which certainly must include these: 2, N. Bourbaki, "The Architecture of Mathematics"; 50, J. Dieudonné, "Modern Axiomatic Methods and the Foundations of Mathematics"; 40, F. Le Lionnais, "Beauty in Mathematics"; and 43, "Architecture and the Mathematical Spirit" by the architect Le Courbusier. The impact, if only in emphasis and in tone, of this school may have bent the curvature of my own writing more than I am aware.

IX ASTRONOMY

Ancient astronomy has stimulated acrid controversy among the authors of modern books detailing its beginnings and development. Therefore I will undertake hardly more than to reiterate my faith in the work of Sir Thomas Heath:

135 T. Heath, *Greek Astronomy* (1932; rpt. AMS Press, 1969).

136 T. Heath, *Aristarchus of Samos* (1913; rpt. Oxford Univ. Press, 1959).

In the book under the general title, after an old-fashioned, reassuringly level-headed introduction, Heath reprints in translation a collection of passages which ancient scholars are reported to have left in the record or, as in the case of Aristotle, have actually done so, in which they express their astronomical theories. Though much of this material is available in fuller contexts, the collection is a convenience, and in certain instances provides a text which is not easy to bring to hand. An example is the criticism which Hipparchus directs toward Aratus of Soli, author of the metrical version of the *Phaenomena*. Hipparchus proves the fact that Eudoxus of Cnidus wrote the account of the heavens which Aratus transformed into epic meter: "Eudoxus gives the same collection of phenomena as Aratus, but he has set them forth with greater knowledge" (p. 117).

In the Alexandrine period Aristarchus of Samos declared himself in favor of a heliocentric hypothesis for the relation of the earth and the planets to the sun. Copernicus was aware of this, so had been Archimedes, a slightly younger contemporary of Aristarchus. There can be no doubt about the singular genius of the Samian. Beside his originality in regard to a sun-centered system, his powers are evident in other calculations, chief of which are his determinations of sizes and distances as they relate to the heavenly bodies. Even Archimedes was not quite capable of handling the notion first propounded by Aristarchus that distances describing the size of the cosmos are *incomparable* with any truly definable physical distance: item 136, pp. 302, 309. This early editorial masterpiece of Heath's is introduced by a long, detailed survey of Greek astronomy, most of which by now has become fairly commonplace among people of learning. There is nothing much in it that has been drastically revised, including the probably fallacious reading of Eudoxus which makes him not so much a Pythagorean geometrician as the proponent of the incredible physics of Aristotle's concentric crystalline spheres as the vehicles for the heavenly bodies. This is a relatively small misfortune.

In importance far beyond any still existing ancient astronomical recitals, is the *Phaenomena* of Eudoxus as versified by Aratus:

137 Aratus of Soli, *The Phaenomena*, ed. and trans. G. R. Mair
      (Loeb, no. 129, with Callimachus, *Hymns*, 1921).

On the basis of Hipparchus's assertion that Aratus went wrong in transcribing Eudoxus only because the poet failed "to make any observations on his own account," we have gained two assurances: one, celestial observations were primary requisites; and two, Aratus, though neglecting the observatory, was following Eudoxus to the best of his ability. This combination of facts gives security to the proposition that early Greek astronomy is to be read at its richest in Aratus-Eudoxus, which looks still farther back toward the observatories of Egypt, where Eudoxus was trained, and *not toward the horoscopic tablets* in the archives of Babylonia.

A theory that Aratus smuggled the doctrines of the Stoics into the poem has made a small uproar:

138 J. Martin, *Histoire du Texte des Phénomènes* (Paris, 1956).

139 Manfred Erren, *Die Phainomena des Aratos von Soli* (F. Steiner, 1967).

Although both of these learned studies cover many textual matters of great interest, I do not find much to support a theory of Stoical teachings having been incorporated in the poem, nor, for that matter, much to support a good many readings favored by the second, item 139. The poem, it is true, does begin with a fine hymn to Zeus. In the prelude and in several individual lines—in the ending of the period on the Altar, for instance (see chap. 6)—the first of the gods is handled with dignity. However, since Zeus figures universally in myth making, and is always, tacitly or directly, toward the center of the stage, as is shown by the coins of many cities, the coincidence with Stoicism seems hardly to be of consequence.

Of greater consequence is the fact that the sky-immortals and their myths range freely in and out of the ancient descriptions of the constellations. The myths, as told in the *Phaenomena,* are arresting, brief narratives; they seem to take on no pattern of philosophic doctrine, but they do present a challenge to the reader to put the meaningful old names of the constellations into a context of mythological narratives.

140 R. H. Allen, *Star Names: Their Lore and Meaning* (1899; rpt. Dover, 1963).

X   MEDICINE

The history of early medicine is in a more fragmentary state than are the histories of the other arts and sciences. A rough equivalent to the central Hippocratic corpus of medical writings is far from inaccessible, since it is included in the Loeb Library:

141 Hippocrates, 4 vols. (Loeb, 1923–1931): W.H.S. Jones, ed. and trans., vols. 1, 2 and 4; E. T. Withington, vol. 3.

The Introductions by W.H.S. Jones, dating from 1923, were innovative in their time, and their general arguments, though not profound, are by no means outmoded. On the other hand Littré's monumental scholarly edition of Hippocrates, while accessible and in demand, is proving to be not so secure in its preferences among manuscripts as has been assumed.

These are not the defeating obstacles, however. What is wanting, it seems to me, is a more assured account of the materials which are at hand. The search for the authoritative individual manuscript on which to build a text is quixotic, because the "Hippocratic" text is the product of a fluid tradition, not of one known author, such as Herodotus. On the contrary, the search for a consensus among texts may be as much as should be expected, and it, in several groupings of documents, is already discernible. The question is, what can we make out of what we already know?

The question is the same as the question which is crucial to the understanding of all of the arts and sciences. What is their origin? If we know the why, the how, and the where, a discipline originated, we know something important about the discipline. If its origins rest on the practice of voodoo or semimagic, science is not in the offing, but if on physical theory, even fantastic physical theory, science has begun to take hold.

These principles emerge clearly in the preliminary chapters of a modest new book—240 pages with fifteen anemic illustrations—which is also a splendidly informed, totally exceptional, completely readable book:

142 E. D. Phillips, *Greek Medicine* (Thames and Hudson, 1973).

The precision with which Phillips summarizes the scattered facts gathered by research into the origins and the development of medicine is elegant; but the situation, as the author himself affirms, remains vague on the question of an exact theory of origins.

The physician in Mesopotamia, though given to attaching sets of numbers to medical oddities, in practice was a shaman wrestling with demons. In Egypt, his tradition was to administer purges; this therapy goes back to misty times, preceding the coming of the Greeks, and to a society about which I feel wholly ignorant. In any event the Egyptian theory was apparently a conviction holding that in order to keep the body in balance, superfluities that build up should be periodically purged away. The Cnidians adopted, fairly systematically, at some unknown early date, the Egyptian theory. Here again is evidence that, as has been observed frequently in this book (see, e.g., Rodopis and Charaxus in chap. 3), exchanges between Egypt and the Aegean area were everyday occurrences.

Since difficulty with origins also plagues the historian of mathematics and astronomy and, more or less, all of Ionian science, it seems that intensive research into the connections of Greek medical science with the contents of the Egyptian papyri would be likely to yield answers where answers are needed most. Medicine is concerned with a subject which submits automatically to empirical observations. Temperatures can be felt, breathing and heartbeats observed, processes recorded. Medicine, the clinical subject that it is, cannot be so elusive as astronomy or mathematics. Admittedly the medical papyri are difficult to read, even literally; even harder doubtless to surround with enough of a context of applicable knowledge to make them understandable. But if they could be read beside the Greek medical notebooks and understood, the world might be made much richer in its comprehension of many aspects of antiquity.

Courageous initial progress toward this end can be seen by anyone who is willing to track down a few handsome but obscure small publications:

143 R. O. Steur and J. B. Saunders, *Ancient Egyptian and Cnidian Medicine* (Univ. of California Press, 1959).

144 J. B. Saunders, *The Transitions from Ancient Egyptian to Greek Medicine* (Univ. of Kansas Press, 1963).

145 I. M. Lonie, "Cnidian Treatises of the *Corpus Hippocraticum*," *Classical Quarterly*, 15 (1965), pp. 1–35.

146 W.H.S. Jones, ed. *The Medical Writings of Anonymous Londinensis* (Cambridge Univ. Press, 1947). Note the two appended *Excursi*.

147 ———, *Philosophy and Medicine in Ancient Greece* (Johns Hopkins Univ. Press, 1946).

Finally there is the report of a recent international colloquy which surveys many diverse aspects of the subject:

148 *La Collection Hippocratique et son Rôle dans l'Histoire de la Médecine,* Colloque de Strasbourg (23–27 octobre 1972), Univ. of Strasbourg (Leiden, Brill, 1975).

In general this group of authorities leaned toward the view that the Cnidians were pressing hard toward an objective science, and therefore also the Crotoniates, while the Coans concentrated on the practicalities involved in handling various diseases. The distinction, however, appears to be of little consequence since in all important respects the schools, as discussed in the colloquy, overlapped one another both in theory and practice. It could hardly be otherwise, granting the mobility of the early Greeks: after all, except in the midst of a rare storm, the island of Cos is in plain sight to the west of Cnidus (see photograph in chap. 6), a matter of a few hours' sailing time with normal winds.

In the colloquy, M. Martiny does, however, associate one of the most spectacular advances in modern medical technique, auscultation, the use of a stethoscope itself, directly to the Hippocratic teachings of the School of Cnidus. The thesis which the great Laënnec defended in 1804 at the end of his training in the Medical School of Paris was entitled: "Propositions sur la doctrine d'Hippocrate, relativement à la médecine practique"; fifteen years later came his two-volume work on the importance of immediate auscultation, a treatise on the diagnostics of illnesses of the chest and heart. A new era had begun. It would be hard for any of us now to imagine a physician entering an examining room without a stethoscope dangling from his neck. For television it would be impossible.

XI PHILOSOPHY

With volume after volume of the materials required for the study of Greek philosophy conspicuously at hand, anyone would think that this cornerstone in our history would be secure, as that for the history of medicine certainly is not. But such is not the fact. Unfortunately the shocks and aftershocks of an explosive scholarship have created treacherous footing in this area. A dominant skepticism as to the intellectual stature of the pre-Socratics, or even their very existence, has been complemented by an openhearted faith in the activities of the Orphics or, if the Orphics are somewhat elusive, of shamans in general.

Commenting on this phenomenon, E. R. Dodds has said that he was "tempted to call it the unconscious projection upon the screen of antiquity of certain unsatisfied religious longings characteristic of the late nineteenth and early twentieth centuries" (item 47, p. 148). While the post-Darwinian spiritual unrest does suggest itself as an immediate cause, the inbred militancy of scholars, such as was displayed most openly in the Italian Renaissance, has doubtless given the compulsion toward controversy in and around Hellenism its great force (see Jacob Burckhardt, *The Civilization of the Renaissance in Italy* (Harper and Row, 1958), 2, 9.

For us the skirmishes are not too important, because in spite of them the documents for a history of philosophy have been put on the table, with exactly the distortions running through them that we should be prepared to expect. The bulk of the materials that are likely ever to be recovered have been gathered, edited, annotated, evaluated, indexed and cross-indexed, in one of the great publications of the modern academic world:

149 H. Diels and W. Kranz, *Die Fragmente der Vorsokratiker*, 3 vols. (Berlin, 1903, 1964).

To this enormously rich and complicated text, a pair of guidebooks that are designed for English readers with no knowledge of Greek supply translations of the principal fragments and under a separate cover an extensive paraphrase of the whole text together with pertinent secondary materials:

150 K. Freeman, *Ancilla to the Pre-Socratic Philosophers: A complete translation of the Fragments in Diels, "Fragmente der Vorsokratiker"* (Oxford Univ. Press, 1952).

151 K. Freeman, *The Pre-Socratic Philosophers: A Companion to Diels, "Fragmente der Vorsokratiker"* (Oxford Univ. Press, 1946).

In expounding so massive a collection of excellent philosophical debris, Kathleen Freeman was faithful, or as faithful as possible, to the work toward which she had directed herself. But therein lay a number of fateful choices, especially in the *Companion to Diels,* in matters of selection and emphasis. As the account stands, the emphasis at the beginning is on Orphism; it mounts toward decadent Pythagoreanism in the treatment awarded Philolaus and, or so I suspect, the later

Sophists. This does not misrepresent Diels. But it does represent Plato and Aristotle rising to full cry against the Ionians and their alter Ionians to the west.

The "unsatisfied religious longings" of the recent generations seem practically to have enthroned Plato and Aristotle as the ultimate adjudicators in matters of philosophic history, the first for his newly appreciated, persuasive otherworldliness; the second for his newly appreciated dominance in the religious traditions of the Middle Ages; and both for their overpowering institutional authority. Consequently, historians have usually oriented themselves at the beginning by taking their bearings from Plato or Aristotle or from both, in the case of Diels, whose purpose was to collect and not to select information: but whatever the purpose, the mass of the two great stars of antiquity has been an overwhelming attraction to the investigator who looks back.

The result is that the Ionians are seldom brought clearly into view; at best they are thought to be hidden somewhere in the turbulence of Academic and Peripatetic teaching. And in actuality, it is not the *Timaeus* with its dubious tangential raptures that bespeaks Plato's mind on the Ionian sciences, but rather the remark he puts in Socrates' mouth expressing disappointment in finding that Anaxagoras was concerned principally with "air, ether, water and *other eccentricities*" (*Phaedo* 98). From Aristotle we get capsules filled with a concentrate derived from a predominant principle, which he calls the *arche,* that he believes is promulgated by any typical Ionian philosopher. By setting the *arches* up—Water, the *apeiron,* Air, Fire, Number, etc.—as if they were absolutes, in no way pregnant figures of speech, not subject to modification and revision, Aristotle is able to demonstrate the superiority of his own construction over these crude Ionian building blocks. See:

152 H. Cherniss, *Aristotle's Criticism of Presocratic Philosophy* (1935; rpt. Octagon, 1964).

I am not denying the many excellences of Plato or the superiority of Aristotle's system over anything that exists in the poor fragments of the Ionians or the Italiote Greeks, although glimpses of something better may be caught in sentences remembered from Eudoxus or carefully marshalled into the pages of a Hippocratic treatise: I am convinced of the superiority of the Ionian method of working from observation rather than from hypothetical first principles. For the difference and for the quality of the achievement which was accomplished far from the schools of Attica, compare any coherent passage from

153 *Eudoxos von Knidos: Die Fragmente,* ed. with commentary, by François Lasserre (Berlin, 1966); and compare, e.g.,

154 *Airs Waters Places* in the Hippocratic writings, Loeb, vol. 1, 66–137.

with appropriate parallels in Aristotle's writings.

If obscure religious longings have distorted the picture of our own past history, of our own very personal spiritual ancestry, I am confident a more objective review of ancient feelings and thinking, rather than the desperate, agonizing intellectual conquest that has been attempted hitherto, would result in recognitions which are genuinely religious in nature. That, at least, is the sense of things which for me arose from the luminous cave of the past. In it there was room for the highest honors for Plato, but also at the same time for such negative counterparts of his as Antiphon and Hippias the Sophists.

However great or however mediocre the reward striven for, religious longings which are so misplaced that, while embracing wizards, they are cultivating a disillusioned modern skepticism to the extent of trying to expunge, in the name of literary science, a number of remote figures from the record, are patently self-destructive. I am still thinking about the near escape of Philolaus, whose adventure among nonexistent creatures, like the sphinxes on grave stelai, is the subject of an essay by Giorgio de Santillana:

155 "Philolaus in Limbo, or: What Happened to the Pythagoreans?" in *Reflections on Men and Ideas* (MIT Press, 1968), pp. 190– 201.

What happened to the Pythagoreans! It is an incredible fact that Pythagoras himself escaped oblivion in the world of scholarship by metamorphosing himself into a shaman:

156 W. Berkert, *Weisheit und Wissenschaft: Studien zu Pythagoras, Philolaus und Plato* (1962); rev. ed. trans. by E. L. Minar, Jr. under the title *Lore and Science in Ancient Pythagoreanism* (Harvard Univ. Press, 1972). See chapter 5.

An event of this sort never could have happened if so much had not been lost. Certainly there must have existed at one time a constellation of writings that originated in the borderlands around the Mediterranean which, had they been preserved, would have made a world of difference in the perspective which we are now allowed to enjoy.

But horizons being as limited as they are, there remains the not impossible imperative to prospect for good ore in the tailings that have survived and have found their way into Diels' collection. We may prosper in such a project by following certain precepts: first, the earlier the fetching back, the greater the quantity of fool's gold that may be expected to turn up; second, the later the hunt descends downward toward Suidas, the greater the accumulation of worthless invitations to a golden Lucianic banquet. Consequently, the standard for selection and rejection remains in the old standbys: Plutarch, and particularly, *De Placitis Philosophorum,* published as *Moralia,* 875D–911C; Diogenes Laertius, Sextus Empiricus, hardy perennials in the Loeb Classical Library. And there is always the possibility of new papyri.

Selectivity rather than helpless dependence on Plato and Aristotle has become the rule in the livelier, and also completely standard, reference books:

157 John Burnet, *Early Greek Philosophy* (1892; rev. ed. Meridian, 1964).

158 G. S. Kirk and J. E. Raven, *The Presocratic Philosophers: A Critical History with a Selection of Texts* (Cambridge Univ. Press, 1962).

159 W.K.C. Guthrie, *A History of Greek Philosophy,* vol. 1 (Cambridge Univ. Press, 1962).

The last of the above is a broad inclusive history; the first is a forceful, pioneering survey in which the Ionian philosophers are allowed to stand up on their feet as advocates of science; the one in the middle has a structure of well-selected key passages set down in English as well as Greek, with a review of each in the light of a consensus of current discussion.

The effect of the ebb and flow of discussion can become wearying. No one wants to be ignorant of new discoveries or new realizations. But there is much to be said for a retreat once in a while into the tranquil libraries of the later Renaissance, where good sense quietly prevailed; Montaigne's, for example, or that of Thomas Stanley, trans-

lator of Anacreon and cousin of Richard Lovelace, in the Inner
Temple, where he wrote his neglected, almost forgotten masterpiece:

160 Thomas Stanley, *History of Philosophy*, 4 vols. (London, 1655–
1662; col. ed. 1687, 1700).

INDEX

DATE DUE

17 Feb 84			
GAYLORD			PRINTED IN U.S.A.

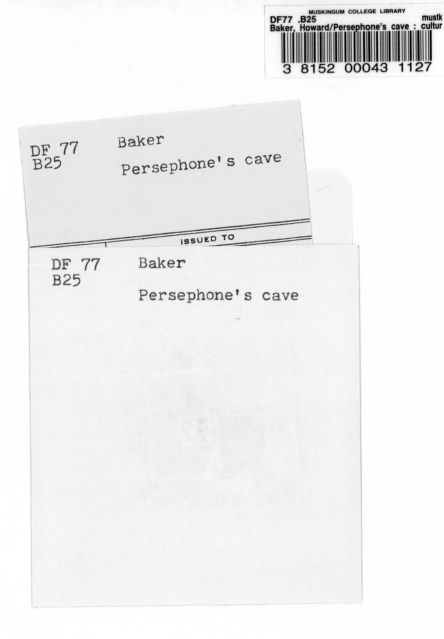

DF 77   Baker
B25
          Persephone's cave

ISSUED TO

DF 77   Baker
B25
          Persephone's cave

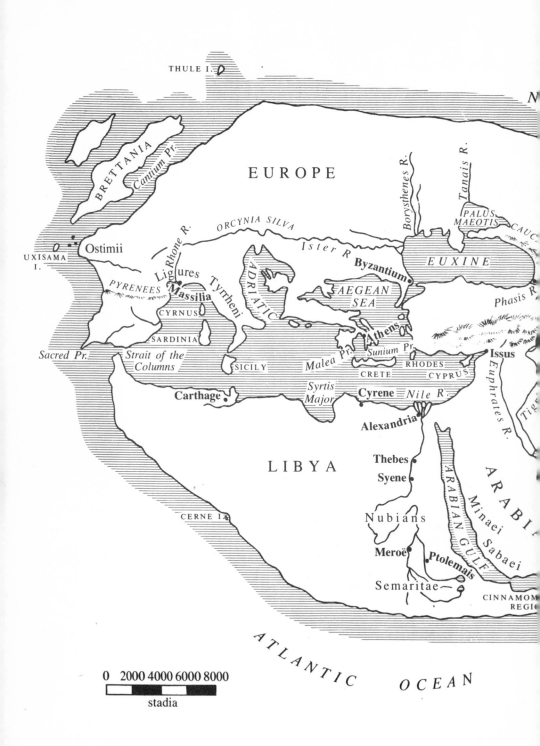

THULE I.

BRETTANIA

Cantium Pr.

EUROPE

N

UXISAMA
I.

Ostimii

Rhone R.

ORCYNIA SILVA

Ister R.

Boryshenes R.

Tanais R.

PALUS
MAEOTIS

CAUC

PYRENEES

Lig ures

Tyrrheni

ADRIATIC

Byzantium

AEGEAN
SEA

EUXINE

Phasis R

Massilia

CYRNUS

Athens

SARDINIA

Sunium Pr.

Issus

Sacred Pr.

*Strait of the
Columns*

SICILY

Malea Pr.

RHODES

CRETE

CYPRUS

Euphrates R.

Tig

Carthage

*Syrtis
Major*

Cyrene

Nile R.

Alexandria

LIBYA

Thebes

Syene

ARABIAN GULF

ARABI

Minaei

Sabaei

CERNE I

Nubians

Meroë

Ptolemais

Semaritae

CINNAMOM
REGIC

0   2000 4000 6000 8000

stadia

A T L A N T I C   O C E A N